ADVENTURES

in

ERROR

By

VILHJALMUR STEFANSSON

New York

ROBERT M. McBRIDE & COMPANY

ACKNOWLEDGMENTS

CHAPTERS I. AND II. ARE, WITH ALTERATIONS, FROM MY SHORT book *The Standardization of Error,* published some years ago by W. W. Norton & Company and now out of print. Chapter III. is but slightly changed from an article that originally appeared in *The American Mercury,* May, 1927. Chapter IV. is adapted from an address which I gave before the American Philosophical Society of Philadelphia, January 2, 1931. About the first ten thousand words of Chapter V. appeared in *The American Mercury* of July, 1927, but much additional information has been added. Chapter VI. is published with slight changes from an article entitled, *That 'Frozen' North* which appeared in *Maclean's Magazine,* Toronto, November 15, 1929.

The publishers regret that owing to Mr. Stefansson's sudden departure on an extended journey he was unable to read the proofs of this manuscript.

Contents

vii

CONTENTS

VI.

BEYOND THE FRONTIER

VII.

OLOF KRARER

VIII.

HISTORY OF THE BATHTUB IN AMERICA

ADVENTURES IN ERROR

CHAPTER I.

THE STANDARDIZATION OF ERROR

IT IS SAID THAT BACON CONSIDERED ALL KNOWLEDGE HIS PROV-
ince. But the sciences of today are so many and complex
that a single Baconian view of them is no longer possible,
and perversions of thought and action result because our intellectual horizon has been narrowed to a part of the field.
From a realization of this have come various attempts to
co-ordinate the sciences to permit a unifying view of the
whole. Comte made one of these a century ago in his
Positive Philosophy. There have been many since.

But if we pause to state clearly the case against the standardization of knowledge, the essential absurdity becomes so
patent that we have to recall the numerous failures to convince ourselves that anyone was ever foolish enough even to
try it.

Consider for instance the physiology of the human skin or
the composition of a dust nebula. In these fields, among
others, the accepted facts of a dozen years ago have become
the error and folklore of today. You standardize knowledge,
and while you are at the job the knowledge changes. Long

3

before the thing can be done adequately it has ceased being worth doing at all.

Then why are we continually attempting this hopeless task? Partly, let us say, from irrepressible human optimism, which leads us to think that any desirable thing is possible. Partly, also, because of unclear analogizing from fields that seem related but are not. One of these analogies is from business. If you have on hand, on July 1st, a pair of socks, assuming honest and successful management, you will have them still on hand on August 1st, or else cash in your till to correspond. But, in spite of unlimited honesty and efficiency, you have no guarantee that an idea on hand on July 1st may not have been simply removed by August 1st without any equivalent remaining. You may have discovered that month, for instance, reasonable assurance that the moon is *not* made of green cheese, without being able to get any clear idea as to what it *is* made of.

The reader may here jump to the conclusion that we are arriving at a philosophy of pessimistic hopelessness. That is not the way of the true philosopher. His ideal is the *tabula rasa*. He sweeps away the systems of others, that he may build his own on a smooth foundation.

Realizing simultaneously the insatiable craving of the human mind for order and the impossibility of bringing order into the chaos of knowledge, we appear to be faced with a dilemma no less distressing than insoluble. But on looking deeper we find the dilemma apparent only. This will become clear when we consider the essential nature of knowledge.

The thoughtless among us may speak, for instance, of a

4

red cow, and naïvely imagine we could prove our point with the testimony of a witness or two. But the philosophers have long ago made it clear that a cow would not be red but for the presence of someone to whom it looks red. Having established that point, the deeper of the philosophers go on to prove that the cow would not only not be red, but would not even exist, were it not for the presence of someone who thinks he sees a cow. In our argument the position is even stronger than this, for we have two lines of defense. First, we agree with the philosopher that you cannot prove of any given cow that it is red, or even that it exists; and then we point out that an idea is so much less stable than a cow that, even were the philosophers wrong about the cow not being red, they might easily be right about an idea not being right, or not existing.

Take an example: The philosophers of the Middle Ages demonstrated both that the earth did not exist and also that it was flat. Today they are still arguing about whether the world exists, but they no longer dispute about whether it is flat. This shows the greater lasting power of a real thing (whether it exists or not, for that point has not yet been settled) as compared with an idea, which may not only not exist, but may also be wrong even if it does exist.

We have now come in our discussion to the point where we see the absurdity of supposing ourselves to have any knowledge, as knowledge is ordinarily defined—or at least we would have come to that point but for lack of space which prevents us from making the subject really clear. However, it doesn't matter from a practical point of view whether you have followed this philosophical reasoning.

Perhaps you are not a philosopher. In that case, and in the homely phrase of the day, I ask you, what's the good of an Englishman's learning, first, that all Americans speak through their noses and, secondly, why they do so, when he has to find out eventually that they do not? What's the good, again, of knowing that central Australia is a desert and that certain principles of physiography make it so, when you may have to listen to an after-dinner speech by someone telling that it is not a desert?

Such things do not always go in triplets of (1) so it is, (2) why it is, and (3) it is not—but that is a common order.

The reader may here protest that we are not getting much nearer our promised emancipation from the dilemma between our passion for system and the impossibility of systematizing knowledge. We have hinted above that the solution lies in finding a new basis for knowledge, and this we now proceed to do.

So long as you believe in them, the nasality of American speech and the desert nature of central Australia are fragments of knowledge capable of being arranged in a system. The trouble comes when you discover that they are "untrue."

This gives the solution of our problem. We must have knowledge that is incapable of being contradicted. On first thought this seems impossible, but on second thought we realize that such facts do exist in the domain of mathematics. Two and two make four.

But why do two and two make four? Obviously because we have agreed that four is the name for the sum of two and two. That principle has been applied in mathematics to such advantage that it is rightly called the science of sciences;

6

and this is the principle which, now at length, we propose to apply to all knowledge. Through it every science will become a pure science, and all knowledge as open to systematization as mathematics.

The trouble with facts, outside mathematics, has been inherent in the method of gathering information. We call these methods *observation* and *experiment,* and have even been proud of them—not realizing their clumsy nature, the unreliability of the findings, the transient character of the best of them, and the essential hopelessness of classifying the results and thus gratifying the passion of the human intellect for order and symmetry in the universe.

Take an example: A man comes from out-of-doors with the report that there is a red cow in the front yard. Neglecting for the moment the philosophical aspect of the case—as to whether the cow would be red if there were no one to whom she seemed red, and also the more fundamental problem of whether there would have been any cow at all if no one had gone out to look—neglecting, as I say, the deeper aspects of the case, we are confronted with numerous other sources of error. The observer may have confused the sex of the animal. Perhaps it was an ox. Or if not the sex, the age may have been misjudged, and it may have been a heifer. The man may have been color-blind, and the cow (wholly apart from the philosophical aspect) may not have been red. And even if it was a red cow, the dog may have seen her the instant our observer turned his back, and by the time he told us she was in the front yard, she may in reality have been vanishing in a cloud of dust down the road.

The trouble lies evidently in our clumsy system of observ-

7

ing and reporting. This difficulty has been obviated in the science of mathematics. A square is, not by observation but by definition, a four-sided figure with equal sides and equal angles. No one has denied that and no one can, for the simple reason that we have all agreed in advance that we will never deny it. Nay more, we have agreed that if anyone says that a square has three or five sides we will all reply in a chorus: "If it has three or five sides it is not a square!" That disposes of the matter forever.

Why not agree similarly on the attributes of a front yard? —making it true by definition that, among other things, it contains a red cow. Then if anyone asserts, for reasons of philosophy, color-blindness, or the officiousness of dogs, that there is no red cow in the yard, we can reply, as in the case of the square: "If it does not contain a red cow, it is not a front yard!"

The author feels at this point a doubtless unwarranted concern that he is not being taken seriously. Or perhaps the plan proposed is not considered practical. But the proof of the pudding is in the eating. The thing has been tried, and successfully—not in the systematic way now proposed, but sporadically. Some instances are well-known and convincing.

Take the assertion that a Christian is a good man. If you attempt to deny this on the ground that Jones, a deacon in the church, ran off with some public funds, your stricture is at once shown to have been absurd by the simple reply: "If Jones was a thief, he was *not* a Christian." A Christian is, not by observation but by definition, a good man; if you prove that a certain man was not good you merely show that he

8

was not a Christian. Thus we have established that a Christian is a good man. It is like a square having four sides.

But if someone asserts that a Bolshevik, a Conservative, or a chemist is a good man, you can soon confute him; for the members of these classes have neglected to define themselves as good. Thus their attributes have to be determined by observation and experiment. It is highly probable that evidence could be brought against many Bolsheviks, and even some Conservatives, to show that they are not good men. At any rate we have here no such clarity of issue as in things that are true by definition—as the four-sidedness of a square or the goodness of a Christian.

Through some experience of arguing this case in the abstract I have learned that its essential reasonableness can best be established from concrete examples. Let us, then, take cases at random from various fields of knowledge.

Consider first the ostriches of Africa. These birds have been studied in the wild by sportsmen and zoologists, and as domestic animals by husbandmen who tend them in flocks like sheep. There are accordingly thousands of printed pages in our libraries giving what purports to be information upon their habits. Besides being indefinite and in many other ways faulty, this alleged information is in part contradictory.

Having studied the bird of Africa, let us turn next to the ostrich of literature, philosophy, and morals. Instead of confusion, we now have clarity and precision. This is because the ostrich of literature exists by definition only. He is a bird that hides his head when frightened. You may too precipitately object that men would not accept universally this definition of the ostrich of literature if it did not also fit the

9

zoological ostrich. The answer is that the definition has never received any support from zoologists, hunters, or owners of the domesticated birds, and yet it has been accepted universally throughout Europe since Pliny's time (about 50 B.C.). It has survived all attacks from science and from the bigoted commonsense of those who did not recognize its true nature. Like the definition of a four-sided square or a good Christian, it has survived because it was useful. Can you imagine any real attribute more instructive than the head-burying of the ostrich-by-definition? As a text for moralists, as an epithet that politicians use for their opponents, as a figure of speech generally, what could serve as well? Our literature is richer, our vocabulary more picturesque through this beneficent bird of hypothesis. He has many inherent advantages that no real bird could have. Since his habits are defined we need not waste time studying him first hand, nor in trying to adjudicate at second hand between books about him that disagree. Since he never existed as a beast he is in no danger of the extinction that is said to threaten the lion and swan.

Consider next what trouble we should get into if we did not have the literary ostrich and wanted to convey picturesquely the idea of that sort of wilful blindness from which we ourselves never suffer but which curiously afflicts our opponents. In pursuit of suitable analogy we might vainly canvass the whole animal kingdom. The ostrich-by-definition is, therefore, not only less trouble to deal with than a real bird; he is actually more useful and instructive than any real bird or beast. When we consider how often he has been used in sermon and precept we must admit that this model creature has contributed substantially not only to the entertainment and instruction of nations but also to the morality and general goodness of the world.

The ostrich is but one of several useful birds of definition. But we must be careful not to confuse these with real birds or their value is lessened. An example is the stork that brings babies. By a confusion of thought which identifies this stork with real storks, and through the pernicious birth control propaganda which insists on rationalizing everything, the baby-bringing stork has ceased to be useful except in conversation with children, in the symbolism of the movie, and in the picture postcard industry.

The wolves of literature are among the most picturesque and useful of our definitions. Zoological wolves go in pairs or families, never above a dozen. It is clear how inadequate this would be for movie purposes, where they should run in packs of scores or hundreds. Even in a novel or short story of Siberia or Canada you need packs large enough for the hero to kill fifteen or twenty, with enough left over to eat, or to be about to eat, his sweetheart. This is readily accomplished by using a wolf of the general type we advocate—having no relation to the so-called realities but possessing by definition all the required characteristics (habit of running in packs of any desired size, willingness to eat, or attempt to eat, the heroine, etc.).

Another useful definition has long been that of Arctic, Canadian, and Siberian cold. The danger and disadvantage of confusing this hypothetical with a so-called real climate are best seen if we compare the facility with which people who have never been in these countries use the weather in conversation, speeches, and books, and contrast that facility with the awkwardness of travelers and natives. An example is a story by Tolstoi. Great as he was, he failed to realize the advantage in simplicity and vividness of postulating that Siberia is always cold, and actually allowed himself to be led into the artistic blunder of having the convicts in one of his novels die of sunstroke. An acquaintance of mine was filming this story. He realized the pictorial ease of "putting over" drifting snow as compared with heat waves—the snow could be managed with confetti and an aeroplane propeller, but how would one photograph heat waves? He realized still more clearly that the public is wedded to the defined, as opposed to the "real" climate of Siberia, and did what Tolstoi would have done in the first place had he been a Californian —he changed the scene from summer to winter, and then froze to death as many convicts as the picture required.

These few examples from among many are enough to show not only that the method of knowledge-by-definition is and long has been in standard use, but also that it has the advantages of being easily grasped, picturesque, and of a higher average moral value than the so-called "real" knowledge. It is inherent in the genesis and nature of defined facts that they can be made picturesque in proportion to the ingenuity of the one who defines them, and as moral as necessary. This is a striking advantage over empirical knowledge, which cannot always be relied on to support the fashion of the time or even the moral system of the community.

It is from this last point of view that there has grown up in many countries of recent years a profound distrust of "facts" and the theories deduced from them. In England the situation is dealt with by the simple and adequate means

12

of paying little attention to the exposition of "new" things. In the United States it has been found that the public listens even to the newest views, and sometimes actually wants to act upon them. This has necessitated the expedient of passing laws prescribing what may and may not be advocated and believed. These American laws are a step in the right direction, but inadequate because they have back of them only specific considerations. Few people as yet realize the general reasons of expediency and broad sanity that underlie the scheme we are here proposing.

Let us consider next a sample or two of knowledge-by-definition that could well be added to our present stock. Just as artificial tongues are built upon spoken tongues but avoid their mistakes, so may we conveniently base our knowledge-by-definition, or absolute knowledge, on what is already believed by some.

Assume, for instance, that all Irishmen are peasants holding land by insecure tenure from grasping landlords, that each has a pig under his bed, that everyone carries shillalahs, that kissing the *Blarney Stone* is the chief national occupation. Having agreed on these things, we could teach them in the schools of all countries. We should then presently all agree (on the basis of common facts) as to what our attitude toward Ireland should be, and the troublesome *Irish Question* would disappear from politics and history.

Think, too, what a charm the new system would lend to travel in Ireland! As soon as you landed you would note the rarity or absence of all the things you had expected. You would meet surprise after surprise, which would not only delight you at the time but give you material for endless

13

letters home and for endless stories to tell when you got back. Thus would be built up an increasing tourist traffic, a source of revenue to Ireland itself and to the shipping and tourist companies of the various nations.

You may think such tourists, on coming home, would upset our system of facts-by-definition about Ireland. Not if that system is once thoroughly established. Consider in that relation the Greek pronouncement that at any time of year it becomes colder the farther north you go. North America is in language and civilization a homogeneous country in which one might think knowledge would therefore spread rapidly, and in which Atlanta, Richmond, New York, and Montreal are, and have been for a century, large and well-known cities that are by observation about equally hot in July. Yet there is even today practically unanimous adherence in all these cities to the Greek definition ("the farther north the colder at any time of year"), and each city believes those farther south to be hotter and those farther north to be colder, though thousands of travelers for a hundred years have found it to be uniformly otherwise. The ostrich with his head in the sand has survived two thousand years and is still going strong. No human being can retain oil, but the hypothetical Eskimo drinks it by the flagon in our books and belief, and is none the worse for it. Then why should not all the world forever believe that every Irishman has a pig under his bed? All parties would benefit. It would be only the hypothetical Irishman that has the pig, and we could by hypothesis arrange that he should thoroughly enjoy it. The real Irishman would get the benefit of the increased tourist trade and surely he ought to be grateful. The tourist

14

would make facile discovery of the non-existence of the pig; that would please him and interest all his friends forever after as a sort of occult knowledge, like knowing privately that Indian fakirs are really no more clever than our conjurers, a pleasing secret now possessed and highly valued by many without detriment to the fakirs or to those who prefer to say they have seen them do marvels. Thus would everyone be the gainer.

CHAPTER II.

THE PLEASURES OF BUNCOMBE

THE MOST STRIKING CONTRADICTION OF OUR CIVILIZATION IS THE
fundamental reverence for truth which we profess and the
thorough-going disregard for it which we practice. This is
the veriest commonplace. The lowest journalism fattens on
pointing it out and the highest clergy prosper in the same
occupation. According to them all, the world is rotten to the
core with hypocrisy and falsehood.

But while they agree on the condition, the physicians of
the world order hopelessly differ on the remedy. Without
disagreeing on the condition, either, we want to suggest
nevertheless that it is a bit naïve of the philosophers to
diagnose from the mere scarcity of truth that the world is
sick with an incurable malady. Is it not just possible that
they cannot cure us for the basic reason that we are not ill?

And if we are not ill, the worries of the moralists should
dissolve into good cheer. Can we, then, be well though the
truth be not in us? Strangely late in the history of philosophy,
we now for the first time address ourselves to that problem.

God and Truth have from the earliest times been the two
ideas that have commanded the greatest reverence. They have

16

been much argued by the philosophers, with many curious parallels and one striking contrast. Typical of the parallels are the long disputes about whether there can reasonably be supposed to exist either an absolute god or an absolute truth. The one contrast is that while the philosophers have discussed at great length whether God is good, they have never discussed whether Truth is good. Is it not a bit suspicious that this is the one thing they have always assumed? And in a world of chaotic philosophies that get us nowhere, is it not high time to ask if there be any sound reason why Truth should be exempted from that fundamental scrutiny to which even the gods have had to submit?

In addressing ourselves to this hitherto neglected question, as to whether truth is good, we adopt in the first instance a test which has long appealed to the common sense of mankind: *By their fruits shall ye know them.*

In defining our subject, we admit at once that the truth may have effects outside of the immediate field in which we shall study it, that of human affairs. It is like the question of soul. For thousands of years the civilization which is intellectually descended from the lands around the Mediterranean has agreed that all men have souls. Usually those who speculated have considered that women have souls also, a few that horses and dogs have souls, and the most generous that all animals have them. But it is only the highest intellectuals and the most benighted savages who have ever conceded souls to plants and sticks and stones. We shall ignore, for the time being, such possible extensions of our subject, and discuss Truth solely in its relation to men (including women).

17

As both definition and defense of our method, we premise, further, that mankind frequently does much better than it knows. Nearly all of us, for instance, can keep in balance as we walk along upright, though the physiologists are still arguing about exactly how we do it. Similarly, the biologists tacitly agree that we know what life is; for they test their definitions of life by measuring them against the reality which they feel they know, though they cannot define it quite successfully.

Go through any considerable number of examples like the preceding, selecting them, if you like, from every sphere of life, and you will gradually reach a firm confidence in the reasonableness of human actions as compared with the flightiness of our theories and the contradictions so frequently involved in our explanations. That may be because (admitting the evolutionary theory and the geological time scale) we, and the pre-human ancestors from which we inherit our traits, have been acting so as to save our bodies and reach our desires for a good many million years longer than we have been speculating on how to save our souls and protect our reputations. And practice makes perfect.

We arrive then at a simple problem: If we ignore all theories and study those instances where mankind has preferred truth or falsehood the one to the other, we shall be in a position to determine which set of choices has been of the greater benefit.

In a later and more rigorous inquiry we may go in for objective proofs, like statistics. Here we shall use only such examples as are well-known to everyone, so that the conclusions we state will certainly be merely the equivalent of the reader's own verdict, set before him in print.

Few things are more generally admitted than that parents, in most cases, love their children and desire their greatest good. These parents may be in error as to what constitutes good, but this is beside the mark, for we are at the moment merely trying to find out what it is they think is for the children's welfare. Of course, if you ask them, they will quote you Truth with a capital, or more likely TRUTH all in capitals. For so have they been taught to protest. But study their actions, which are a surer guide than their words.

THE CASE OF INFANTS

To put it bluntly, most loving parents take the greatest care to surround children not with truth but with deception.

We cannot deceive children before they are born, so we do the next best thing and practice every deception about them. We conceal, not only from children but also from grown persons so far as possible, how babies come into the world. The marriage is announced, and even made a public occasion, but thereafter everything is mystery. Pregnancy is concealed by an artful dress, the expectant mother hides or goes to a remote place. In some classes of society it is rather a breach of etiquette if the doctor talks openly about whom he is going to attend that night. There is a blare of publicity after the birth, in which, however, only a few things may be told—the weight and sex of the child, whom it resembles, and in a very general way how the mother is progressing. But the fact that the child looks red and wrinkled, that its

19

eyes do not focus, and several other details about it, are of so private a nature that many mothers discover these and other more "intimate" things only in their own children. And certainly to most fathers the new-born looks as surprising as it looks unpleasant. That, by the way, is a fact every parent must conceal—it would be dreadful if anyone were ever to find out what a disagreeable shock his first-born was to him.

The reader may here want to stop and argue with the author that all this is but decent and proper reticence—which if he does he pleases the author very much. For there would be nothing to argue about. The author, too, feels that this is how all these things should be. He certainly would hate to break any such taboos. But let us not argue one way or the other. To do so would be unscientific. We should pursue our inquiry with a steady view to just one thing: Is it true that the majority of people feel and do as stated? From that survey will emerge a general conclusion as to which it is that men really prefer in practice, truth or falsehood.

The systematic deception of the child usually begins almost at the moment of birth. The instrument is speech, most fittingly, since our studies will show that this is the favorite means of deception throughout life. At first, the child does not understand any words, and balks the mother thereby. However, she makes capital of this dilemma by seeing to it that her baby shall chiefly hear (and therefore learn) only incorrect speech. This is known as teaching the child "baby talk."

There are certain standard forms of baby talk which, through wide usage, are not completely deceptive; as when the child is taught to say that papa has gone bye-bye when the meaning is that papa has gone out. Accordingly, most mothers invent a special jargon so that each child grows up with several dozen sounds or combinations of sounds which are either not words of any language or else are real words with perverted meanings.

As the child grows up he discovers that he has been deceived in the first speech taught him; and thus he gets an early and practical lesson in one of the main concerns of life —how to deceive others.

As soon as the child has acquired a vocabulary by which he can be misled, people begin to deceive him in ways that increase in complexity with his growing faculties. Many of these are specially devised by his mother and family and do not lend themselves to sociological study, for they are seldom placed on record. But there is a general system, one broad aspect of which is stories, especially classics, that fall under the heads of fairy tales and folklore.

There has come to my attention a very practical way of determining what people really think of the place of folklore in the education of the young. As there has been prejudice to guard against, I need to describe the manner of my investigation before I come to the matter of it.

In a very tentative and general conversation I casually introduce the subject of bolshevism. In three cases out of four there is an immediate hostile reaction, and then I go no further, for my desire has been to get an opinion on a reported bolshevik undertaking, and a person who bristles at their very name is certain to be opposed to anything they sponsor. Correspondingly I get in some cases reactions of favorable

21

enthusiasm, and these are equally hopeless, for they would naturally support any part of the bolshevik program.

In the few cases of seeming freedom from bias, I proceed to retail, without vouching for it, what I have heard about certain educational experiments conducted in the Soviet Union. It really makes no difference about the truth of these reports, for a person scientific enough to be neither strongly pro- nor strongly anti-bolshevik is also intelligent enough to consider a hypothetical case and give the same sort of verdict he would if it were a real one.

It is said, then, that the Soviet powers believe in the maxim of Paul about proving all things and accepting only those that can stand the most rigid investigation. I do not know (I must say, since the subject has been brought up) whether the bolsheviks are trying to discourage baby-talk, insisting that mothers shall speak a real language even to the youngest child; but it has been represented to me that from the time the child begins to speak the government makes an effort to see that it is told only the truth.

One of the first things western mothers tell their children is about Jack and the Beanstalk. The Russians feel reasonably certain that there never was such a Jack or Beanstalk. Accordingly, neither that fabled youngster nor the fabled plant is ever mentioned, I am told, to the up-to-date bolshevik-sponsored child.

But, says the Russian, there are in real life things quite as interesting and marvelous as Jack and his stalk; for instance, a child named Tom instead of Jack, and surnamed Edison. Nothing very marvelous is reported about this Tommy while he was small. But when he became a sizable boy, or perhaps even later, he got an idea about how a string could be heated till it became red and even white, and how this string could be put in a glass bottle and hung up to give a light much brighter than any lamp that ever existed up to that time.

The Soviet educators are said to maintain that by applying the same ability and ingenuity to telling the story of Tom and the glowing string that has been used in popularizing the adventures of Jack and his Beanstalk, you could create an equally vivid story, equally entertaining and, they contend, more beneficial since it is "true."

In the case of a child taught to believe in the Beanstalk, it becomes necessary to tell him later (or else to let him find out for himself) that it never existed. Some psychologists claim that there is an injurious mental shock involved when a child's faith is shattered. What the Soviets emphasize is that if Jack had been real the child's interest would not have had to cease at the age of five or six, but might have continued growing until the larger boy gradually mastered all the history and later grasped the achievements of Jack. If, then, instead of Jack and the Beanstalk, you begin with Tom and the red-hot string, there is no shock, they argue, no dead halt, no shifting of interest from one thing to another, but instead a growing delight in the whole adventurous life of Thomas Alva Edison that finally develops into a grasp of all the sciences with which he was concerned.

I seldom get this far in my second-hand explanation before my listeners stop me with rhapsodies on the glories of the imagination and diatribes against the bolsheviks who now for the first time are seen by these previously impartial people to be insidious foemen of the soul.

23

This counterblast used to floor me and I would stop at that point; but more recently I have developed a flanking operation. People strong on the beauties of the soul are nearly always great admirers of Maeterlinck. So I apparently change the subject, falling in with their praise of the imagination and asking if they think its subtle beauties are anywhere more evident than in the great son of Belgium. There is usually agreement, and soon we are communing ecstatically together about his book on the bee.

The next step is to ask the champions of the imagination whether they remember that Maeterlinck says near the beginning of that book (which we have just agreed is one of his greatest works) that he has long since given up trying to invent anything half so marvelous as the truth. Oh, yes, they remember that, but they always understood it to mean Truth with a capital letter, which is something very different from a fact, and apparently means anything you are so fond of that you are prepared to stick to it whether it is true or not. But a little discussion about the sort of truth which Maeterlinck says he is trying to present in the Bee, and the sort which the bolsheviks say they are trying to present about Edison, shows that both are of the same kind. This conclusion results in no increase of admiration for the bolsheviks but a noticeable decrease of liking for Maeterlinck, who apparently has been cheating some of his readers into thinking that he was telling them Truths when he was only telling facts.

Usually the outcome of the conversation is a feeling of how blessed are we whose imaginations have been stimulated and delighted by Little Red Riding Hood, Bluebeard with his many wives, and tales of that sort, and what an eclipse of the imagination is spreading its shadow over Russia, where even little children have to be told the truth.

The Soviet campaign against folklore in general has been paralleled by an American campaign for Santa Claus in particular, which shows the differing temper of the two countries. Santa, it is well known, drives reindeer. Now it happens that some friends of mine own a hundred thousand reindeer in Alaska and have been trying to find a market for them. Other friends of mine own and edit *The Kansas City Star,* one of the most respectable and respected newspapers in the United States. Theodore Roosevelt, after he had been President, thought it an honor to be one of its editors: and the standards of personnel, management and policy are quite as high now as then. My Alaskan friends are, in ideals and character, not below the level of even the *Star.* However, they were not at that time as well-known, nor was their standing in the community possibly of as direct business value to them. You might, therefore, suspect them of using Santa Claus to help them find a reindeer market, no matter what they thought of the Saint himself. But surely the *Star,* whose business sense is as keen as its ethics are scrupulous, would not touch the enterprise unless its editors were sure of two things: that Santa was all right, for otherwise the *Star* would not associate with him even for profit; and that nearly everybody else thought Santa all right, for otherwise the *Star* would not profit by associating with him.

The campaign was planned to deceive the children of Kansas City into believing that the real Santa with his real gift-bearing reindeer had entered into an arrangement to arrive in Kansas City some weeks before Christmas and to be on exhibition there. The *Star* organization were his alleged representatives and the part for which I was requisitioned by the Lomen Reindeer Corporation was to write to the kiddies a letter telling how I had visited Santa in his northern home and what message he had sent by me to the children of the United States. My letter would be printed on dozens of front pages, aggregating millions in circulation, for this was a nation-wide campaign handled by newspapers or department stores in many of the larger cities, such as Cleveland, Brooklyn, Denver, Oklahoma City, and I have forgotten what other places. The letter I wrote was deceptive, though not literally untruthful. It was printed by all the papers engaged in the Real Santa campaign, and between me and a thousand other willing collaborators who all felt we were doing the nation's children a real service, we fooled them so thoroughly that the *Star* (to come back to that worthy paper) was able to stage a parade through the streets of Kansas City that was even larger, it was said, than the American Legion could muster when they held their National Convention in the same city the year before. The entire police force was needed to control the crowd. Some other cities did almost as well.

I have heard much comment on the campaign waged by the *Star,* and by the like-minded papers of other cities, and none has been unfavorable. I believe the mayor of Kansas City thanked the *Star* for a great public service—or something of that sort. But mayors do such things rather perfunctorily—whatever is done by a prominent enough citizen or foreigner, at that they publicly rejoice. But tradesmen are usually more hard-headed, and their chief organizations are discreet and particular to be always on the side of the common weal. But higher than any of our non-religious bodies in its ideals and aims is likely to be the Parent-Teacher Association of the city. Listen, then, to what they said in a display proclamation which occupied, in suitably large print, nearly a whole page of *The Kansas City Star* on Christmas Day, 1925:

To *The Kansas City Star:*
May we express our congratulations and appreciation to *The Star* on the wonderful success of its enterprise in bringing Santa Claus and his reindeer to Kansas City and acting as the host, friend and guide of the children's Christmas saint.

We believe all Kansas City and our neighboring towns share with us in our felicitation. It is nothing new for *The Star* to be generously mindful of the children at Christmas time. We have not forgotten *Snow White, The Seven Swans* and *Peter Pan!* But this year Santa Claus and his reindeer have been brought "in person," have paraded our streets, visited our schools and hospitals and have taken their Christmas cheer directly to the children and to the older folk as well.

The Old Spirit of Christmas has been revived and stimulated, and everybody has been made happier and better by this Yuletide visit. With this Christmas Spirit in our hearts, we now think it most fitting to thank *The Star* publicity for it unique and happy achievement.

27

TO SANTA CLAUS AND HIS HOST: A MERRY CHRISTMAS AND THANK YOU

Merchants Association:
Parent-Teacher Association:
Chamber of Commerce

You agree with them, heartily, Gentle Reader, I am sure. And so do I. The pudgy Saint with his sleigh load of gifts and his eight reindeer is part of the glory and romance of childhood. You and I, when we were small and believed in him, saw with our mundane eyes nothing more than a jolly old man in a red coat with a crinkly smile and a flowing beard; the more blessed youngsters of today (thanks to the Lomen Corporation in Alaska and men of humanity and vision in our cities who cooperate with them), become personally acquainted with Dancer and Prancer, and Donner and Blitzen, and all the other members of the famous team. They ride in the sleigh with Santa and they ride on the backs of his deer. They are thrilled by the no longer simulated (as in our day) interest of their parents who now stand shivering with cold and quivering with delight as they are shoved about by policemen to make way for a Santa-and-Reindeer parade as large and enthusiastic as ever marched behind a young lady that swam the channel or a young gentleman who flew the Atlantic.

Best of all, this apparent faith of the elders enables us to stretch the faith of the younger generation a year or two

28

longer than was possible before the Lomen concern thought of providing real reindeer to make the mythical Saint more real. We used to lose such beliefs when we were five, but today the Parent-Teacher Association, the Merchants Association, the Chamber of Commerce, and the *Star* are able to stretch the faith of Kansas City at least till seven—two years of happy unreality given to thousands of children in that one city alone. And so in many other cities. Multiplying the clear gain, two years for each child, by the total number of children affected, we have an aggregate of millions of happiness-years added for this nation alone. When the fashion spreads to other countries and continues through the years, the total gain to the world will become incalculable.

Preserving the faith of children was the main purpose of the Santa campaign, but the more enterprising newspapers used the opportunity to benefit older readers as well. The Denver paper (which we will not name, for some people mistakenly consider it wrong to deceive grown-ups) erected an imitation snow house near where the reindeer were kept (I think it was at the municipal buildings) and employed an Eskimo, who had never before seen that sort of snow house except in movies, to explain to visitors that he and other reindeer herders of Alaska dwelt in that kind of snow house when they were at home. So far as I could judge, and I was in Denver at the time, every grown person, from Unitarian to Rotarian, swallowed that as readily as the children did the Santa part, and with as much satisfaction. Such beliefs have a moral as well as an entertainment value. It certainly makes you more content with a hall bedroom if you can visualize the Alaska Eskimos shivering in huts of snow.

29

But this about Alaska snow houses and the preservation of the faith of adults, has been a digression. We must proceed with our systematic inquiry into the planned and benevolent deception of the growing child.

THE CASE OF THE GRADE SCHOOL

We aim in this book at no more than establishing a reasonable presumption either in favor of truth as opposed to deception or else in favor of deception as opposed to truth. We shall not, therefore, attempt a study of our educational system as a whole but shall take a few cases that are typical.

The Teaching of History: Under this head we shall consider two general problems and then a few specific instances.

One of those disadvantages of facts which their advocates usually admit, is that they are complicated. Another is that in most cases people cannot agree as to what are the facts. Simplification and standardization are therefore necessary, especially for the young. This is universally conceded.

Not till the prospective historian starts graduate work in a university does he usually begin to have any conception of how debatable are most of the things that he has been taught as a child. The disillusionment then continues rapidly until he feels like selecting as the best definition of his specialty the one usually credited to Napoleon: "History is a set of lies agreed upon." But (and this is significant), in spite of the high average moral tone of our populations, few historians become crusaders against history. The simplest, and I believe the correct, explanation is that they think that, on the whole, deceiving children does them good.

30

When we entered the 1914-18 war, we suddenly discovered that most of our school histories were anti-British. Many of them were forthwith changed to pro-British, without a murmur from anyone except a few people who (we all agreed, as soon as they began to protest) were either pro-Germans or Pacifists. But the War, after we got into it, was so short that before it was over there was not time to oust all the anti-British propaganda from the texts. I had the instructive experience of being in a city where a violent newspaper controversy sprang up between correspondents, some of whom advocated anti-British history but most of whom favored pro-British. The ground of the pros was that we ought to stand by our former allies, that there might soon be another war, and that we should bring up the younger generation strong for English-speaking unity, because that was the natural basis of the coming alignment. Some argued specifically that we might be able to annex Canada if we used the same sort of histories as the Canadians and therefore grew up to the same beliefs. Even the Hearst papers, which then opposed this view and anything else that seemed to favor the British, later came out for the principle and advocated an English-speaking union.

The voices which suggested an impartial history were few and weak. Thus did what we believe to be the sound common sense of the people manifest itself. For next after patriotism comes a right world outlook. We must know in advance what country to favor in time of trouble. And how can the needed unanimity be secured in a democracy except by teaching the youngsters to like the right country so that they may vote correctly when they later come to decide tariffs, treaties and wars?

Much proof of what no one doubts is tedious and we have gone far enough in the argument. Certainly if you are pro-British, you will see at once that teaching love for British ideals, respect for British institutions, cannot help but benefit any country. If you are not pro-British, you can arrive at the same conclusion by substituting in the discussion the name of whatever country you most admire. Call that country X. You will then at once see the advantage of teaching the rising generation to be pro-X, or *proex*—to coin a much-needed word.

The reader may here object that even if it is agreed that history teaching in the schools should be chiefly for the purpose of laying down principles to guide us in life, it does not follow that we have to teach children to be in favor of any particular country or set of countries. Perhaps you are a pronounced isolationist and think we are strong enough to go it alone, then this strength would be increased by the solidarity we would gain if we learned in school to dislike all other nations and later ran our government and shaped our private actions so as to get them all to dislike us. That is an old and much-advocated principle: that real unity can be attained only in the face of a common enemy. Very well, then, you are not a Proex but an Antex, and you must go about trying to get the schools into your hands. Let the best men win! It looks just now as if it would be the Antexes.

Coming to specific problems of truth in history, we need little but a catalogue to see on which side we stand. Supposing, just for argument, that the biographers of Lincoln could

32

prove, as some of them have tried to do, that he was of illegitimate descent, would you then want that taught in the schools? The conclusive arguments against are: (1) Such teaching would attack the Home, the most precious of all our institutions; for Lincoln is our greatest national hero, and having him illegitimate, even if only back in his parents' or grandparents' generation, would be a destructive influence. (2) That teaching would also attack the institution of National Heroes. Lincoln is our greatest hero; nothing is more beneficial than to have heroes to look up to; we would not look up to Lincoln quite so much if he were in any degree illegitimate; therefore we ought to hide the fact, if it were a fact. (3) Nothing could be gained by encouraging children to attach scandal to the names of great men. (4) It would be in bad taste to teach in school about the illegitimacy of anyone. On the basis of these and many similar reasons, all decent people will agree that the question of whether Lincoln was illegitimate should never be mentioned in the schools.

To be on the safe side, the author states here emphatically that the biographers who favor the legitimacy of Lincoln, even unto the third and fourth generation, have, in his opinion, much the best of the argument. For this book might possibly fall into the hands of minors.

It is maintained by some that it would do no harm for adults to know the fact, if it were a fact, that Lincoln was illegitimate. Their reasoning is that character is formed in infancy and that the perverting influence of a truth, no matter how improper, is negligible in adults. We agree with that contention, and the more readily because it is in harmony

33

with the conclusion at which we are fast arriving (a conclusion, by the way, at which you could arrive still faster with less reasoning): The purpose of child training is to build character, and all education should therefore trend toward that goal. The truth should be admitted into the curriculum or kept out of it by that test alone. Facts of a disturbing nature should be permitted, if at all, only when characters have set beyond the reasonable possibility of change.

The importance of discretion in history teaching was once brought forcibly to my attention when I was spending a summer in northern Vermont, and found in use three miles away across the Canadian line in Quebec, school texts in which the War of 1812 differed so much from the war in the Vermont histories that you would hardly believe it was the same war. You can readily see how wise that was on both sides. Imagine the discord that would be introduced into the teaching of Canadian patriotism if they used Vermont histories, and similarly what havoc a Canadian history could work, if tossed into our school system like a stone into delicate machinery. Nor is there any halfway course possible. If you were to cut out all the contradictions, there would be little left of that particular war; neither would the leavings be any good for inculcating patriotism or other moral virtues into either Canadians or Americans. Obviously things had best remain as they are.

Or would you ever hint in the history courses that Sir Galahad never had a bath? That Tristram's courting, so touchingly described by Edwin Arlington Robinson, must have smelled pretty strong even at arm's length (except when the wind was just right)? That some of the most revered

34

saints of the Church made vows never to bathe and never to be unkind to the lice that swarmed over them? And that the only two great bathing eras of known history were the ancient period which historians call the decline of the Roman Empire, when civilization was going to the dogs, and our modern period, when the Fundamentalists tell us we are all going to the Devil? Would not such teaching suggest that there may be a connection between clean bodies and unclean living? And what could be worse for æsthetics or for the soap trade?

The fact was, of course, that Tristram liked, the smell of his sweetheart, and she liked his, both being used to it, and that the sinners as well as the saints of the Middle Ages really enjoyed what we would call the stink of foul linen. The past was not necessarily such an unpleasant time for those who lived in it (in view of their tastes). But, even after dwelling on that, most of us will remain convinced of the superiority of our own taste, and will continue unwilling that historical studies shall in any way encourage those of our youngsters who seem to have been born with medieval propensities for dirt.

Indeed, what possible good end could be served by letting such facts (if they be facts) gain currency through history teaching? Would patriotism, good manners, or good morals profit thereby? Would such teaching build character? Certainly not, and the present course is the right one: to say nothing about bathing in the Age of Chivalry, but to imply always that cleanliness is the natural state and passion of man —excepting rare miscreants who come to school inadequately washed behind the ears.

35

And so we might go on, canvassing our histories and our moral, political and æsthetic judgments till we arrive at the conclusion that in school texts at least the truth needs to be very judiciously handled.

The Teaching of Physiology: If the truth be a tricky thing in history, it is no less so in many other "branches" taught in the first eight grades of school. For instance, consider physiology. We need not dwell on sex, which most of us instinctively and rightly feel must not be thrust upon the young, but will instead continue under this head the discussion with which we ended the section on history.

Cleanliness may seem to lie in the field of æsthetics, but it has the most practical value. You would be ostracized socially if people knew you did not bathe; you would be worse off than if you had halitosis and four-out-of-five pyorrhea. Personality courses, books on etiquette, and the efforts of the Hamilton Institute combined with Pelmanism would be of little avail to gain you preferment. Listerine could not remove the odor nor Pond's Cream make your countenance seem agreeable. So at least, we believe, and so the rising generation must be taught to believe, or cleanliness may depart from among us.

But it is now said by some of the physiologists (doubtless untruly) that nearly all the supposed scientific arguments for bathing are fictions and fallacies. *Item:* The skin does not excrete any appreciable amount of harmful substances from the body, nor do the pores "breathe." Therefore your system is not purified by "keeping the pores open" and one argument on bathing-for-health disappears. *Item:* A chief function of the skin is to protect the body; poisons, such as mercury, cannot enter your body through a skin proofed with its own secretions, but will seep through if the natural lubricants have been washed away with warm water, soap, or other methods. Therefore your health is, in this respect at least, the safer the less you bathe, and another of the standard arguments vanishes. *Item:* The skin's own secretions keep it softer and in better condition than any substitute yet discovered. This is a deserved pat on the shoulder for the Lord who made us, but a rather stiff jolt for the cosmetic manufacturers. *Item:* The body odors come chiefly from three areas or parts of the body (that are too taboo for mention even here). Keeping these clean goes nine-tenths of the way toward freeing you from odors that other normal humans can detect, and changing your underwear every day, or even every other day, would go the remaining one-tenth, thus removing that argument for bathing.

And so on for many arguments more, the sum of which is that if you have a healthy skin it is safe enough to bathe if you like; but with eczema and certain other diseases you must not bathe if you want to stop the blotches from spreading, or to sleep for the itching at night.

Now just assume, for argument's sake, that all the above (or to be conservative, say half of it), is true. Then ask yourself, would you be in favor of having little children of the dirty-ear stage find out about it? The slogan was, in the generation of our parents: "Cleanliness is next to Godliness." But the investment in soap and in the allied industries has grown faster since then than the property of the churches, and the soaps advertise more. Today the sales talk sways the nation, and it is doubtful if godliness even approaches cleanliness in popularity. We must fight harder, therefore, to keep such physiology out of the schools, than any fundamentalist has yet fought to keep Darwinism out of the colleges. And we shall succeed, backed as we are by the advertising funds and the publicity genius of the whole soap industry from Bon Ami to Zap.

But there is one disquieting thought: The interests of Listerine and the perfumers are opposed to those of the soap and bath towel manufacturers. Europe, too, may seek to control our cleanliness, as it does our politics, by its insidious propaganda. But, fortunately, it will be disunited. It will be England pleading that odors be removed with Lifebuoy against France urging that they be covered up with Houbigant. These may kill each other off. Then there will be apathy and discord at home among our Napoleons of business. Some will stand aside from the struggle, for great houses, like Colgate, make soap as well as perfume. The underwear manufacturers will be against both, and so will the laundries, for they will want us to get rid of odors by frequent changes of linen. Frequent launderings wear out clothes and thus benefit the cotton planters of the South and the wool ranchers of the West.

The issue will be doubtful if the battle ever starts. We, the great public, having once been won over from France and the perfume to England and the tub, should try to prevent the issue from ever rising again by keeping the unæsthetic new physiology out of the schools.

Furthermore, especially as this book may fall into the hands of minors, the so-called new physiology is doubtless all wrong. So let us continue circulating the story about the page in Venice who was clothed in gold leaf for a pageant and who died of suffocation because his pores could not breathe. Let us never forget suggesting, when we see a lad whose face is covered with pimples, that he has doubtless been neglecting his wash basin and soap. And let us soft pedal the fact, if it be a fact, that abstinence from bathing is frequently prescribed by the most expensive skin specialists.

The Teaching of Geography: The teaching of this science brings out a new consideration—the reticence customarily practiced in it, while no less benevolent than in the other subjects, is based on motives new in our discussion and results in benefits of a different kind.

When facts are played down in geography teaching it is not usually because they would be in bad taste or otherwise detrimental to the character of the scholars, but rather because they are too complicated. The teachers are busy and overworked, and the pupils have limited time for the curriculum, for some of them may have to quit school soon and go to work. A complicated idea takes a long time to teach, it is hard to learn and difficult to remember and understand. From both the giving and receiving end, simplicity is therefore desirable, but facts have usually the unfortunate defect of being complicated. In the practice of teaching it is therefore often necessary and sometimes desirable to ignore them. We can best and most sympathetically understand this if we take a case where we have been ourselves deceived, for we shall then be able to testify from personal knowledge that we have benefited, or at least that we have suffered no harm.

The best geographical example under this head is per-

39

haps one of those upon which we touched briefly in the first section of this book—that, other things being equal, the farther north you go the colder it gets, no matter what the time of year. We shall develop that topic more fully than we did before, exploring some of its more instructive and entertaining ramifications.

First we need perspective from the history of geographical science. As in many other cases, we owe the beginnings of learning in this field to the Greeks. They may have borrowed from earlier civilizations, and probably did; but they formulated the doctrines and cast them into the molds in which many of them are still set. One of their chief achievements was that they worked out the laws of temperature distribution over the earth substantially as we learned them in the grade schools up to a few years ago, and roughly as they still remain in the minds of the general public.

Already five hundred years before Christ, the Greeks knew that the earth was a sphere. They understood the migration of the sun northward over the earth in summer and southward in winter between what they called, and what we still call, the tropics of Cancer and Capricorn. They also determined the polar circles beyond which the sun does not rise in winter nor set in summer. This was dividing the earth into five logical zones. The Greeks and the rest of mankind lived, they said, in a zone that was temperate. But if you crossed the Mediterranean and were to travel south into Africa you would get too near the sun and come first to a section unpleasantly hot, then to one intolerable, and last to a burning region where no living thing, either plant or animal, could exist by reason of the fierce downpour of the

40

sun's heat. This was the Torrid Zone. Going north from Greece you came similarly first to lands unpleasantly cold, then to others intolerable, and last to a permanently frozen region "where life is as impossible because of the freezing as it is in the Torrid Zone because of the burning." South of the tropics there doubtless was another temperate zone and this might be inhabited—probably was, in fact, though we should never know except by inference, as no one could ever cross the burning tropics. And at the south end of the earth would be a second frozen zone.

Thus from their doctrines of beauty, simplicity, and symmetry, and from the principles of logic the Greeks evolved laws of temperature distribution which are so easy to explain and understand that if you had never heard of them before you could have grasped both them and their necessary implications from a description no longer nor better composed than mine that you have just read. Such a natural law is a boon to teacher and student alike. No wonder, then, that it held its ground from more than four hundred years before Christ to more than fourteen hundred years after, as John Kirtland Wright has recently proved in a long and scholarly work published by the American Geographical Society of New York: *The Geographical Lore of the Time of the Crusades.*

That we do not still have in the schools these Greek temperature laws in all their pristine simplicity is due to two of mankind's most troublesome qualities, cupidity and skepticism. In the fifteenth century Western Europe was greedy for the riches of the Far East, and the road to Cathay, traveled by Marco Polo and his predecessors and successors, had

41

been closed by Mohammedan victories over the less bigoted Mongols. It is usually easy to disbelieve anything that crosses our desires, and so doubts began to arise as to whether the tropic lands were really burning hot and the tropic oceans boiling. Henry the Navigator gets most of the credit for cooling off the burning zone by sending out ship after ship that went farther and farther south along the West Coast of Africa, each returning with fearful tales of what they had seen or imagined, but most of them nevertheless returning and thus giving hope that others might go still farther. At last a ship did sail to where the sun stood overhead without cooking the sailors alive. Indeed, she returned with the story that the days had not been hotter right below the sun than they were on some occasions in Portugal.

So began the "Conquest of the Tropics," and so ended the simplicity of the Greek laws of temperature distribution. Every work on meteorology of college grade now tells you that the highest temperatures registered by thermometers in the shade, under weather bureau conditions, are not recorded in the Torrid Zone at all; but in the Temperate (!) Zones. Probably the highest in-the-shade records so far taken are those of Death Valley, California, about 900 miles north of the northern edge of the Torrid Zone—136°; almost certainly the highest temperatures that can be recorded in Africa are in the Sahara Desert, also north of the tropics. If there are higher temperatures south of the Equator we feel sure they will not be near the Equator, but near the tropic of Capricorn or else (more likely) in the South Temperate Zone.

These principles are now known to all authors of text

42

books, but they are still able to maintain a degree of simplicity in the lower school grades by implying it is average temperatures that matter, and by saying nothing about extremes. The fact is that averages count for some things and extremes for others, and that both are important. It is not, of course, the average cold of January that sometimes destroys the fruit in the South, but the one extreme night; similarly it is not the average heat of July that kills by sunstroke in New York but the one extreme day. Extremes are really more important, in that sense, than averages; but averages are much simpler and more teachable. It is so complicated to explain and remember that extremes may be high where averages are high, that extremes may be high where averages are low, and that extremes may be low where averages are low. We would certainly have to lengthen out our school courses if we went into such hairsplitting, and our millions of potential workers would be kept out of the mills and factories even longer than they are now. Besides, the complexities of facts are bewildering and confusing to the average mind, and never give the feeling of enlightenment you have when you grasp a simple principle which throws a flood of logical light on a previously haphazard world.

It is unfortunate—or perhaps fortunate—that we have not space to go deeply into the history of the way in which the simple Greek law of temperature distribution has been gradually broken down by explorers who went to remote places and came back with stories of conditions that did not fit into the theory, and how the scientists toiled at fitting together the mosaic pieces till they finally evolved an explanation that does fit all the facts. But we must give at least a brief sketch.

The investigation that has been going on since the days of Prince Henry the Navigator started from the simple Greek proposition: There is no cold and the greatest heat on the Equator, no extreme of either heat or cold in the North Temperate Zone, and no heat but merely intense cold at the North Pole. The first slight exceptions to this had, of course, been noted long before Henry's day: The mountain tops are cold. Other discrepancies due to sea breezes, ocean currents, and many other things soon followed, but they were, on the whole, not very difficult to explain as exceptions to the rule. True enough, the altitude one was taken to be a universal exception; mountains were said to be colder than their surroundings in any zone at any time of year, and it became a popular saying that climbing a few feet up was like traveling a good many miles north.

All exceptions other than altitude were explained in the Middle Ages, and down to our day, as an inroad of conditions from one zone into the territory of another—the Gulf Stream warmed the British Isles because it came from the tropics, the Labrador Current cooled Newfoundland because it came from the Arctic, and so on. New Yorkers still speak of sunstroke waves as coming from the Equator, even on occasions when the press reports few or no deaths south of Washington and the weather bureau shows that Boston is hotter than Richmond (those who think about it at all probably supposing that the heat arrives by some special conveyance through the upper atmosphere). By similar acceptance of theory and lack of reasoning, cold winds are still spoken of as coming from the North Pole.

Serious trouble for the classic theory first developed when

44

travelers returned from the Arctic with their reports. John Davis, whose name you find on the strait west of Greenland, said, for instance, that he had been far within the so-called Frozen Zone "three divers times" (1585-1588) and that he had on occasion found the weather there "as salubrious as ever I did in the Isles of De Verde"—which was certainly amazing, for those islands lie in the region supposed until Prince Henry's time (after 1400 A.D.) to be lifeless "because of the burning."

Both before and after Davis there were, however, conflicting reports from the Arctic explorers, those of the hero kind speaking (with modest reserve) only about the cold, while those of the commercial type, like Davis, dwelt on the surprising heat. On the whole there was reason for the textbook writers to side uncompromisingly with the Greeks (particularly in elementary education, where simplicity is most desirable), so long as any travelers continued to support them.

The balance was more seriously disturbed than ever before when the weather bureaus entered the field, and the U. S. Weather Bureau, for instance, began to report from Fort Yukon, Alaska, which is within the Arctic Circle, temperatures and humidities like those which kill people in New York. After that the classic simplicity of the zone in which it is "always cold" could be maintained only by ignoring the records. This has been done with remarkable success, for the textbooks stating or plainly inferring that it is never warm in the Arctic were in extensive use in American schools for more than twenty years after the Bureau at Washington began to publish at government expense Arctic temperatures

45

ranging up to 100° in the shade. You can verify this by going ten years back in the geographies used by the schools of your own neighborhood—not in every case, but in most.

There are some texts still in use which imply that it is never warm in the Arctic, but many have felt themselves compelled to present the following complicated explanation of Arctic summer temperatures (after stating that the old law does hold for three-quarters of the year): Practically all the heat comes from the sun, some arriving at any given spot directly in the form of light, some transported there by various agencies, such as winds, ocean currents. The amount of heat (light) delivered straight from the sun to a unit of the earth's surface on a summer day depends primarily on how nearly vertical the sun is and for how many hours it shines; but secondarily it depends on other factors, such as clouds or dust in the atmosphere, the color of the surface the light rays strike, and so on. The resulting temperature, as observed either by a thermometer or by the human sensory organs, is further modified by how long a night, during which heat was lost, has preceded the day, and by how much "cold" was stored in that locality by the preceding winter. In some places that are mountainous, such as Greenland, this winter chill has been effectively stored in the form of snow, which not only throws back the light rays without giving them a chance to turn into heat but also neutralizes those that have become heat by using them to lessen its own cold; other places, such as the ocean, have also stored the "cold" effectively, and cancel the heat of the summer with great success. Therefore it is never very hot on mountains in the Arctic, nor on the ocean; and it is probable that if you spent a summer in a

46

tent on an ice floe at the North Pole out-of-doors you would never observe a temperature higher than twenty degrees above freezing (say 50° or 55° F.) measured five feet above the ice. It would of course be much hotter if you put up a windbreak and then let the sun shine on a dark tarpaulin spread on the floe.

But there are in the Arctic, the explanation would continue, thousands of square miles of low land not very near either to mountains or to the sea. Over these it is far colder in winter than at the North Pole (because the air above the Pole is warmed by the heat radiated by the ocean up through the floating ice). Winter winds are therefore frequently warmer when they blow from the north than from some other direction, and in some places the coldest winds are southerly. This extreme cold makes a heavy precipitation impossible, and the average snowfall of the Arctic lowlands for twelve months is therefore less than the average snowfall of Virginia or Scotland. This little snow dissolves quickly in the spring, and after that the sunlight strikes a dark surface, which helps it turn into heat. Nor is there much cold stored anywhere near that can become effective to neutralize the sun. What cold had been stored up by the snow is gone, except as it is held in a little water on or near the surface. What has been taken up by the ground through last winter, and through the centuries, is securely imprisoned there; for the first few inches which thaw near the surface become an insulating blanket that confines the rest of the chill and makes it as powerless to affect the temperature of the air as if it were hundreds of miles away.

On the Arctic prairie that is remote from mountains or

47

the sea, one factor, then, far overshadows all others in determining how hot any given day shall be. This is the quantity of heat received each hour from the sun at that place, multiplied by the number of hours. Now, at the Equator the sun can deliver heat no more than twelve hours out of every twenty-four, giving the tropical prairie an equal length of time in which to cool off. But on the prairie north of the Arctic circle the sun shines the whole twenty-four hours, delivering less heat per hour than at the Equator, but more per day, and without any night in which to cool off. There is, accordingly, a period in summer, varying in length according to where you are in the Arctic, during which the sun delivers to your locality about the same heat per day as at the Equator. *This is the rule,* for it is based on the broadest principles; the places where it does not work out are exceptions, for narrower or special reasons. And it is a fact that there are many places on and near the Equator where the hottest day in a hundred years does not equal the hottest days of the same century at many places in the Arctic that are equally high above sea level.

Few will deny the interest of the preceding facts; but, says the really sensible man, the world is full of interesting things, and we certainly have not room for them all in the textbooks, nor time for them all in the schools. The practical value of this curious Arctic lore is very small to the average man, who stays at home or, at the most, goes to Paris; though it is undeniably highly useful to those few individuals who travel to the Arctic and who want to know in advance what sort of weather to expect, warning them to take fly dope instead of furs if they are going on a Midnight Sun excursion to Fort

48

Yukon. But even for the excursionist, facts are not an un-mixed blessing. If you know about the heat and the mos-quitoes in advance, you will not have the pleasure of dis-covering them; the fly dope may save you from stings, but it also spoils the after-dinner value of the tale about how foolish you were and how badly instructed *before you went north,* which sort of story is the only really satisfactory way of putting your listeners both firmly and pleasantly among the uninstructed where they belong. And even from their point of view, too much advance knowledge is rather a bore, for what is the drawing-room value of that which everybody has learned in school when compared with: "Jones, you know, the Famous Traveler, told me once that when he was in the Yukon, etc."

Facts are tedious, anyhow, and we should think carefully before agreeing that the simple and edifying Greek rule shall go by the board. Consider just a few of the entertaining and instructive things, some of them with no mean character-building value, that would have to go, too.

Item: All the ideas would have to go that are similar to the familiar kindergarten ditty that has been sung by mil-lions of little Americans and which goes something like this (there seems to be no standard version):

> "Frosty little Eskimo,
> In your house of ice and snow."

and so on, till the final line:

> "For in Greenland there is nothing green
> to grow!"

49

We might be able to salvage the house of ice and snow temporarily, though it is a bothersome fact that of something over 14,000 Eskimos in Greenland, by the last census, less than 300 had ever seen a snow house. But the "nothing green to grow" would not last very long under the combined attack of the unromantic geographers, who insist on pointing out weather bureau records, and the historians of Greenland, who will tell you that the country was a republic from 986 A.D. to 1261 (a good deal longer than the United States has yet been a republic) and a dependency of Norway and Denmark thereafter; that they had churches and monasteries administered from European archbishoprics (you may have seen the Greenlandic church ruins in the movies some years ago, as background for the King of Denmark hobnobbing with Eskimos). The historians will point out that a European civilization could not have existed in Greenland during the Middle Ages except for stock raising. The colonists had cattle, with as many as a hundred head in a single barn. They lived in considerable part on milk and milk products, and wove cloth from their own sheep, making garments which you can examine today through photographs in many books or study in the museum collections of Europe. Both cattle and sheep raising are now again practiced in Greenland, and have been for many decades. That means hay, and hay means meadows with that "something green to grow" which is denied by the kindergarten.

Such are the facts, but what of it? If we pressed them upon children while they were at the impressionable age, we would so change their mental picture of Greenland as to rob it of every charm it has so long had for us. What substitute would they find for the delicious thrills and chills that creep up and down our spines as we look with the mind's eye upon a world of permanent white silence and peer into Greenlandic snow houses where Eskimos shiver (doubtless without their teeth chattering, else it would not be so silent) as they devour (again silently) the blubber that enables them to eke out their miserable existence. And then there is the character-building value of thinking what a marvelous thing is the human spirit that continues its fight against the powers of darkness and cold even up there on the frozen edge of the world. On the other hand, too, how fortunate we are who live in a country of warmth and green grass—and schools. Take away, if you must, the good old picture of the North that is always cold; but consider first what it is you are going to give our disillusioned children in its stead. Surely it will have to be something better than cow pastures and a few ruined churches. We already have at home enough of the one and many of the other.

Teaching Through Educational Movies: While our love for children makes us conceal from them anything that may be injurious to their welfare, the same affection leads us to strive for their instruction in whatever we consider beneficial. But in this field we are sometimes misled. I have in mind a special case, parents who were greatly incensed at a movie called *Nanook of the North,* which, although not true to the native life of the Eskimos, had been shown in their children's school and recommended as true. But these parents were wrong, as will appear.

To begin with, the *Nanook* story was at least as true as that of Santa Claus, of which those parents approved. It was the same sort of partial truthfulness, only greater. Real as well as Santa reindeer have horns, four legs, and are driven before sleighs in harness, though not such sleighs, quite, nor in such harness as the ordinary Christmas pictures show. They run on the ground, not through the air; they are very swift, though not quite so speedy as Santa's. There are in the world old men, too, who would like to give a present to every child at Christmas if they could, though there is no old man that actually succeeds in doing it. Thus the Santa story, while fiction in a way, does represent truths.

Similarly with the movie, *Nanook*. There are Eskimos in Hudson Bay where the picture was taken, and the people you see on the screen are Eskimos, which is more realism, right from the start, than you have ever had in a Santa Claus picture. The country you see, too, is the real Hudson Bay. True enough, not even the coldest month up there averages as cold as *Nanook* tells you the whole year averages (35° below zero), but then you must have something exceptional in a movie or it would not impress. You are told, too, that the Hudson Bay Eskimos still hunt with their primitive weapons, and this is justified. For it would spoil the unity of the picture to tell the truth about the weapons, though it is an interesting fact in itself that the forefathers of the Eskimos shown on the screen have had guns for generations, as the Hudson's Bay Company has been trading into the Bay since 1670. Moreover the titles do not actually say that the Bay Eskimos hunt with primitive weapons *only*, so you can take it any way you like. Doubtless the producer meant nothing more than to say that the children (who are certainly Eski-

52

mos) still play at hunting (which would be hunting of a sort) with bows and arrows.

No real Eskimos, in my belief, ever hunted seals through the ice in the manner shown in the picture, nor do I think a seal could be killed by that method unless he were a defective. But it is true that certain Eskimos in other parts of the Arctic (about half of all there are) do know how seals can be killed through ice. That the Hudson Bay Eskimos, with whom our producer had to deal, did not know such methods was no fault of his, and he would have been deficient in resource if he had allowed that to stop him. Neither are there libraries in Hudson Bay where he might have borrowed a book that described the method so he could have studied it up and taught it to the local natives. There he was with an expensive movie expedition, the picture just had to be taken, and audiences in the South would demand to be shown what they had heard of—Eskimos sealing through the ice. And so a method was developed (perhaps by the Eskimos themselves along lines roughly indicated by the director) which photographs beautifully and gives as much feeling of enlightenment to an audience as if it showed the real technique that does secure seals.

I have gone to *Nanook* many times for the purpose of observing the audiences. In several cases some movie fan has noticed that the seal ostensibly speared in the picture is stiff and dead, clearly planted there. But that, it seems to me, is all the realism you could expect in a play. You would not demand that Fairbanks really kill all his adversaries, though you do appreciate seeing a bit of good swordsmanship. And in *Nanook*, what seal but a dead one could possibly be ex-

53

pected to allow himself to be speared in the manner shown?

Another thing I have found *Nanook* audiences complaining about is that they had heard somewhere that Eskimo snow houses are warm and comfortable, while the *Nanook* picture shows the occupants shivering as they strip for going to bed, and there are clouds of steam puffing from their mouths and nostrils. These erudite fans are still more troubled when they see the movie title which says that the Eskimos must always keep their snow house interiors below freezing to prevent them from melting, for they have read a book by someone who has lived in a snow house and who has explained the principles of physics by which, when the weather is cold enough outside (and no weather was ever quite so cold as the *Nanook* country is supposed to be), the snow does not melt though it is comfortably warm inside— say, as warm as the average British or Continental living rooms in winter. But the answer is simple, and the producer is quite justified by it: An Eskimo snow house is too small for inside photography, and the light might not be good enough. So to get the best light and plenty of room for the camera man, half the house was cut away (like the "sets" you see in the movie studios), and the poor Eskimos were disrobing and going to bed out of doors. But it would have spoiled the picture to introduce such technical details. Hence the producer had to explain the shivering people and their visible breathing by the harmless pretence that snow house interiors have to be colder than freezing to prevent the walls and roof from thawing.

And so on for the whole picture.

It was the very fact just stated and others like them which

54

made my friends angry. That may have been because the realities of the picture were not so charitably interpreted to them as we have done above. It is possible to make the same facts look a good deal worse if you try.

But no charity is needed, and only a proper understanding of the case, to reconcile any parent to a movie like *Nanook* and to its presentation in the school. For the Eskimo, properly understood, is really the grown-up's Santa Claus. We love the world of the imagination. Santa, fat, jolly and generous, portrays certain things and qualities as we would like them to be. But in the world of fancy we need contrasts; ugliness as well as beauty, wickedness as well as goodness. For the proper effect, we need not only Heaven, but Hell also. It may be pleasant to think how fortunate you will be if you go to Heaven, but that is nothing compared to the satisfaction you get from a reasonable prospect of being able to keep out of Hell.

What we mean, then, is that the Eskimo is really a sort of reversed Santa; and that since Hell has begun to fade, the Arctic is our best substitute. For somehow grown people, even those who cannot visualize Hell, seem to be able to believe not only that Hudson Bay is in the Arctic but also that the Arctic averages thirty-five degrees below zero, as the picture says the Hudson Bay country does, and that it has all the other distressing attributes.

In fact, the Arctic, peopled by Eskimos, is much more practical for our purposes than any inferno ever was when peopled by tormented spirits. No picture of spirits ever gets us like one of a wretched flesh-and-blood Eskimo who shivers from one year's end to the other. Away up there, crouched

55

in his foul, unventilated house, drinking oil, he has a power to make us remarkably contented with poor lodgings, a careless landlord, and meals at Childs'. In our little backyard with its one wretched tree we think with a pleasant compassion of the stunted little Arctic Mongol who has never seen even a bush. And then, to make his usefulness complete, we remember in summer when we are perishing with the heat that Nature has her compensations! She mercifully sees to it that her chilled children of the snows shall at least escape sunstroke and the after effects of too much Coca-Cola.

And how could you get these and other similar benefits from the Eskimo and the Arctic if you did not encourage such pictures as *Nanook of the North,* and the books that correspond? And what better time than the impressionable years of childhood in which to acquire ideas that are going to have such high consolatory and moral values later?

Perhaps, Gentle Reader, you had arrived at the truth about Truth before you saw this treatise. If so, you will know, or you may have guessed by the trend of this inquiry, that neither side is going to have it all its own way. At first Truth (in the sense of facts) seemed to be getting the worst of it, being so frequently immaterial, inexpedient, even immoral, and nearly always in such bad taste. But the last argument from geography has shown the merits divided, with, generally speaking, the "practical" advantages in favor of the facts, but the idealistic ones against them. We are likely to feel here an immediate concern that in a crass and materialistic age the "practical" side will prevail. Not necessarily, for we may be able to show the higher practicality of idealism.

We will admit now, partly to save the trouble of a formal canvass, that the rest of the argument from the schools will go, on the whole, against us; or, rather, against the conclusions deduced. The fact is, our position is not really at all what it has seemed to be. We keep another, and so far unhinted, solution in reserve.

A Glance over the Other Studies: A critical study of psychological teaching would not go against the preceding conclusions from history, physiology, geography, and the educational movies, but in fact decidedly in their favor, more especially as the newer developments have tended so strongly toward an undesirable, and, in fact, degrading materialism. Psychoanalysis and especially behaviorism come near being a total loss from the point of view of character-building. But chemistry has scarcely any bad aspects unless you happen to be a pacifist, objecting to gunpowder and poison gas. But even so, what is that when measured against soap, a product of chemistry on which rests that perfect cleanliness revered today even beyond godliness? Physics, too, is on the right side, especially those theories of it that are neither so puzzling that the ordinary man can make nothing of them, or else are clear in statement but seemingly lead to impossible conclusions—which can, nevertheless, be experimentally verified. For it is so valuable to be able to lay one's hands somewhere on views that seem either silly or impossible and can nevertheless be proved. Reasoning from them gives such

57

force to analogous religious views which it does not happen to be possible to verify.

Going ahead thus to canvass the rest of the grade school and high school sciences (for we have inadvertently progressed on our argument a little beyond the grades before we knew it) we shall come to the provisional conclusion that about forty per cent of the truths of education are good and should continue to be encouraged, about forty per cent are bad and should be ignored or suppressed, and the remaining twenty per cent are all right in themselves but too complicated and should be reserved for those who continue their education into the universities.

Since our love and care prompt us to make the education of our children their best and most logical preparation for the life which we admire, it is not really necessary for our present examination to go beyond the common and high schools, for they are a sort of abstract or synopsis of the world as we both think it is and want it to be. Still it will do no harm to take another case or two.

In politics, for instance, would you want the whole truth told about every candidate? You can test that out with a few simple reactions. When it was whispered around, for instance, that Harding was partly of negro descent, was it your first inclination to try to discover if the charge were true or not? On the contrary, you almost certainly took no thought of truth or falsehood, but were offended and angered by the bad taste and poor sportsmanship of whoever it was that started the yarn. In the case of Wilson, would you have favored it (even as a Republican) if there had been openly circulated some of the things which (as a Republican) you firmly believed about him? Bad sportsmanship again, and bad taste; you would not have done it and are glad no one did. Even in the case of so innocent a thing as President Theodore Roosevelt's bad eye, said to have resulted from a boyish sparring bout, would you, as a Democrat this time, have favored any campaign use of it whatsoever? Once more, bad sportsmanship, bad taste, an emphatic no.

In the August, 1927, number of *Harper's Magazine* Dr. Joseph Collins, famous as a physician in all literary circles, had an article on *Should Doctors Tell the Truth?* It will not take a reading of that article, nor anything but a backward glance of the mind over our own experiences, to make us agree with him when he says: "The longer I practice medicine the more I am convinced that every physician should cultivate lying as a fine art." Nor do we quarrel with the general conclusion that while a physician should tell the truth in certain cases, lying is usually the kinder, the safer, and therefore the better way.

And what of the every day social relations that are more important than our business or professional contacts to most of us? Consider the one remark: "How well you are looking!" Can you imagine the sort of place this world would be if that little exclamatory sentence, or its equivalent, were not working overtime in every country? I know my own case. Ever since I can remember the declaration: "You are looking better than when I saw you last," has cheered me greatly. It was not till a year or two ago that it first struck me that if this had been uniformly true all these years I ought to be looking remarkably well by now. But even so, I am still able to take a little comfort in this serial fiction.

59

In view of the benevolent nature of the many sample reticences we have considered, all of which and many more like them are sure of a heavy vote in their favor could this nation, or any other civilized country, be polled on the subject—in view of this and much more that could be said in favor, is it not rather strange that most of us have allowed ourselves to fall victims to that cynical outlook on life which considers the deceiver, almost necessarily, wicked? You see how absurd that is, particularly if you think back over the cases of your own deception. As a child you may have deceived your parents occasionally to get out of a licking; but far oftener, I am sure, you did it to save their feelings, so they would not be offended or worried—on the well-known and sound principle that "what you don't know don't hurt you." And, in later life, was it not usually the same? In school you bluffed partly for marks, of course, but very often, almost oftener than you realized, to save the feelings of a kindly teacher who trusted you and would have been so disappointed had he known. In married life, too, you deceive, oftener than not (I am sure the married will agree) to save the feelings of the other party. In fact, the conjugal relation calls for the highest known percentage of benevolent reticence. There are, for instance, certain situations that do not seem to irk the technically aggrieved parties, even when they know about them, so long as they are able to keep up the appearance of not knowing. And what is more, that public which always takes an interest in the marriage relations of other people, does not think it reprehensible for the technically aggrieved party to know about the dereliction and still do nothing, so long as he does not know that the public knows he knows.

60

In fact, next in importance after the systematic deception of children by parents, comes the amiable deception of husband and wife by each other. That is not only in the nature of things, but proper according to the highest standards, since the family is the social unit and the home the strong citadel of our institutions.

CONCLUSION

We have now come to a point where we can survey the whole ground and draw reasonable conclusions from the facts set down. The irresistible main decision is against the rest of the philosophers and against all their philosophy. This is as it should be; for what would be the profit of a new philosophy if it failed to destroy the old? The philosophers may, of course, rise to counter-attack; but what do we reck of that? For we have the public with us, since we have come to a conclusion which justifies what they always have done, what they dearly love doing, and what they are at heart convinced is right—though they did not know it, any more than the perfect athlete knows how he balances when he walks.

The conclusion is, then, that like religion, truth is neither good nor bad. There are good religions and bad religions, good truths and bad.

Generally, though, or at least more often than not, truth is, in practice, bad—especially in the fields of æsthetics, ethics, morals, character-building, and business (which last we have not stopped to argue since it is so self-evident).

We pointed out in the first section of this book the necessary imperfection of all the sciences except mathematics.

61

Since nothing is true there by observation or by any evidence, but merely by agreement, it is obvious that truth in mathematics need never be bad—since we are not obliged to agree on it if we do not like it, and nothing is bad unless it is something we do not like.

Though we have not covered the field exhaustively, we may agree that truth is good, usually, in engineering, chemistry, physics, and the allied sciences. It is good in astronomy and geology whenever it does not conflict with religion. It is good about as often as bad in sociology, psychology, physiology, biology, and several of the related sciences, for in these about half the time it appears to support present-day manners, current morals and the prevalent religion. In history, civics and many such fields it is always open to the gravest suspicion. In the training of very young children as a general thing it should be rather carefully avoided.

THE NECESSARY REFORMS

Having arrived at this conclusion, we must profit by it. At first sight it will seem that, since we have found the truth bad as often as not, the thing to do would be to proclaim our emancipation from its tyranny. But that would be forgetting the more important part of our findings—the benevolent nature and salutary effects of at least a good half of all the deception there is. How could you carry on a Santa Claus campaign, or remain happily married, if you said openly that you were going to deceive whenever you thought it best? It is only in prestidigitation, where "the quickness of the hand deceives the eye," that you can safely tell people that you are going to fool them. In spiritualist seances, in praying for rain, or in forecasting a year without a summer, what effect do you suppose you would produce if you said to everybody that you were doing everything for its mere psychological effect on them?

We can well take our pointer as to what to do from a famous general who has announced publicly that he is going to explain in a book just how he himself and his associates invented and circulated some of the most effective (or outrageous) lies of the Great War. In connection with this announcement he has had two things to explain, and he has made an explanation that is not only satisfactory in his case but admirably suited to broader uses.

Asked how he could, without shame, admit such lies as he proposed to admit, he replied in substance that if you are justified in using shrapnel, poison gas, torpedoes from submarines and bombs from airships, you are justified in using any means at all. The main concern is to make the nation at home and the soldiers in the field a unit for the war, and you cannot do that unless you at least convince them that there is good reason to fight. The more convinced they are the better they will fight, and what propaganda does is to make them more convinced. This argument is so familiar that it deserves no further amplification.

The General's second defense was against the accusation that he had said himself that he expected another war within twenty-five years from the last, and that such a war could not be won without propaganda. How, then, did he justify himself in giving away his country's secrets of just how its citizens were fooled in the last war? His reply was that the

63

remedy would be very simple. All you had to do was to say: "Yes, quite right; we fooled you in the last war. But times have changed and that sort of thing would not work now. Besides, we would not fool you even if it served our ends, we have become so honorable." Having said this, you could go ahead and fool them not only with the old methods but, in some cases, with the very same tale. All you will have to do in the last case is to explain: "The story which we invented in the last war must have given the enemy the idea, for now they are actually doing what we then accused them of."

We may well adapt the General's ideas to a wider field. The leaders of thought among us must continue to proclaim their devotion to Truth, in order that they may be able to get people to believe and act upon those things that are for the general welfare.

The conclusions and recommendations at which we have arrived will receive informal support from most thoughtful and all public-spirited persons. But will that be enough, especially in view of the solid front presented by the old-school philosophers, who still hold that the Good is the same as the True, and that the True is whatever corresponds to facts? It should be enough, for we have an initial advantage in the cogency and popular appeal of our reasoning. By considering the very same facts as the old philosophers, but merely selecting them more judiciously and approaching them from the opposite, or scientific, angle (of reasoning from facts to principles), we have discovered (what has long been instinctively felt) that many facts are bad; and have demonstrated that the Good cannot be synonymous with every

64

kind of fact, for that would make good synonymous with bad, which is nonsense. The Good, we have thus demonstrated, has no necessary relation to facts at all, but is ultimately determined by the sound instincts of the majority.

The ancients, it seems, anticipated our findings in a measure; but that is natural, and strengthens our position, for we are only trying to go back to the first principles of Nature, and they understood Nature better than we, being closer to her and yielding a freer rein to their instincts. They expressed their conclusion in the saying that "The voice of the people is the voice of God." The triumph of the same idea was poetically forecast by Tennyson when he spoke of an epoch in which "The common sense of most shall hold a fretful realm in awe."

Can we secure the triumph which Tennyson foresaw, the need of which we have shown, without a special organization to attain it? Pondering the question, it does not seem that we need any wholly new organization, but rather a federation of those existing agencies that believe in acting on our principle—the principle of the sound common sense of the majority. Consider what we have to start with: The Fundamentalists would take care of religion, the American Legion and the Liberty League would see to patriotism and would safeguard the status quo, the Anti-Saloon League, the W.C.T.U., and similar organizations would look after the prohibition of alcoholics (and other prohibitions, as needed); the Society for the Suppression of Vice, the Watch and Ward Society, and their kind, would protect our literary and other morals. And so on through the list.

Of course it will never do for the benevolent organizations to continue acting separately, each for its own end. They must unite. The Fundamentalists must agree to support the Legion and League on patriotism, and they must return the favor by a united Anti-Darwinism. All of them must get behind the next Clean Books Bill, and so on till every organization to promote the common good has the support of every other.

Such union will be strength, but there will be more power in reserve that may be called on when needed. Suppose, for instance, that the schools are threatened. The toy makers, the printers of fairy tales, and the educational movie people will see to it that Noah and his Ark remain in our religion, Jack and the Beanstalk in our folklore, and the permanently frozen Arctic in our geographies. The politicians will arrange that the histories shall continue to be reticent and the soapmakers will look out that the physiology of the skin does not get too well understood. Back of all such individuals, corporations, or groups, will be the sound morality and the good taste of the community, taking care that mere facts shall not lead us too far astray.

CHAPTER III.

ARE EXPLORERS TO JOIN THE DODO?

THERE ARE FEW WHO WILL NOT ADMIT THAT EXPLORATION IS A Good Thing (we do not here deal with those who question its economic importance, and so on). In this chapter we offer proofs that exploration can remain durable after the last island has been discovered.

With so much recent flying over seas previously unknown, and no land discovered on any of the flights, the commentators are beginning to worry about the end of the romantic Age of Exploration, and the possible extinction of the Columbus family. Are there to be no more explorers, they ask, or, at least, no more Great Explorers?

Waiving the question of whether it matters much if the tribe of Columbuses does perish, we have encouragement, of a sort, in a study of the inside history of exploration, by which we see that nearly all the most famous explorers came into their greatest fame through misunderstanding, or through the planned or accidental fruits of publicity. That is good news for those who want us to have Great Explorers in future. For there is always room for more misunderstandings, and surely the arts of publicity are not on the wane.

67

The Columbuses should, therefore, be able to flourish among us yet awhile. Their last fade-out will come only when mankind ceases to delight in being humbugged.

For those who want new Columbuses hereafter, there is nothing more encouraging than the story of Christopher Columbus himself. If there were any such thing as an abstract greatness in discovery, then surely *the* discoverer of America would not have been Christopher, but the first human being who stepped ashore on the continent, or who first saw it from a distance (I rule out of court the beasts that were ahead of the humans, since the institution of fame has never been developed among them).

This first human discoverer came thousands of years ago, and may have been a Negrito or some sort of Negroid person. He may have resembled a kind of Chinaman, or perhaps he was a good deal like some modern Europeans. (In that case the Nordics would assume, *a priori,* that he must have been a Nordic, or at least an Asiatic proto-Nordic, in whom their coming greatness was already foreshadowed.) One more assumption is that the discovery probably took place across Bering Straits or along the Aleutian chain, though some contend that it may have been from island to island across the South Pacific.

But we are really perverting the meaning of "discoverer" by this talk of Negro or Mongol, for by immemorial practice the use of that word is confined to Europeans. No place is discovered until some European finds it. It might be safer to narrow down still farther the meaning of "discoverer," for there are books claiming that a kind of European (in the sense of coming from Europe) really found North America

68

in very ancient prehistoric times. These would not have been adequate discoverers, for they probably resembled Eskimos, and no one would suggest that a place was discovered when the first Eskimo found it—even if he came from Europe.

We do not arrive at a proper competition in claims of discovery until we begin to discuss whether the Irish found America. They have enough political and other prominence —in fact, they are the next most fashionable whites after the Nordics. Still, merely being Irish is not enough, for what we really mean by a Great Discoverer is a European who was hurrahed while living or at least haloed reasonably soon after he died. The Irish discoverer, if there was one, does not meet these requirements. The Irish themselves never tried to make much of him until recently, when they became ambitious for setting up a rival to Columbus. Greatness does not sit very securely on even the most deserving dead man unless, as said, he develops a cult soon after his real or alleged deeds.

After the Irish, we come to more formidable discoverers, for we know their names and they have the advantage of being Nordic—Gunnbjorn, who first of known Europeans sighted the American island of Greenland, probably around the year 900; Eric the Red, who colonized Greenland following 982; and his son Leif the Lucky, who visited the American mainland in A.D. 1000. There are no scholars and few intelligent laymen who dispute the records of Eric and his son Leif, but still most of them agree that they were not the real discoverers of America, even though the Papacy followed soon and effectively in their footsteps by establishing churches in Greenland about 1050, maintaining them for

69

400 years, and encouraging the knowledge of the Western World to spread throughout Europe by way of the learning that bound together the medieval monasteries.

Christopher Columbus is *the* discoverer of America chiefly because he and what he was supposed to have done got the right advance publicity. Marco Polo and others had reminded Europe afresh of the riches of the East. Desert raiders, fairly well press-agented for those days, were making more dangerous the overland routes which had always been difficult. Prince Henry the Navigator and his group had finally worked out an eastward seaway by rounding South Africa, but the way was stormy and tedious. Everybody wanted an easy and cheap eastward route. For centuries many had been trying and the public interest was constantly getting more and more inflamed.

Then, at the psychological moment, Columbus sailed westward for the East, with all his other publicity advantages strengthened by fashionable royal backing. He struck land, and at first everybody thought he had discovered a short route to the wealth of the Indies. A little later doubts arose, about which people argued violently, and the arguing was quite as good for advertising as the previous harmony of acclaim. Before the legend died that Columbus had found Asia, other legends about gold and jewels and fountains of youth had grown up to take its place. There never was a let-down of publicity until colonies developed, and America became wealthy in her own right.

As a result of the centuries of advertising that thus went before the rise of historical scholarship, it is hopeless now to try to disturb the preeminence of Columbus by publishing the truth about all the discoverers who preceded him. Folk-lore has gathered about him until he is almost as safe in his historical shrine as if he had never existed, like some god or demigod. When a well-known character is securely mythical he has such permanence as our world can give. Hercules is more famous now and his achievements are more widely known than ever they were in the days when a handful of Greeks believed in him. Little Red Riding Hood is better known than Queen Elizabeth, more safely immortal than Mary Baker G. Eddy. If fame depends on any achievement at all, it depends only on publicity achievement.

Greatness in the field of discovery can be acquired today or tomorrow by the same publicity methods that worked for Columbus. That such modern greatness happens to have been secured most often by men who deserved well and worked honestly, is really beside the point. For others who deserved as well and worked as honestly are now forgotten, or else were never known to the public at all.

The most striking case in point is that of Admiral Peary. For integrity, ability, courage, persistence, and many other admirable qualities, he had few equals. He discovered or elucidated several laws of nature that are of permanent value to science, and he widened the horizon of geography. Theories of the wind circulation of the globe, for instance, hinge in considerable part on Peary's work in Greenland. Now that we are flying, and especially when we begin to fly more with dirigibles, to understand the winds has become crucially important. Peary is a world benefactor in helping us to that understanding, but it is reasonably certain that his fame will not thereby be appreciably increased. Geographers are nearly

71

unanimous in holding that his biggest achievement was determining that Greenland is an island. Also, his demonstration that the north end of Greenland, now called Peary Land, is free of snow in summer, and that it supports plant and animal life the year round, was a death blow to the old theory that if lands were only far enough north they would be sure to be covered with ice. But in spite of all these things, Peary's greatness has been made to depend almost solely on his having been first to reach the North Pole. With all his real worth, Peary would not have become an immortal had the North Pole not been a well-advertised place. He rode in on its publicity.

A side issue is that the public will not usually consider a man great unless he has done something which it can visualize. Children play with tops and we have all seen vehicles running on wheels, so we think we know what is meant by the axis of the earth. We translate axis into axle, visualize a top or a wheel, and imagine that we understand about the North Pole. It is one end of the axle on which the earth spins like a top or wheel. Accordingly, we think we can understand and value properly the achievement of the man who first got there.

But what most people knew about the North Pole until recently was an understanding as far from reality as it was clear. By an artificially simplified theory of the nature of the earth, they had arrived at the conclusion that this pole had many remarkable qualities beside being the end of the axle of the earth. It was discussed as if it were the coldest place on earth, the center from which the cold winds were distributed, the hardest place to reach, and the one toward which the magnetic needle pointed. It was supposed to be at least five poles in one—Cold Pole, Wind Pole, Pole of Inaccessibility, Magnetic Pole, and North Pole. We now know that the coldest place is more than a thousand miles from it, the wind center nearly a thousand miles, the hardest point to reach about four hundred miles away, and that the magnetic needle points toward a district in Canada that is much closer to the nearest railway station than it is to the North Pole.

However, during the long time when the North Pole was still supposed to possess the qualities of all the other poles, it became so famous and acquired such a hold on the public imagination that if you were now, by knowledge and argument, to strip away from it one by one all of its supposed attributes of greatness you would not detract appreciably from its fame—just as Pike's Peak remains the most famous mountain in Colorado although more than twenty peaks in that state alone are higher—just as Hercules will always be more famous than any real strong man—just as Columbus will remain the great discoverer of America no matter how many earlier discoverers history may soundly establish.

Peary seems to have agreed with Cicero that to be ambitious for the immortality of your name is among the greatest of human virtues. Furthermore, he wanted the glory for his associates and for the flag of his country. So he went to the North Pole and became immortal. It was not the most difficult of his achievements nor the most important scientifically. But it had the necessary advance publicity, and the proper follow-up.

In fact, the North Pole has a superfluity of popular reputation, enough to make many explorers famous. Byrd will

73

probably become immortal for having been the first to fly there, and Amundsen for having been the first to fly there in a dirigible. No motor vehicle yet devised is likely to travel effectively over the floating ice north of Spitsbergen, but if such is built it is likely to make its driver semi-immortal for having been the first to visit the North Pole by automobile. This Pole is doubtless reachable by submarine, and the first man who goes there that way will become still another fixture in history. And so on for several firsts by new methods.

These will all be international immortalities. National immortalities will fall to the first Frenchman, the first Japanese, the first Siamese.

If you want to find out how much glory a man gets for doing a hard thing that is little advertised, just check up on the credit Amundsen received for flying over the Pole of Inaccessibility. That pole is at least as much harder to reach than the North Pole as the top of Mount Everest is harder than the highest point yet climbed. But, you will discover, the applause of the world for Amundsen's Inaccessibility Pole achievement was only a faint echo of what he received a few hours earlier for the North Pole. Although he was the first man to do the most difficult thing possible on our earth from the point of view of exploration, he got out of it far less than for being the third man to visit an easier place that was better advertised.

True enough, this North Pole flying immortality does not depend entirely upon the publicity of the North Pole. Some of it rests in considerable part on the publicity value of the airplane. Unless it be swimming,* nothing has a better press now. Just imagine the vaudeville salary of the first man to swim to the North Pole!

Close beside the North Pole and the airplane in publicity value is femininity, as used recently, for instance, in the Channel swims. Thus we may one day have immortality for the first woman who goes to the North Pole, then for the first mother of a family, and eventually, when we get a little more advanced, for the first divorcee. And think of the first visit to the North Pole by Siamese Twins! (A later set of them could be the first to marry there, perhaps in an airplane.)

If and when the public gets fed up on the North Pole we could no doubt, by suitable publicity, convince them that the Pole of Inaccessibility is really more interesting because more difficult. Hereupon vast glory will come to the first man to fly there in an airplane, to the first to walk there, the first to motor there, and so on. Then would come the first debutante to go there, the first mother of a family, and so on, with no limit other than that set by the arts of publicity.

A further encouraging thing about geographic discovery is that people are forgetful of details, although they remember generalities.

After more than three hundred years of heralded search, the Northwest Passage has become permanently famous. Then it was discovered by Sir John Franklin in 1846, but nobody knew about that and gold medals were awarded to

* This was written when Gertrude Ederle was being showered with ticker tape. Neither she nor the ticker stood quite so well three years later.

75

Sir Robert McClure for discovering it in 1853. The world resounded with McClure's glory for a while.

The great public had forgotten about even McClure, but still remembered that there had been a search for a passage, when, in 1903, Amundsen sailed west from Norway. Three years later, when the job was done, some newspaper man misunderstood Amundsen's announcement that he had navigated the Northwest Passage and put a story on the wires that he had discovered it. The public hurrahed for the discovery even louder than they had done in the case of McClure half a century before, and most people think even now that Amundsen discovered the Northwest Passage. Why not, if Columbus discovered America?

That it is not the first discovery, but rather the best advertised discovery that counts, was proved to me from my own career. For, in so far as I am known at all, I am generally known as the discoverer of the "Blond" Eskimos. But the first traveler to report a strangely blond people in the Arctic was not I, but Nicholas Tunes 256 years ahead of me—in 1656. This seems to have been in Baffin Island, far from my locality. But in my own district, without attracting much attention, European-like Eskimos had been reported in the following order: by Sir John Franklin in 1824, by Dease and Simpson in 1837, by Captain Charles Klinkenberg in 1906, by Captain William Mogg in 1908, and lastly by me in 1911. The report that created a furore was my second, given out in 1912.

That none of these reports about a European-like people in the Arctic produced an appreciable stir in the world was apparently either because the public did not know of the possible romance behind them, or else failed to make the proper connection. They certainly did know of the romance in 1911, but they failed to see its relation to my report, even though it was published in the London *Times*, a paper that commands much attention. But in 1912 the same report was dressed in newspaper extravagance and joined up by the re- porter with the tragic drama of the colony of 5000 Europeans who disappeared from Greenland in the Middle Ages. There was better reason for connecting the report of Tunes with the lost colony than with mine, and at least a reason equal with mine of 1912, for connecting those of Franklin, Simp- son, Klinkenberg and Mogg, and my own report of 1911, but it simply was not done. The achievement of making the same discovery was presumably a little less each time it was made, yet more glory resulted from the last one than from all the others put together—because the right publicity note was struck

The connection once made with a topic of high publicity value (involving also a misunderstanding similar to the supposition that Amundsen had discovered the Northwest Passage), the "Blond" Eskimo story swept the world and has not yet been forgotten after fifteen years—in fact, shows no signs of fading.*

In view of how often America, the Northwest Passage, and the "Blond" Eskimos were discovered before the hero came along who got the maximum publicity out of each, we have little reason to be depressed, thinking that the glamor of dis- covery is about to fade. When the first man has climbed Mount Everest, the first woman can do it, and then the first

---

* This was written in 1927. The press version of the "Blond" Eskimo story, as opposed to my book version, is still going strong in 1936.

mother of a family; when the first airplane has flown over Everest, there is still room for the first dirigible. You can go to Northwest Australia this year and visit a black family who have never seen a white man; next year you can capitalize the same family by taking a woman to see them, for they will never before have seen a white woman. Then will come the turn of the first mother of a family, who really should take one of her children with her. There would be a tremendous thrill in the cannibalism angle. To make the front pages it would not be necessary to have the baby actually cooked and eaten.

It may seem for the moment absurd that we shall ever be as excited again as we were recently over the North Pole, the Northwest Passage, or the "Blond" Eskimos. But the wisest guessers frequently guess wrong, and especially about news. During the last several years I have read many estimates of the journalists of New York; none of them have failed to put Mr. Carr Van Anda high as a judge of news, and most of them have put him at the very top. Yet, in 1912, Mr. Van Anda said to me that, with the North Pole found and the Cook-Peary controversy settled, the Arctic would never again occupy much space on the front pages of the New York papers. But in 1926 he either himself directed or was present while someone else directed that the entire front page of the New York *Times,* along with several of the inside pages, should be given over to the North Pole, first for the second party to visit it and a few days later for its third visitors.

I doubt if Mr. Van Anda would prophesy as confidently today as he did in 1912 that twenty years from now the North

Pole will occupy little space on the front page. And who knows but the public may forget Amundsen as they did McClure, so that a new discoverer of the Northwest Passage may ride in on a new wave of hurrahs? Some explorer with a good press may be able to get the same result sooner by flying the Passage, or swimming it. A new man may in time get new renown out of my "Blond" Eskimos as I did out of Franklin's. The "Tunnit" remains of Labrador were discovered for perhaps the tenth time in 1926, and the tenth discovery (if it wasn't the twentieth) won more glory than any preceding it. Judging from past records, those "Tunnit ruins" could be found again with even greater *kudos* about 1946. And so on for many thrilling discoveries.

It is, then, the best of discovery methods to find a thing over again after just enough years so that the public has nearly, but not quite, forgotten. Next best, as a perpetual device, is to search again and again for a thing never found. The interest created is not so intense as in the case of a repeated discovery, but there is the compensating advantage that you can search perhaps three or four times more often—you get passable results say once every five years for the repeated search method; effective rediscoveries need at least twenty-year gaps.

One of the best examples of perpetual search and resulting publicity is the quest for an Arctic continent.

Through various theorizing it had been pretty well established a century back that a great land mass spread across the northern polar sea. It was the Arctic Continent or Polar Continent. The corner towards Europe and America had been found and was called Greenland. The corner towards

79

Asia had been seen by natives looking north from northeastern Siberia but had as yet no well recognized name.

Just for walking to the North Pole it seemed best to climb upon the continent at the Greenland corner. But sailing might be easier, and there was known to be a lot of water north of Alaska. So it appeared logical to sail up through Bering Straits, coast along the east side of the land seen by the Chukchis. This would presumably take you into a deep bay. When you got to the head of it you would just anchor your ship in some harbor and walk the rest of the way to the Pole.

Meantime the land seen by the Chukchis had also been seen by the British—by Kellett in the ship *Herald,* so that an island was named after the ship and a greater land seen to the northwest after the captain. A modicum of fame resulted from this discovery.

The first attempt to pick up the east coast of Kellett Land and sail north into the polar bay was by the American De Long in 1879-81. Instead of sailing much, however, he was caught among eddying floes that with the autumn frost solidified around his ship and carried him drifting to the northwest across a corner of the theoretical continent, amputating Kellett Land—the piece now called Wrangel Island. The expedition made notable discoveries and was successful in adding to our knowledge as well as to the record of well-conducted adventures, but it ended in personal tragedy for De Long and a third of his men. Some of the interest which the world gave De Long was through the bearing of his work on the discovery of the Arctic Continent.

A series of notable attempts to walk over Greenland to

the North Pole was made by Admiral Peary. The result was one of the greatest geographic achievements of the last hundred years, the determination that Greenland does not run to the Pole, but is an island. De Long had made a small amputation; Peary now made a large one. The Arctic Continent had contributed materially to his fame.

The work of many expeditions to the north of central and western Asia, notably the voyage of Nansen, cut farther into the theoretical continent and the chance became small it could contain the North Pole. In 1909 Peary marched from Ellesmere Island to the Pole, the whole distance over floating ice, and took a sounding at the Pole showing the water two miles deep. No shore of the dwindling continent was therefore likely to be very near the Pole. Peary thought, however, that he had seen land to the northwest of the north tip of Heiberg Island, which might, of course, be a foreland on the continent. This was named Crocker Land.

So the two greatest explorers of their time, Nansen and Peary, had profited materially in popular acclaim and in more enduring reputation through the bearing of their work on the Arctic land mass concept.

The interest in the elusive polar land had grown enough by 1905 that an Englishman, Harrison, organized an expedition the chief purpose of which was to search for the continent to the north of Alaska. He might have done something, for he was a good man himself and had with him one of the finest northern travelers, Hubert Darrell, whose quality can be measured from Hanbury's book, *Sport and Travel in the Northland of Canada,* London and New York, 1904, one of the great travel stories, an account of an expedition shared

81

in by Darrell. But there was now a whaling fleet at Herschel Island. Whalers and Eskimos alike were sure that anyone was crazy who tried to travel afoot over the sea ice to the northwest, and, strangely, were apparently able to convince Darrell. Harrison stuck to his ideas but could get no one to go with him. Therefore, his book, *In Search of a Polar Continent,* London, 1908, has in a way a deceptive title—the search was never started. But it had a good name. The Polar Continent, through being much sought after and never found, had become a thing to conjure with.

There was a receptive popular audience when there appeared in Washington a scientific study by R. A. Harris which, in the opinion of the author and of many others, came near proving that there was a continent. The land's dimensions and the situation of its corners were pretty well determined by deductions from what he thought to be reliable tidal observations taken at a few northerly points.

Between wish thinking and mathematics the continent grew substantial and for the first time had a name, Harris Land. The other names had been for just corners—Greenland, Kellett, Crocker; this was a name for the whole land, now shrunken but still spoken of as a continent. In size it still more or less deserved the name.

Our 1913-18 expedition had somewhat better luck than Harrison's. The whalers and Eskimos were not able to talk us into believing that we could not travel over the sea ice far from land and live by hunting. Between sledge journeys and the drift of one of our ships (the *Karluk,* Captain Robert A. Bartlett master), we made further inroads upon the continent. More serious, we took soundings of 1386 meters without bottom near some of the farthest points we reached. However, to the northwest of the Ringnes Islands where, on one occasion, we were forced to turn back less than 100 miles from shore the soundings were only around 500 meters, and there seemed possibility of land.

Between driving Harris Land from some of its outposts north of Alaska and finding what might be signs of it northwest of the Ringnes Islands—between these achievements our expedition got a whole lot of *kudos* out of the Arctic Continent.

A year after we started our work in the sea north of Alaska, Donald MacMillan attacked the problem and sought the theoretical continent under the name of Crocker Land. He started out from Cape Thomas Hubbard, Heiberg Island, whence it had been seen and tentatively located by Peary. MacMillan returned without seeing land but there was no assurance that it might not be hidden a little way beyond, for the expedition had taken no deep soundings near its farthest. It was, therefore, possible to speculate after the return that perhaps the farthest point might have been over very shallow water, the land therefore possibly only a bit farther on, concealed by clouds.

So between our shallow soundings, MacMillan's absence of them, and Peary's report that land had been seen, there was an interest growing keener with the number of searchers and the publicity of each.

The interest remained keen and there was much talk of the undiscovered continent when Amundsen, Ellsworth and Nobile flew in 1926 from Spitsbergen to Point Barrow by way of the North Pole. They saw no land and would have divided the theoretical continent into approximate halves but for the saving report that for portions of the journey between Peary's farthest (the North Pole) and Alaska the weather had been so thick that they had not been able to see what lay beneath. This, said the commentators, still left a chance that they crossed fairly wide stretches of low snow-covered land. The continent still lived.

In 1927 Wilkins and Eielson flew 550 miles northwest from Point Barrow and took at their farthest point the deepest sounding ever recorded in the polar sea, 5440 meters. The flight itself removed land possibilities through a wide space. The sounding was a cause of further discouragement to the geographers, but the public didn't mind. So far as they were concerned the Continent was merely elusive, rather clever at hiding itself.

In 1928 Wilkins and Eielson crossed from Point Barrow to Spitsbergen. They went some 200 or 300 miles out of their way to avoid the North Pole, for three assigned reasons—they wanted to avoid the sections which had been visited by previous explorers; they did not want to be suspected of a play to that gallery which was still interested in the North Pole; and they wanted to cross the area within which, for reasons we have just given in dealing with the Peary, Stefansson and MacMillan expeditions, there seemed the best chance of finding land. The newspaper files show there was a great deal of speculation as to whether they might find the Arctic Continent. There was also talk of checking up on the observations of Dr. Cook who had reported one or more lands to the west of the course he described himself as having followed back from the North Pole in 1908.

Wilkins took a course which was for a time approximately halfway between the areas explored by our 1913-18 expedition and those seen by Amundsen. Then he swung toward skirting the district explored by MacMillan, and so on to Spitsbergen, without seeing land. However, he was forced to admit that for portions of the flight they, like Amundsen, had been unable to see what lay beneath. The speculators said there still remained the possibility of the Arctic Continent. There was talk that somebody really must go and settle the question of the Continent.

Between what is reasonably inferred from the soundings and from the visual report of travelers there is, however, small chance now for an undiscovered land in the Arctic bigger than Cuba. Islands from that size down are possible, though not probable. But the interest in what is now beginning to be called the lost continent still continues. There will probably be plenty of talk about it next time anybody flies. Anticipating discussions have already speculated on the chance that the next flyer may discover "a lost continent the size of Cuba."

As we admitted in the beginning, there have been in the search for the continent no such storms of excitement as there were from at least two of the discoveries of the Northwest Passage, after McClure's report (third or fourth discovery) * in 1854, and Amundsen's (fourth or fifth) in 1906.

* It can be argued that the first European discovery of the Northwest Passage was by Thomas Simpson (with whom Peter Warren Dease was associated) in 1839. If this be not admitted, then the claim falls to John Rae who worked both before and after the Third Franklin Expedition, on which the Passage was also discovered. Thus the McClure discovery in 1853 was either the third or fourth.

85

But on the whole the theoretical continent has given a pretty consistent performance for a hundred years.

I have myself been in parties, of three in one case and of four in another, that discovered large islands, rich with vegetation, birds and animals, which had never been seen before by human eyes, press agented or otherwise exploited. We were thrilled, of course. It was one of the great experiences of our lives. But to judge by outward appearances, there are friends of mine who have been even more thrilled by "discovering" hamlets in Brittany that were "absolutely unknown to Americans." And I think they really had at least an equal right with us to the thrill, for I imagine that discovering polar countries never seen by human eyes is today easier than the discovery of a Brittany village previously never seen by Americans.

Adventure, in the last analysis, is measured by the thrill it gives to the discoverer, and later to those who hear about it. You can predispose the world to any desired thrill by suitable advance publicity. A deliberate campaign would be too long and expensive, so you should choose for discovery something well advertised already, as, for instance, the word and idea "ray." We have long had the rays of the sun, and they have been very popular. Then there are the X-rays, radium rays, and many others, until the world is now ready to be thrilled by anything that is called a ray. It is also important to have a good adjective for the ray you are going to promote. "Cosmic ray" is the best to date—see what it has done for Millikan. If you can find a name a little better than

86

cosmic, people will go daffy over the discovery of your ray. (Death rays are perennially successful.)

Thus we arrive at a heartening conclusion: the tribe of Great Discoverers will not become extinct until the Age of Advertising has passed.

CHAPTER IV.

TRAVELERS' TALES

o

WHAT WE NOW CALL A FISH STORY THE ELIZABETHANS SPOKE
of as a traveler's tale. I shall discuss whether there are many
fish stories among the travelers' tales of today, whether they
have an important effect on the sciences which gather their
data in part from the reports of explorers, and whether we
ought to do anything about it. These questions are more
important in our time than in Elizabeth's, for the explorers
were mere travelers then. Now they all claim to be scientists
or at least to be the leaders of scientific expeditions.

I address you both as an expert and as Exhibit A. For my
own expeditions have been insistently, if not so very effectively, publicized as scientific; and I am one of the travelers
who, by my own contention and the claims of my friends
and backers, should be taken as a scientific explorer.

I begin, then, by discussing the extent to which my own
books and other protestations are to be taken seriously.

In a way this exposition is the direct result of a talk which
I gave in 1907-8 before the Century Association of New
York City. It is my necessary introduction to repeat in con-

densed form what I said there and to tell you what the Centurions thought about it.

So far as I remember, I began by explaining to the Century Association that I was an exceptionally reliable witness, and particularly so with regard to the Arctic. My father and mother had both been born on the north coast of Iceland on the very edge of the polar circle, and that furnished me with a useful background. I myself had been born in Manitoba where winter temperatures run down to 55° F. below zero, which is about as low as they get on the north coast of Canada—as a matter of fact lower than any official record, for the lowest of these to date is —52°. I had read the northern literature from infancy and had always been so soaked in it that my first published article labeled scientific (apart from a brief linguistic study) was "The Icelandic Colony in Greenland," *American Anthropologist,* April-June, 1906. In North Dakota I had seen blizzards as bad as any I had experienced on my first Arctic expedition, which I was then describing to the Century, and the prairies of my childhood Dakota, when snow-covered in winter or green in summer, were much like the Eskimo prairies of northern Canada, so that I had been quite at home in the Arctic from the first, gathering information more reliable than if I had been a nervous visitor who was frightened by conditions different from those of his childhood—as might easily be the case with, say, a Frenchman.

Such preliminaries being disposed of, I launched into what I still believe was to the Century Association a convincing first-hand picture of how things are with the Eskimos of the Mackenzie River.

I told how I was taken into an Eskimo home where 22 people and myself lived in one room through the middle of the winter and where my life with the people was intimate throughout the year. I enjoyed being there and they apparently enjoyed having me with them. I entered both into their routine and into the spirit of their beliefs, so that they began to discuss things with me or in my presence quite as freely as if no stranger had been near. In fact, no stranger was near—I had become as one of them.

On the basis of this I regaled the Century with many amusing and allegedly important contributions to the ethnology of the Mackenzie Eskimos. I shall here review only one topic.

One of the Eskimos, Memoranna, wore an eagle feather on the left shoulder of his reindeer-skin coat. I asked him once why he did this and he said there were two reasons:

In Memoranna's childhood the people of his native village had been more numerous than now; and, besides, there were many visitors. Athletic games were common and the people took off their coats perhaps when wrestling or running foot races, throwing them in a pile. Every coat was of deerskin and most of them had the same trimmings, but they were not all of the same size or workmanship and some were newer than others. It was, then, important that when the games were over each man should be able to find his own coat. "Therefore we each had a mark on our coats. One man would have a weasel tail in the middle of his back, another perhaps a strip of wolf skin on his sleeve. I had an eagle feather on my left shoulder."

The second reason for these marks was that when everyone was dressed alike and when there were hundreds together you could not recognize a man unless you saw his face. But with the eagle feather on the shoulder of the coat anybody could tell that the wearer was Memoranna.

The chief reason why I repeat all this is that at the end of my talk Dr. Franklin H. Giddings, Professor of the History of Civilization at Columbia University, a foremost figure in American sociology, came to me. He had been making a study of property marks, he had been much interested in this particular contribution of mine, and he was satisfied of its accuracy not only because of my careful methods of observation and my intimate life with the people but also because it fitted in with his studies of the origin and development of property marks among primitive people.

This address of mine before the Century was based on a year with the Eskimos of the Mackenzie River. I returned north in six months and spent four years more, making five all together. In the last of those years I finally acquired such a control over the language that I could speak with the people almost as freely as they spoke with each other. Then at last I learned that the eagle feather was a talisman, with no intentional property mark connection.

Some weeks after I learned this I met Memoranna and asked him why he had deceived me four years ago. He replied in substance that he had been almost brought up as a cabin boy on whaling ships and had besides associated with missionaries, so that he knew the white man's point of view. If an Eskimo told his real beliefs, a sailor would call him a damn fool and a missionary would explain how wrong and wicked they were. Through long experience he

91

had learned the kind of explanation a white man likes; giving that kind saved a lot of trouble. He had not meant specially to deceive me; he was merely treating me as just one more white man.

There are within the social sciences few more broadminded or with a keener sense of humor than Professor Giddings. Still, it is my impression that he felt just a little bit more enlightened and pleased when he heard the original incorrect property mark explanation of the eagle feather, which agreed with his own theories, than he did when later I told him the final and as I still believe correct explanation —which did not fit into his sociology quite so neatly.

If this property mark tale were an isolated case it would not be worth repeating, but it is typical of my work. The impressions and conclusions of my first year in the Arctic were, I now think, mostly wrong. Luckily for me I did not publish a book at the end of the first expedition but placed the diaries of it in storage with the American Museum of Natural History of New York City. They remained there during my second expedition of four years and while I wrote my first published book, called *My Life With the Eskimo,* 1913. They remained there also during my third expedition of five years and while I wrote my second book, called *The Friendly Arctic,* 1921.

It was only in 1922 that I got out the diaries of the first expedition and studied them as the basis of my third book, *Hunters of the Great North.* In the introduction to that volume, I said: "As I look over my diaries I shudder to think how vastly I might have augmented the already great misknowledge of the Arctic had I published everything I

92

imagined I had seen and everything I thought I knew."
You may think this autobiographical preface strange. But
I shall presently be dealing with names far more eminent
and respected than my own, even with those holding membership in this oldest of the great scientific societies of America, and I need myself as the thin entering wedge for a general discussion.

The introductory remarks closed, I turn to what I intend
as a criticism of the social sciences in so far as they depend
for their data on the findings of explorers.

If I were giving a course of lectures, and had at my dis-
posal ten evenings instead of one, I should like to consider
under three heads the misinformation contained in the
books and reports of travelers. The first would be intentional
misrepresentation, the deliberate drawing of the long bow;
the second would be that unintentional misrepresentation
which results from careless observation or from misplaced
confidence in witnesses; the third would be that subdivision
where the traveler states as a fact which he has observed a
thing which he cannot possibly have observed but in which
he believes because it conforms to, or is part of, a belief which
he holds and has never questioned.

Since I have only one evening, too short for me although
it may be too long for you, I shall not merely confine myself
to the third heading but shall discuss only a few typical cases
under it. What I said awhile ago, then, about property marks
does not belong to our subject and has its use merely as part
of the introductory approach.

We turn, then, first to a large body of false testimony
which is nevertheless a small subdivision of the last third of

our subject, and consider some of the things that have been testified to about animal and plant life in that small but typical sample of our world, the Far North.

The foundation of European belief about the distribution of life over the earth was laid by the Pythagorean Greeks, if not by someone else from whom the Pythagoreans borrowed the idea. Essentially it was that terrestrial life depends on heat from the sun. This heat, when it is of a degree called warmth, permits life in a belt called the temperate zone. To the south of the temperate zone there was, according to orthodox Greek belief, a burning region where the rocks were red-hot and the oceans boiling. North of the temperate zone was a region frozen solid. One of the ancient authorities has it that in the North life is as impossible because of the freezing as it is in the South because of the burning.

It is not a part of my northern specialty to review what is so well-known to historians, that from the Greek learned period before Christ to the age of Prince Henry the Navigator, and therefore through almost 2000 years, it was nearly or quite the unanimous opinion of the learned world that no human beings would ever cross the lifeless, burning and boiling tropics. It is more within my field as an Arctic explorer to point out that the accepted Greek belief was at one time that because of the cold no living thing could exist north of Scotland. Then the Irish discovered Iceland, 600 miles north of Scotland, and the Icelanders, or someone else, discovered Spitsbergen, another 600 miles still farther north.

The average January temperature of Reykjavik is about the same as that of January for Milan in Italy or Philadelphia in Pennsylvania, and the tourist companies which contract with their passengers to show them pack ice are forced, some years, to carry them 200 miles beyond Spitsbergen to keep their promise. But at every advance of knowledge, which in this case has been the northward advance of travel, it has been discovered with profound surprise that life was there ahead of the traveler. The interpretative scientists have been driven to every expedient of logic to explain the contradiction between what they believed and what they saw. This effort, in turn, has been the foundation of much false testimony by those of them who were explorers.

Take the case of perhaps the most solidly famous and respected of the British polar explorers, Sir Edward Parry. He landed on Melville Island the summer of 1819 and found musk oxen grazing there. This was startling, but had to be accepted. Presently he went into winter quarters, practically hibernating with his men for several months. When they emerged in the spring they saw musk oxen. Hereupon Lieutenant Sabine, himself later a distinguished explorer in his own right but acting for the time as naturalist in the publication of the scientific results of Parry's voyage, wrote as follows:

"They (the musk oxen) arrived in Melville Island in the middle of May, crossing the ice from the southward, and quitted it on their return towards the end of September." *

This was accepted by the entire learned world because it fitted in with two of their preconceptions—that Parry and Sabine were reliable witnesses, and that the Far North was

* Appendix X, Natural History, (p clxxxix), *Journal of a Voyage for the Discovery of a North-West Passage, 1819-20*, by William Edward Parry, London, 1821.

95

by nature hostile to animal life. It had been believed earlier that no animals could exist, at any season, as far north as Melville Island. Now, when they had been found to be there in summer, the scientists executed a strategic retreat by saying: "The beasts make a summer foray deep into the Arctic, but they flee from the winters to the hospitable shelter of the temperate zone." The theory of the complete absence of grazing animals from this part of the Arctic was thus replaced by an elaborate theory of seasonal migration.

For a quarter century after Parry's first voyage there seems to have been practically if not complete unanimity among the explorers and the stay-at-home scientists alike that the musk oxen, in spite of short legs, made each year a 1200-mile round trip between the winter shelter of the forest on the North American continent and the summer stamping grounds in Melville Island.

Lieutenant Sherard Osborn, who both shared in and wrote books about the Franklin Search, appears to have been the most thoughtful of those officers. Yet in 1856 he published *The Discovery of the North-West Passage* . . . and assumed in it that the grazing animals of the islands north of Canada migrate south to the mainland in the Autumn to return each Spring. But in 1857 he published a second edition with a new Chapter, XVII, on "The Migration of Animals Theory." For the views there expressed he says he has been "nearly excommunicated as a heretic." In this chapter he points out the manifest theoretical absurdity of the postulated migrations and cites a little testimony he had been able to get which tended to show that there was no migration.

Thirty years later Greely was sure that the musk oxen of

the Arctic islands do not migrate south * and most observers are now agreed that they do not move from one Arctic island to another at any time in any direction. Yet there are still in use in the English-speaking countries, among others, textbooks of recent copyright which retain the Parry statement and the Parry explanation—that the musk oxen migrate and that they do it because they need the shelter of the forest against the severe climate of the northern winters.

When the scientists were finally converted to believing that the musk oxen do live in the remote Arctic permanently, they and the travelers cast about for some more explanations —the philosophical scientists are continually busy trying to reconcile new knowledge with ancient theory. They now hit upon something clever. People had believed, they explained, that grazing animals could not exist without grass, and that was why they had thought there would be no such animals in the Arctic. They were right in part; there was no grass. What they could not have foreseen was that in the Arctic the place of the flowering plants is taken by mosses and lichens. The musk oxen live on mosses and lichens!

The musk ox still lives on mosses and lichens in the usual reference works; he is mounted with his mouth stuffed with them in the usual museums. This is in part because many explorers have supported the philosophizing scientists by testifying that lichens are verily the food of the musk ox.

But many explorers have denied this flatly. Greely said†
". . . in no case did I ever note the musk-ox feeding on the latter vegetation (lichens), although in many places near

---

* *Three Years of Arctic Service*, by Adolphus W. Greely, New York, 1886, p. 221.
† Op. cit., p. 105.

Conger the ground was covered with scanty, minute lichens for acres in extent." Roderick MacFarlane says* that musk oxen live mainly if not wholly on flowering plants, and I have said the same.†

But the traditional belief is still being advanced by explorers as testimony and as observed fact. For instance, a statement implying that musk oxen do live on mosses and lichens was issued within the year by the Northwest Territories and Yukon Branch of the Department of the Interior of Canada, for they published a photograph of musk oxen with an accompanying letterpress which said that they were here shown grazing on mosses and lichens. I wrote at once to a friend, O. S. Finnie, who is official head of this department although not personally responsible for the picture and description. I asked him how did they know that these animals were feeding on lichens and whether their botanists could not (by examining the original photograph and perhaps enlarging it) determine what plants were really visible along with the animals. Finnie then submitted the photograph to A. E. Porsild, the distinguished Danish-Canadian botanist and specialist in Arctic flora, whose verdict came in a letter of February 27, 1930:

"There is a firm and rather hard turf composed chiefly of grasses and sedges with a slight admixture of flowering plants. Most predominant is the Alpine Foxtail grass (*alopecurus alpinus*) which probably has a higher food value than any other Arctic grass. With the foxtail grow a few sedges (*Carex*). In the

* Charles Mair and Roderick MacFarlane: *Through the Mackenzie Basin,* Toronto, 1908, p. 175.
† Vilhjalmur Stefansson: *The Friendly Arctic,* New York, 1921, p. 584.

98

foreground to the right are flowers of the Alpine Chickweed (*Cerastium alpinum*). A few twigs of a decumbent willow (*Salix*) show in the center of the photo."

Not only these recent Canadian Government observers but also many scores of normally honest travelers have, then, testified, because of a solidly founded belief, that musk oxen live exclusively or mainly on a food which in fact they rarely eat—and then probably not by choice.

One of the most interesting of the systematic fabrications about the polar regions is within the observational domain of the exact sciences, although its effects are noticed chiefly in the social sciences. This is the statement that at a certain place a certain observer has noted that the midnight sun was visible for a given number of days in summer and that correspondingly the noonday sun was invisible at the same place for the same number of days in winter. All statements ever made to this effect are false. They could not be true anywhere in the world unless at least one important fact were changed and some laws of nature altered or abolished. The fact needing change is that the sun would have to be contracted down to a pinpoint; the laws needing change are those governing refraction.

A medieval writer, Jordanes, says: *

"In its northern part (of Norway) live the people Adogit, who, it is said, in the middle of the summer have continuous light for forty days and nights, and likewise at the time of the winter solstice do not see the light for the same number of days and nights."

* Fridtjof Nansen: *In Northern Mists*, London, 1911, Vol. I, p. 131.

On this Nansen comments * to the effect that there can never have been any such place. For, says he, if the sun was visible at midnight 40 days in summer then it never disappeared at all in winter. Or if it was invisible 40 days in winter then it was visible 63 days in summer.

Nansen conjectures for the writers of this immediate group, the commentators on northern Norway, that they had heard for a given place that the sun was invisible for a certain number of days in winter and had then added a gloss (in conformity with Greek theory) to the effect that the midnight sun was visible for the same length of time in summer. Nansen seems to believe, then, that had the writers themselves been residents of northern Norway, or had they spent a year well beyond the Arctic Circle, they could not have written as they did. In this judgment Nansen is not at his best as a student of human nature. Nor does he show thorough familiarity with the writings of his contemporaries, for there are on record a number of them who without question have seen with the eyes of the body that the periods of the sun's invisibility and visibility are unequal, but whose mental eyes have been holden so that they thought they had observed the periods to be equal.

We could go into a long catalogue of instances but shall actually use but a single example which, although typical in a sense, is striking for three reasons among others: that the witness is a Russian and therefore a member of a northern people who ought to understand northern conditions, that his general scientific work is looked upon by his colleagues as good, and that he has undoubtedly spent long

* Nansen: Vol. I, p. 133.

periods within the Arctic Circle. The quotation we are about to give was published on pp. 581-2 of the *American Anthropologist,* for October-December, 1929. The author is Waldemar G. Bogoras, who says:

"The north polar circle forms the southern border of the area which has in midsummer the continuous day and in midwinter the continuous night. And so, for instance, on 68-70 degrees of north latitude, we have in the polar zone three or four weeks of continuous night in winter and as many weeks of continuous sunshine in summer."

Unaware of the laws of refraction and forgetful of what they knew concerning the brightness of the twilight before sunrise and after sunset, Europeans throughout the Middle Ages and down to our time have assumed generally that darkness comes in the Arctic when the sun dips below the horizon. This belief is popularly translated into saying: "In the Arctic there are six months of daylight and six months of darkness." That most people hold this belief is shown by the frequency with which the idea appears in school texts, in serious newspapers, and in the humorous journals. The average reader supposes the humor to rest upon some basis of fact when an Eskimo wife who sits up to await her husband's homecoming starts scolding and he replies: "Why, my dear, it is only half past October." The father of a baby with the colic walks the floor with it through the night and is then referred to as being on a six months' tramp. A funny paper tells that Macpherson operates his business from San Francisco during the summer and from Point Barrow during the winter. You want to know why he goes north in winter and are told he conducts his business a good deal by telegraph and uses the Barrow office six months to get the benefit of night rates.

That great universities and leaders in science are still teaching the view on which the humorists base their quips, was brought in upon me through a talk I gave at the Explorers Club in New York. There I cited one traveler after another who had reported from various places within the Arctic Circle, some of them far north, that they had observed the sun to be fully visible in summer and wholly invisible in winter for equal periods. These men, I contended, had reported what neither they nor anyone else can ever have seen.

A few days later a troubled voice called me on the telephone for an appoinment with regard to a situation àt Columbia University. On arrival he proved to be a student in a course on meteorology. He had heard my talk and had reported to his instructor my saying that there was no spot on earth where the days of the sun's complete visibility and invisibility could be equal in number. The instructor had not been impressed, and had pointed out that the author of a book they were using in the class, Robert DeCourcy Ward, Professor of Climatology in Harvard University, likely knew what he was talking about when in defining the zones he said:

"In the polar zones, the sun is below the horizon for twenty-four hours at least once in winter, and is above the horizon for the same length of time at least once in summer."

I had Ward's *Climate: Considered Especially in Relation to Man* in its 1908 edition. Sure enough, on p. 20 were the lines cited by the Columbia instructor. I procured a "Second Edition, Revised" which says in a note dated August 1917:

"I have taken the opportunity offered by the publication of a second edition of this volume to make some revision of the chapters on 'The Characteristics of the Polar Zones' . . ."

In that edition I found, unchanged, the statement we have quoted.

Professor Ward had, then, taken special thought of his chapter on the polar zones and had nevertheless repeated himself verbatim. No wonder the Columbia instructor was also firm.

Some textbooks, with a pretense to meticulous accuracy that makes them more effectively deceptive than others, will contain such statements as: "Among the Eskimos there is continuous darkness for three months." There are, of course, no Eskimo settlements that have continuous darkness for even three days, or one day.

The textbook writers are in a vicious circle. Embryo explorers learn from school texts about the continuous Arctic winter darkness; they come back some years later from an Arctic expedition with testimony of having observed the said darkness, and this testimony becomes in turn the basis of new incorrect textbooks. A case is Elisha Kane, the most famous of American polar explorers before Peary. He reported having wintered at a place where there was no trace of daylight in a clear sky at the winter solstice. For comment on this it suffices to quote Captain George E. Tyson, who says: "Have passed Rensselaer Harbor, where Dr. Kane wintered during 1853-55. I am surprised that in the latitude of Rensselaer Harbor (N. Lat. 78⅔°) he should have found the darkness so intense as he describes it. It was not totally dark with us at high meridian at any time in clear weather...." *

In Heft 1/2, 1930, of the international scientific journal *Arktis,* Dr. Wilh. Meinardus of Göttingen, has published a diagram of the distribution of daylight and darkness within the polar regions throughout the year which shows not only that Kane (as Tyson implies) must have had a lot of daylight at noon on the shortest day of the year but also that no polar explorer except members of one Nansen and one Peary expedition have ever been so far north (or south) in midwinter that they could say accurately that there was no trace of daylight in a clear southern sky at the solstice. Yet there are dozens of explorers who have said so in books or reports which have been believed. Many of these were as respectable and respected as Nansen or Peary. They were not liars; rather they were observers and reporters who had been hypnotized by a belief.

It may be said in the defense of these travelers that when they said "no daylight" they meant "only a little daylight." But would we similarly excuse a chemist after an autopsy if he said "no trace of arsenic" and really meant "only a little arsenic"? Explorers are putting themselves forward as scientists. If we are to take them seriously and at their own evaluation, we should require of them the standards not only

* Tyson's winter latitude, to which he here refers, was 81⅔° N. For our quotation see Tyson's *Arctic Experiences,* New York, 1874, p. 195.

of truthfulness but also of precision that we require of chemists or astronomers.

It follows naturally from what we have said above how ridiculous it is to suppose, as many school textbooks still assert or imply, that you have "six months of daylight and six months of darkness at the North Pole." If you mean by daylight what Captain Tyson means in criticizing Dr. Kane, then we have at the North Pole more nearly four months of darkness (from October 6 to February 5) and eight months of daylight (from February 6 to October 5). If, on the other hand, you mean ability to read ordinary print throughout a clear day out-of-doors, then the division must be something like 5 months of darkness and 7 months of daylight.

A further corollary is equally plain. It is that we are being misled when it is constantly being stated or implied that there is less daylight per year in the polar regions than in the tropics or temperate zone. You can perhaps defend that old view if you say that by daylight you mean the quantity of sunlight delivered per unit of earth's surface per year, but that is not really at all what we mean when we say daylight. For instance, you will hardly say that daylight is lacking when there is so much of it that you have to wear colored glasses to protect your eyes and must be careful to sleep in dark places so as not to go snow-blind while in bed. Judged by ability to read print out-of-doors, there is more daylight at an average Arctic station per year than there is in the temperate zone or in the tropics. (We are not here entering into niceties of how dark it is in Arctic mountain canyons or how light on snow-clad tropical peaks.)

There was a time when it was commonly believed in

105

Europe (by those who did not identify travelers' tales with fish stories) that the people of a certain remote land had ears so conveniently large that in sleeping they used one for a mattress and the other for a quilt. This we now consider a strictly medieval belief. But it is thoroughly modern to believe that Eskimo women carry babies in the hoods of their coats. We shall cite you eminent men, many of whom are living, who have asserted that they themselves have seen Eskimo women carry babies in their hoods, but first, departing from the main chronological order of our discussion, we give the testimony of the man indisputably the best authority on this subject.

Knud Rasmussen was born in Greenland of a Danish father and a mother who was part Eskimo. He was brought up by the Eskimo women somewhat as our Southern babies are by their Negro mammies. He was raised bilingual, his two mother tongues Danish and Eskimo. He associated with Danes in the house and played with Eskimo children out of doors. In due course he was taken to Copenhagen where he went through that university and other training which has made him both a well-equipped scholar and a cosmopolitan gentleman.

Quite apart from his childhood, which is in this connection the most significant period, Rasmussen has spent more time in the countries inhabited by Eskimos than any other man who is ordinarily classified as an explorer. He is the only one of us explorers who has visited every Arctic Eskimo territory and practically every Arctic Eskimo people from the east coast of Greenland to the west coast of Alaska and to the East Cape district of Siberia. He is primarily an anthropologist and geographer. For his sound work in these fields, and especially for his interpretation of the Eskimos to the learned world, he has been awarded gold medals by nearly every important geographical society in Europe and in the United States.

On the basis of the studies for which Rasmussen has really deserved these medals, he says about the belief that Eskimo women carry babies in their hoods: "The women in Greenland have never in the past carried their children in their hoods, nor do they do so now. . . . the child is decidedly not (carried) in the hood, as that would simply choke the mother." (Letter to Vilhjalmur Stefansson, 3rd May, 1930.)

Now we turn to the history of the belief. The early travelers through Eskimo lands described from most if not all districts a custom whereby women's coats were made especially roomy in the back so that a baby could be slipped up under the coat and supported by a belt. The child was then held by the coat and belt against the small of the woman's back. Usually in removing the child the mother would undo the belt and let the baby slide down, but the neck of the coat was naturally made roomy to enable the child to breathe and sometimes the mother would reach in that way and pull it up and out. It is not impossible, but was at least geographically rare, that mothers inserted the baby into the coat from above. But whatever the method of ingress or egress, the baby, according to early northern books, was always carried inside the body of the coat, never inside the hood.

Since there are now living men who hold distinguished

professorships in great universities and others of equal rank who say that they themselves have seen babies carried in hoods, I am planning one day to write almost a book on this subject, citing, so far as my researches allow, practically every traveler who has said anything about how Eskimo babies are carried. Here I give only a few typical cases, generally men who are not only entitled to respect but who have received it from the learned world.

Taking them chronologically, the first writers examined are the following:

Hans Egede: *A Description of Greenland,* first published in 1757 (pp. 132 and 148 in the London, 1818, edition).
David Crantz: *The History of Greenland,* London, 1767. Vol. I, pp. 138 and 162.
Hans Egede Saabye: *Greenland . . . in the Years 1770 and 1778,* London, 1818, pp. 13 and 259.
Vol. XIX of the *Continuation of the General History of Voyages,* Paris, 1770, in which there is a "History of Greenland" by an anonymous author.

All of this early Greenland evidence agrees with Rasmussen—the manner in which the child is carried and the coat in which it is carried are described in almost the same terms as he uses.

But there existed a stream of contradictory testimony. Henry Ellis published his *Voyage to Hudson's Bay* at London in 1748. There you find on p. 136:

"The Difference between the Dress of the Men and the Women is, that the Women have a Train to their Jackets, that reaches down to their Heels. Their Hoods are also larger and wider at the Shoulders, for the sake of carrying their Children in them more conveniently on their Backs."

On pp. 495 and 496 of Sir Edward Parry's *Journal of a Second Voyage*, London, 1824, the hood-carrying is weightily reinforced.

Between Parry's time and about 1855 I have found the following references:

BABIES CARRIED IN HOODS:

G. F. Lyon: *The Private Journal*, London, 1824, p. 315.
John Franklin: *Narrative of a Second Expedition in the Years 1825, 1826, 1827*, London, 1828, p. 118.
John Rae: *Narrative of an Expedition to the Shores of the Arctic Sea in 1846 and 1847*, London, 1850, p. 39.
John Richardson: *Arctic Searching Expedition*, London, 1851, Vol. I, pp. 252 and 369; also *The Polar Regions*, Edinburgh, 1861, p. 306.
Berthold Seemann: *Narrative of the Voyage of the H.M.S. Herald during the Years 1845-51*, London, 1853, Vol. II, p. 53.

BABIES NOT CARRIED IN HOODS (BUT CARRIED INSIDE COATS):

Captain W. A. Graah, *Narrative of an Expedition to the East Coast of Greenland*, London, 1837, p. 118.
Thomas Simpson: *Narrative of the Discoveries on the North Coast of America*, London, 1843.
Joseph Bellot: *Memoirs of Lieutenant Joseph René Bellot*, London, 1855, Vol. I, p. 186.

Around 1850 there was living in Greenland a man who knew the Greenland Eskimos at least as well as even Rasmussen does now. This was Samuel Kleinschmidt, born of

109

missionary parents and brought up there until he had learned Eskimo as one of his mother tongues. He was then educated in Germany and went back to Greenland to spend the rest of his life, much of which he devoted to the preparation of an Eskimo-German grammar and an Eskimo-Danish dictionary.

In some Eskimo dialects *amaut, amaun,* or some variant of that word is the name of an enlargement for child accommodation in the back of a woman's coat, or it may be the name for an entire coat which contains this enlargement. In many districts the nursing mother wears a coat of no special design but one simply large enough so the child is well accommodated. The name of the coat is still *amaun.* This is, then, a word referring to the purpose for which the coat is used, not to its design. *Amaun* is never used as the name for a hood, of a woman's coat or of any other garment.

In *Den Gronlandske Ordbog,* Copenhagen, 1871, p. 24, Kleinschmidt defines the verbal form *amarpok,* "carries a child on her back in a roomy coat designed for that purpose"; and the noun form *amaut,* "such a coat for carrying the baby." Thus we see that while most of the travelers had by this time been converted to the Ellis-Parry hood carrying and were testifying that they had themselves observed it, Kleinschmidt, working as a missionary and scholar in his native Greenland, had either never heard about the belief that children are carried in hoods or else considered it so absurd as not to be worth noticing in his dictionary.

In 1927 Schultz-Lorentzen published a dictionary which in many respects is an improvement on Kleinschmidt's. At that stage, as we shall show in a moment, the books were favoring by a substantial majority the Ellis-Parry view, at least if you merely count noses among the testifiers. Greenland books, among others, were favoring it and on p. 16 of the Schultz-Lorentzen dictionary we find: *amaut,* "fur jacket with hood for carrying child."

But this is really an ambiguous definition. If you think already that babies are carried in hoods, you will read that meaning into Schultz-Lorentzen's words; but if you think that babies are not thus carried, you will understand him to mean that the coat is for carrying the baby and that this coat also has a hood. It is therefore fair to him to cite some of his allied definitions: *amaq,* "child carried in fur jacket with hood"; *amarpa,* "takes him on his back; carries him on his back"; *amarpoq,* "carries a child in fur jacket with hood."

From about 1855 down to about 1888 the evidence of explorers who had traveled among Eskimos is divided as follows:

BABIES CARRIED IN HOODS:

Charles Francis Hall, 1865.
Isaac I. Hayes, 1867.
Dr. Henry Rink, 1877.

AMBIGUOUS:

A. W. Greely, 1886.

BABIES CARRIED INSIDE COATS:

No testimony during this period.

Now we come to what makes our discussion really worth while. It is that one of those who report Eskimo babies carried in hoods is Franz Boas, Professor of Anthropology in

111

Columbia University and President of the American Association for the Advancement of Science.

Boas is, if not the most eminent living anthropologist, which he very well may be, at least the most distinguished of those who are also Arctic explorers and who have made some specialty of Eskimo studies (we classify Rasmussen here as a traveler or geographer rather than as an anthropologist). Moreover, the Smithsonian Institution, through which Boas published a book on the Eskimos on Baffin Island and neighboring districts, is in one sense at least our foremost scientific body. It is then significant that on p. 556 of the *6th Annual Report, Bureau of Ethnology,* 1884-85, in the Section, *The Central Eskimo,* by Boas, we have:

"The women's jacket . . . has a wide and large hood reaching down almost to the middle of the body. . . . If the child is carried in the hood, a leather girdle fastened with a buckle is tied around the waist and serves to prevent the child from slipping down. . . ."

Boas spent a winter with the Eskimos at Baffin Island and undoubtedly had hundreds of opportunities of seeing how the women carried their babies. He was there for the purpose of studying just such things and there is no doubting his sincere desire to record and interpret rightly everything he saw.

But Boas had in a considerable part of his Eskimo work the collaboration of a man who testifies directly against him, a man, too, of keen observation, shrewd judgment, and much longer experience among Eskimos. This is Cap-

tain George Comer, who lives at East Haddam, Conn., co-
author with Boas of *The Eskimo of Baffin Land and Hudson Bay,* Bulletin of the American Museum of Natural
History, Vol. XV, 1901. On the subject of the belief that
Eskimo women carry babies in their hoods, Captain Comer
says:

". . . (The statement that) Eskimo women carry their babies
in the hood of their garment is perfectly absurd. . . . Once when
I spoke of the child being carried in the hood it made the women
laugh." (Letter to Vilhjalmur Stefansson, May 22, 1930.)

This discussion has been based on the easiest reading of
Boas, which is that he means to say the Eskimo babies
are carried in the hoods of the women's coats. However,
the part about the leather girdle serving "to prevent the
child from slipping down" may be taken to show what
Boas really meant was that the child is carried not in the
hood, but inside the coat as described by Rasmussen. For an
examination of Baffin Island women's coats in museums, or
an examination of the pictures from Boas and others which
give the women's coats of Baffin Island, will show that if a
child (or anything else) is in the hood, then there is no
chance of its sliding down along the woman's back whether
or not she wears a girdle.

Continuing our studies, we have made the following
classification of the reports on the Eskimo manner of carrying babies by travelers later than Boas.

BABIES CARRIED IN HOODS:

Lucien M. Turner (Bureau of Ethnology), 1894.
David Hanbury, 1904.
E. W. Hawkes (Canadian Dept. of Mines), 1916.
Donald MacMillan, 1918.

BABIES CARRIED INSIDE COATS:

Alfred H. Harrison, 1908.
John W. Kelly (U. S. Bureau of Education), 1890.
Fridtjof Nansen, 1893.

AMBIGUOUS:

Ejnar Mikkelsen—expedition 1906-08 (book undated).
John Murdoch (Bureau of Ethnology)—reports them carried in coat for those Eskimos he visited but says that among the eastern Eskimos (whom he had not visited) the baby is carried in the hood—1892.
Josephine Peary—describes method of carrying, showing that child is really carried in coat; but she calls it the hood—1893.
Henry Rink—same as above, description correct for carrying in coat but speaks of it as hood—1877.

You may think that in spite of the distinction of some of the advocates, the carrying of babies in hoods has by now been relegated generally to the domain of folklore and that this discussion has therefore grown academic. But until within the last twelve months several of the foremost up-to-the-minute authorities have in reality been influenced to believe that the baby hood-carrying is a fact.

For with Rasmussen and Boas in knowledge of the Eskimo we might well group Diamond Jenness, Chief Anthropologist of the Canadian Government at Ottawa, who, as anthropologist on the staff of the expedition which I commanded from 1913-18, spent three years in studying the Eskimos from western Alaska eastward along the north Canadian coast as far as Coronation Gulf. Since then, through his continued studies and official position, he has been in close touch with anthropologists and with the development of Eskimo research. On March 29, 1930, he wrote me in substance that, although he was convinced those early travelers who had testified that babies were carried in hoods in the districts which he had himself later investigated were mistaken, nevertheless he was willing to believe other travelers who said that in certain districts which he had not visited the babies were so carried. It was only when Rasmussen and Comer testified about those very districts in which Jenness still credited the hood-carrying that he realized the belief had a folklore nature outside his own territories as well as within them.

There is plenty of evidently correct testimony that Eskimo women do carry certain things in their hoods. Among things frequently mentioned are cigarettes (in recent times), needle cases, dolls or other playthings for their babies, and small stolen articles. Why is it not, then, reasonable that they might carry babies similarly?

The reply is that the admittedly hood-carried articles are light. A baby is so heavy even at birth that (as Rasmussen points out) it would choke, or at least seriously incommode, the mother if its weight reposed in the hood. (Babies are carried on women's backs until they are three or four years old, making the weight increase considerably each year.)

115

The second paragraph in rebuttal will be that most testimony represents the babies in the hoods as usually naked, at least while very young. If you study the construction of the hoods on women's coats in any of our museums, you will find not only that a weight in them would press against the mother's throat with choking action, but also that they are so open at the top that a naked baby would necessarily suffer a great deal from cold, at least in winter, even if it were not frozen to death.

It may be suggested that when Boas, for instance, speaks of a hood he is actually referring to the enlargement farther down in the coat which makes it commodious, as described by many travelers and easily seen in museums.

The reply is that this might not be a bad defense argument for Greenland, where the women frequently have coats without hoods, but that Boas is dealing with Baffin Island and other neighboring districts where the women's coats, at least usually, have hoods. Since Boas does not describe the coat he has in mind as having two hoods, we are inclined to feel that by hood he means what the rest of us do.

Then it may be advanced that there are motion pictures and other photographs in existence which show Eskimo babies actually in the hoods of women's coats. This would serve as good argument, if not full proof, were it not that we know the circumstances under which those photographs were taken, which are that to oblige the photographers, or for pay, the women consented to place the babies in the hoods for the time of as much photographing as the explorer needed to show graphically on his return what he believes to be the custom of a primitive people.

116

In other words, we are driven to the conclusion that the many travelers who have said they have seen Eskimo babies carried, as a matter of widespread custom, in the hoods of women's coats, have all testified to having seen things they did not see. The merited eminence of some of these unreliable witnesses comforts the rest of us who, led by faith, have said or implied in print that we have seen certain objectively non-existent things. For it is not only misery but error that loves company. People like Dr. Franz Boas and Sir Edward Parry are very good company indeed.

The importance of the babies-in-hoods case is in that it shows strikingly the danger to which the social sciences are exposed when they include the testimony of explorers among their data.

There are bound to be many in every scientific audience who feel that the misrepresentations and misstatements of their own science are as serious as any that will fall within the domain of the geographers and anthropologists. They may be right, which, if they are, makes the case more interesting. What we cite are then not exceptions but fair samples of the body of knowledge.

I have, in reality, never met any specialist who thought that fully half of what is now being taught in the schools about his subject was contrary to fact or definitely misleading; but that proportion fits my opinion with regard to my specialty and I shall use the last few minutes of my time in dwelling upon it.

The first reason for there being abroad fewer "untrue facts" about the Temperate than the other zones is that ours is a temperate zone civilization and that to our fore-

117

fathers (and, to an extent, ourselves) the two regions of unrestrained imagination were the tropics and the Arctic. Five hundred years ago the percentage of misinformation was no doubt approximately the same with regard to the zones north and south of the North Temperate, but of late books and ideas about the tropics have become relatively correct. For the crossing of the tropics has been a commonplace these 400 years, while the crossing of the Arctic was not accomplished until within our own time and is not yet a commonplace, though it soon will be.

The tropic myths have been dispelled by the frequent journeys of investigators and by the necessities of commercial development. The Arctic myths have not been dispelled by these or any other causes, or at least not to the same extent. Moreover, the human mind appears to crave some district where the fancy may roam. Our favorite character of the imagination is Santa Claus and we are perhaps right in feeling subconsciously that it is fitting and necessary for him to reside in an imaginary world. Moreover, our present attitude towards explorers makes them the grown-ups' equivalent of childhood's Santa Claus. The explorers, then, need an imaginary world for a satisfying background.

I might confess here that to the extent that I am successful in talks such as this, I feel as if I were stealing candy from a child when I make it increasingly difficult for the rest of the world to swallow the good old hokum about the Arctic. Fortunately, I have never been very successful.

But it is equally fortunate that I am not very serious about Truth—fortunate at least for me. I am no Jeremiah declaiming against iniquity. I like to contrast my benevolence with

the misanthropy of the satirists, and I go on now to point
out the amusing but effective ways which the scientific organizations, some of them nearly as lofty and respected as
the American Philosophical Society, have discovered for
keeping Santa Claus in his Arctic so that all may be well
with the imaginary world.

One of the branches of our government is the Geological
Survey and another branch is the Signal Corps. Lieutenant
P. H. Ray, of the United States Army, discovered on the
Signal Corps expedition to Point Barrow (1881-2) that
"willows" 20 feet in height grow a little way inland
from Barrow, more than 200 miles north of the Arctic Circle.
But it is out of character to picture such large vegetation
in the Arctic, and so the Geological Survey now comes to
the rescue by issuing through the journal *Science,* the official
organ of the American Association for the Advancement
of Science, and through *Science Service,* a statement that
in the great triangle north of the Endicott Mountains in
Alaska (an area larger than that of the great Commonwealth
of Pennsylvania) there is no tree-like growth bigger than a
lead pencil.

Before any of us were born the Hudson's Bay Company
had a trading post called La Pierre's House, on the Bell
branch of the Porcupine River, and at Fort Yukon, where
the Porcupine enters the Yukon. Ever since then missionaries, traders, and white men and women of nearly every
condition and description, have been traveling up and down
that river or residing upon it. Now the United States Bureau
of Education, among its other contributions to the Santa
Claus background, tells that one of its agents will go north-

ward and associate on this river with Indians who are un-touched by the white man's civilization. The implication is that some of them will never have seen a white man until the Bureau representative gets there. Really he will find there Athapaska Indians speaking English with a Scotch accent, their inheritance from the Orkneyman "servants" of the Company.

We have been listing a few of the notable contributions from scientific departments of the American Government to our knowledge of the Arctic. There are naturally similar contributions from the governments of other countries. We close our remarks on this subdivision of our topic with a note on the Antarctic which appeared in *Science* on February 27, 1925:

"The Minister of the Colonies, by a decree dated December 30, has created a large game sanctuary in France's Antarctic possessions . . . the principal animals protected are polar bears, walrus, sea lions and penguins. The French naval station in Madagascar will be responsible for the patrol of the new pre-serve."

In this French decree we seem to have the first published reference to walrus south of the equator. The polar bear cita-tion is even more remarkable, for up to this time there had been discovered in the Antarctic no land mammal, small or big.

The walrus in southern waters has apparently not been reported again since the French government's original note; but the polar bears, once introduced (and protected by gun-boats in Madagascar only a few thousand miles away) have been doing well in our Antarctic mental world. True, they appear as yet with comparative rarity in print; but they appear frequently in pictures—not in photographs, of course, but in drawings. A sample contribution was a cartoon of the *New York World,* spring 1930. Formerly in such drawings, penguins by themselves had symbolized the Antarctic; now they were joined by the polar bear. Father Knickerbocker was shown standing at the New York waterfront to welcome Byrd home from his southern adventures. The boat conveying the hero toward shore was rowed by a crew of polar bears and steered by penguins.

These same late years that have been so propitious to the Antarctic have seen a reciprocal enrichment of the Arctic. As there had been no bears in the South so had there been no penguins in the North. Or, rather, there had been a sort of penguin, the Great Auk, which became extinct a century ago. It would manifestly add charm to have penguins, and so they have been appearing more and more frequently in references to the North. As with bears in the South, they are most frequent in drawings. There is, however, a growing demand for photographs of them. It happens to me, for instance, with increasing frequency that lecture committees bargaining for talks on the Arctic request that I shall use movies, or at least stills, showing penguins.

I get friendly advice, too, after my talks—what I said was interesting and they didn't realize before they saw my pictures that there are flowers in the Arctic. But why did I not also show the penguins?—they are so solemn, so funny and so human.

Next after the official Government agencies in the Santa Claus propaganda, with regard to Arctic and Antarctic, may be ranked our great universities. Few of them are greater (and I remind you again I am not trying to be satirical) than the University of Chicago. In the spring of 1928 that university informed us through what appears to be an official press release that a graduate student of theirs, Cornelius Osgood, was going to live on Great Bear Lake. They said:

"If he is successful, young Osgood, . . . will be the first white man ever to live in the Great Bear Lake region. Two missionaries who tried it in 1912 were slain by the natives. Armed only with rifles, cameras, note-books, recording phonograph disks and a sleeping bag to withstand the 79 degrees below zero weather, Osgood will seek to win the confidence of the natives, living their lives, helping in their work and eating their food. . . . The only other white men who have penetrated the district are Steffanson, the Arctic explorer, and his companion D'arcy Arden, a famous figure of the North, and a Northwest Mounted Policeman who captured the murderers of the missionaries."

The stodgy fact is, of course, that John Franklin wintered at Fort Franklin on Great Bear Lake a hundred years ago, that the Hudson's Bay Company operated on the lake thereafter, that Richardson and Rae, three quarters of a century ago, built their Fort Confidence on Great Bear Lake, and that white men too numerous for easy cataloguing have been there off and on ever since. I was so overborne by this knowledge that when I was there in 1910-11 I lacked the courage, or something, to claim I was the first white man ever to winter.

The bit "Steffanson . . . and his companion D'arcy Arden"

122

will be news to him, as it is to me. We never met at or near Great Bear Lake. I believe he began his long residence in that district a year or so after I left there. The lake is big, however, and the country is big—he may have been to the west somewhere in 1910 without my knowing it.

It is perhaps heaping Pelion on Ossa to prove further the thesis of this paper, that even scientists will constantly and solemnly report, as having been observed, things for which there is no foundation but an inherited belief. I might have resisted the temptation except that a beautiful example has just fallen into my hands.

In Canada, Dr. F. G. Banting, Professor of Medical Research, Toronto University, Nobel Prize winner, is the country's foremost scientist in that more people know his name than that of any other Canadian scientist now living. The Canadian Government has deservedly recognized his position by what the papers say is a lifetime stipend. There is in Canada now an organization called the Canadian Geographical Society, a purpose of which is the increase and diffusion of knowledge of Canada. I shall list for you a few of Dr. Banting's observations on a summer trip North, as chronicled in Volume I, No. 1 (May 1930), of the official organ of the Society, the *Canadian Geographical Journal*:

1. "The thickness of the pans (of sea ice) varied from twenty to forty feet, depending on whether they were one-year-old or two-year-old ice."

Many Northern explorers, prominent among them Nansen, have studied the time required for the thickening of sea ice. Their reports are of the order that the first winter's

123

freezing is from seven to nine feet, that of the second winter adding one to three feet, the third perhaps less than a foot.

2. "On the surface of the older pans were pools of fresh blue water, while on the year-old pans the pools were of salt water."

"Pans" several years old and those a year old will both have on them pools of water fresh to the taste in summer, if the spray has not reached them. It is ice much younger, only a few weeks or months old, that has salty pools.

3. "Varieties of saxifrage, fireweed and stunted willow spring up beneath the snow and ice."

Probably what Banting means is that during the winter they had been under snow, as plants are in Minnesota. Some of the spring processes may conceivably quicken a little while the snow is still above the plants, but, if so, how could Banting learn this on a summer trip? Since he distinguishes between ice and snow, what can he mean by their springing up beneath the ice? What ice other than snow would there be?

4. He lauds Franklin and his men who, on Franklin's last expedition, "in tiny sailing vessels, ventured through these perilous waters."

Franklin's *Erebus* was 370 tons and his *Terror* was 340 tons, large to date for ships which have gone in among the islands that are north of Canada. Amundsen's *Gjoa,* by which he navigated the Northwest Passage, was 47 tons. The largest of the six ships of my own third expedition was the *Karluk,* 247 tons; the smallest, the *North Star,* about 30 tons.

5. "In protected spots the flowering mosses of various colors . . . reminded us of a summer day at home."

Either Banting here made some startling discoveries or he was a bit confused as to the nature of mosses. Not a few works of reference divide plants into flowering and non-flowering, putting the mosses on the non-flowering side of the fence.

6. "During these blizzards the land animals huddle together with their backs to the storm and allow the snow to drift ' around them."

Banting must have been thinking of cows and horses down Ontario way. The ordinary report of hunters and naturalists is that both caribou and musk oxen feed into the wind and are more likely than otherwise to travel into it.

7. ". . . thunder is so rarely heard that the natives are frightened by it."

I know people in New York who are frightened by thunder, and have seen the like farther south.

8. "The married women wear larger hoods which are used for carrying the baby."

125

We have earlier in this paper dealt with the question of whether babies are ever carried in hoods.

9. ". . . the Eskimos live in igloos made from blocks of hard snow."

We consider this under two heads:

(a) If Banting means that an Eskimo calls his dwelling an igloo, then he is of course right; the Eskimo word *iglu* means dwelling. A lot of people in a lot of countries live in dwellings.

(b) If by igloo Banting means a snow house, then he should not have said "the Eskimos." Certainly there are Eskimos who live in snow houses in winter; but it is equally certain that the number of Eskimos who have never lived in a snow house is larger than that of those who have lived in them. This statement goes not only for the 20th century but, so far as we believe, for the 19th, 18th, and 17th centuries at the least. In fact, there are good reasons to consider that the snow house was geographically more widespread in 1900 than it was in 1600.

10. ". . . the native has *no* natural immunity."

The only necessary comment is to say that the italization in this quotation is ours.

11. "In a country where there is no sunshine for three months of the year the people are dependent on their food for their vitamins . . ."

126

The inference seems to be that if there were more sun-shine these remarkable people would not have to depend on food for any of their vitamins. The recipient of one Nobel Prize for endocrine studies may then well be candidate for another in comparative racial physiology and in deficiency diseases.

12. "Perhaps the most important introductions (from whites to the Eskimos) are the darning needle, which has been the greatest help to the women in making the clothes and boots, and matches for igniting their lamps."

The testimony of many travelers has been that Eskimos felt it a hardship to sew with copper or bone needles which almost necessarily were too large for their purpose. Ac-cordingly, the needles which the Eskimos most valued when the whites arrived were those that were smaller than darning needles. No. 1 needles are much smaller than darning size but are, nevertheless, about the largest that I have found the Eskimos of my territories to value at all appreciably. No. 3 was a rather large needle for most of the seamstresses whom I have known, who did most of their sewing with size 5 or smaller. So far as my experience goes, it has been a standing marvel with white women, and with white men used to sew-ing, that the western Eskimos sew with such small needles. I do not recall ever seeing one use a darning needle for any-thing but darning or sewing heavy cloths, like tenting.

As to the preciousness of matches to the Eskimos: I have reported that the Stone Age people of Coronation Gulf, with whom we spent the summer 1910, often got their camp fires lighted with blocks of iron pyrites quicker than we did ours with matches. On days of strong wind pyrites has particular advantages, so that it seemed to me the Eskimos needed matches less, and appreciated them less, than they did many of our other contributions to their way of life.

The issue is not so clear with the matches as with the needles. It is ludicrous to claim that darning needles supplied a keenly felt want. Whether the matches did is in the field of legitimate dispute.

To guard against misunderstanding I close this discussion of the Banting paper by reminding you, and insisting upon it, that I am on the whole one of his great admirers. It appears to me that his career and character are both of a high order. That is my point. We get from eminent and deservedly respected men substantial contributions of misinformation useful in maintaining the general unreality (or shall we say poetic quality, imaginative charm?) of our world outlook.

Before introducing the next example of how the great stand with us shoulder-to-shoulder in the battle to keep the world unreal, we mention that the North Pole of reality lies in a deep ocean and is removed some 400 miles from the nearest land. During a hundred years there have been numerous explorers studying this ocean. No one has during this century, or at any other time, seen an iceberg within 300 miles of the North Pole; few have been seen within 600 miles. We know, too, the conditions under which icebergs are formed. So it appears both from well-established theory and from uniform observation that there are not and cannot well be icebergs anywhere near the North Pole.

Now we come to a statement that could not be introduced to you more impressively than by a simple recital of facts. The publication is the September 20, 1928, number of *Science*. The original author of the statement is Sir James H. Jeans, who, according to *Who's Who,* is M.A., D.Sc. from Oxford, LL.D. from Aberdeen, F.R.S. and secretary of the Royal Society. He is quoted with implied approval by Robert A. Millikan, who, according to *Who's Who in America,* is A.B., A.M., Ph.D. from Columbia, studied at Berlin and Göttingen, is D.Sc. from Oberlin, Northwestern, University of Pennsylvania, Columbia, Amherst, Dublin and Yale, and LL.D. from California, as well as holder of the Nobel Prize,

And this is what Millikan says, quoting Jeans: "Our position is that of polar bears on an iceberg that has broken loose from its ice pack surrounding the pole."

Millikan and Jeans consider, then, that icebergs come from the vicinity of the pole. But if you could take a census of icebergs as we take a census of the human population of the United States, you would find more of them in the temperate zone than in the Arctic; if you could determine the population center of icebergs as we determine the population center of the United States, you would find this center is nearer the British Isles, where Sir James lives, than to the North Pole. Or, speaking astronomically, since Jeans is an astronomer, it would be as correct to imply that Saturn is the center of our solar system as it is to imply that the North Pole is the center of icebergs.

Jeans tells us in a recent work on *Cosmogony* that light, which goes eight times around our earth in a second, requires 140,000,000 years to reach us from the farthest celestial

129

object that our telescopes now show. With his intellect and with that marvelous tool of the intellect, mathematics, he probes these depths. The while he probes the vulgar on-looker speculates as to how accurate Jeans may be about those distant reaches when he is so far from being accurate about things that are, comparatively speaking, within a stone's throw of his house.

It may be said that many people have heard of icebergs who have never heard of sea ice, and that Millikan and Jeans were perhaps just catering to their audience in using the better-known word. For it is a common view that scientists, addressing the laity, have an obligation to translate their rigorous phrasing into the looser forms of common speech. But when Millikan referred to the iceberg as "broken loose from its ice pack surrounding the pole," he was, according to *Science,* giving not a popular talk but an "Address before the Society of Chemical Industry, New York, September 4, 1928, on the occasion of the conferring on Dr. Robert A. Millikan of the Messel Medal in honor of his work on the structure and relations of atoms." We are too polite to believe it was necessary to talk down to that audience.

Jeans and Millikan were no doubt really thinking of floe ice when they said iceberg. Their precision of speech would then be like my referring to Halley's planet or calling the moon a nebula. An iceberg differs as much from sea ice as a comet does from a planet.

The iceberg is formed on land; floe ice at sea. The iceberg begins as snow and gradually acquires the semblance of common ice through time, pressure, etc., while sea ice forms directly from liquid water. The iceberg has been fresh since

130

it started; the floe ice began salty and, if fresh now, has attained that state through a long process. The ice destined to be a berg gradually approaches the sea; the floe ice was on the sea from the start. These are but a few of the differences.

It is possible, however, that Jeans and Millikan were not confusing an iceberg with any form of sea ice. For it appears to be the view of the average scientist who is not a geographer that the northern polar sea is just filled full of icebergs. For instance, practically everybody whom I ever heard objecting to the use of submarines in the northern polar basin will say that you are bound to collide with icebergs even if you can navigate deep enough so that there is no chance of colliding with sea ice.

It may be said, finally, that since Jeans is an astronomer, and Millikan a physicist, you can't expect them to know much about the earth. But why not? I find in several of Jeans' books which I own, and have even read, that he talks a lot about the earth in general. He analogizes from earth to moon and to various other bodies. And Millikan should know something of land, sea and air, for he and his agents scale mountains and go aloft in aircraft to study his later rays, sometimes crossing oceans to do so. Meteorology and geography should be to him, then, not wholly alien professionally.

The fact is, of course, that this whole reasoning is beside the mark. Jeans and Millikan, leaders in science, are simply acting, too, as leaders in that great effort where we all collaborate, the struggle to keep the world unreal.

Or, declining to close with a negative statement, we affirm

131

that all the way through from my telling the Eskimo method of property identification to Millikan's telling of icebergs breaking loose from an ice pack surrounding the pole— through that whole gamut we multitudinous scientists are champions of a higher knowledge which I have advocated in *The Standardization of Error,* knowledge derived from facts-by-definition.

There is a perhaps subconscious awareness that lands near home are getting dull through excessive familiarity and it may be this feeling which prompts many who are not scientists to join them towards keeping the ends of the earth from becoming too ordinary. There are many examples in recent polar exploration and we take a few.

The New York newspapers carried one day a statement that Byrd had flown over the North Pole and that the temperature of the air had been 10° F. above zero. Now that is a commonplace temperature, without fascination; for every state north of the Mason and Dixon Line has had it, as well as a good many states farther south. This cheapening of the North Pole needed counteracting. Accordingly, there was an editorial the next day to the effect that in properly evaluating Byrd's achievement we must remember that the flight was performed in cold so intense as to be unimaginable to New Yorkers.

The reports from most of the winter flights in the Arctic or Antarctic have been that the planes flew in warmer air than on the ground. There have been instances where they flew at 40° or 50° warmer; in one case the temperature was 79° higher at the plane than on the ground below. Reports of this kind we neutralize in our discussions by assuming,

132

without citing figures, that (because high mountains are snow-capped and for various other reasons) the heroic polar flyers contend during their journeys with temperatures even colder than those endured by their earth-bound predecessors who explored by dog and afoot.

A danger well-known to the air mail between New York and Cleveland, too well-known in most parts of the so-called temperate zone, is that of ice forming on wings to make the plane heavy and, what is more serious, to change its aerodynamics so that it becomes unmanageable. This occurs in what the people of New York and Cleveland think of as cold weather. Accordingly, in our discussions of polar flying we just assume that because it is much colder the danger to the flyers, through ice formation, must be that much greater than on the New York-Cleveland winter run. This gets by 90 per cent of the readers and is one of our most effective devices in keeping the polar districts unreal. The fact is, of course, that ice forms on wings chiefly at temperatures between freezing and fifteen degrees below that point (between 30° above zero and 15° above). When it gets colder you have comparatively little icing trouble with a plane.

The Arctic and Antarctic have their chief social usefulness as proving grounds for heroes. The stay-at-homes are thrilled by that courage, that devotion to the aims of science, which leads men to expose themselves to the terrors of a frozen and lifeless wilderness. In order that the said terrors shall have their maximum appeal to the reading public there should be a good many of them. One of the things commonly dreaded is illness, and it is therefore desirable to have it believed that

133

the polar risks include the greatest possible number of diseases. Recent deficiency-disease study has been helpful through showing that one at least of the vitamins can be produced by sunlight falling on the human skin. Obviously, then, the members of exploring parties are going to suffer great deprivation, are going to be in imminent risk of their lives, because of the long absence of the sun in winter. This belief has been utilized in two chief ways: You take along ultra-violet lamps and then make a great play on the fore-thought of a commander who enlists the newest powers of science towards protecting from disease the members of his courageous band. Or else you have the expedition go into the field without the lamps, and then work up a suspense on whether by cleanliness, regular exercise, amusements, and strict medical supervision it may turn out possible for the men to retain their health until the sun comes back after the Long Polar Night.

On the whole, disease scares have been managed satis-factorily by the public relations departments of at any rate the larger expeditions; but until just recently there was a serious exception. It had been found by many explorers, and had been so often reported as to reach the public conscious-ness, that head colds and the related diseases of the pulmo-nary passages were rare on polar journeys. Some said they had been practically absent. For instance, it was reported on one of the British expeditions that nobody had a cold for several winter months, that everybody then caught cold from germs which emerged when boxes of clothing were unpacked, and that when this flare-up was over no more head colds ap-peared through the rest of the year.

Obviously the polar explorer is deprived of half his chance to be courageous if the life and the climate are represented as normally healthful. The growing awareness that cold prevents colds had to be dealt with. Simplest was, no doubt, to counteract this through the old belief that cold produces colds. Notable help in the campaign was received from the cough-drop industry.

CHAPTER V.

STANDARDIZED WOLVES

THOSE WHO WANT TO BELIEVE THAT WOLVES DO NOT RUN IN packs should read only the first two-thirds of this chapter. For believing in wolf-packs, read the sections "Crumbs for Believers" and "Wolves for Posterity." The section "Wolves and Babes" can be read safely by believers and non-believers, for these are an entirely different (though standard) species and the nursing complex, save for one classic exception, seems to be confined to Hindu wolves.

To read all sections may prove not merely difficult but also confusing—may we hope even befuddling.

Everybody knows that wolves run in packs. One of the standard definitions of pack is: "A large number of predatory animals, such as wolves, banded together for the purpose of hunting their prey."

That used to be an undisputed statement of the case. But now there is an argument about whether any wolf-pack ever really existed, with the scientists nearly all on one side, the general public nearly all on the other, and the sportsmen divided about half and half.

On the affirmative side we have the undoubted fact that

136

"everybody knows," especially in Russia, that wolves do run in packs. If you want to refresh your mind as to what Russian wolf-packs are believed to be like, you can do so easily and pleasantly by turning to Willa Cather's *My Antonia,* page 63. The people Miss Cather is going to feed to her wolves are the very diet to which Russian wolves are most accustomed—a wedding party. There are six sleighs drawn by three horses each and carrying from six to twelve passengers. There is starlight on the snow and the road is through a forest. The first distant wolf howl does not drown the tinkle of the sleigh bells or the laughter of the wedding guests. But the rallying cry is answered from many sides, the leaders of the pack draw nearer, and fear grips every heart. The bride sobs on the groom's bosom and the drivers lash their horses to breakneck speed. The rear sleigh upsets, the passengers sprawl out over the snow and the wolves are on top of them in a moment. The screams of horses being eaten alive are more dreadful than the shrieks of people whose entrails are being torn out. The cries of terror from the remaining sleighs are as loud as the cries of pain from the dying. The wolves are silent now—they have other work to do.

And so the story goes on for sleigh after sleigh in Miss Cather's story, and in all the typical stories, until only the bridal sleigh is left. About forty or fifty people and fifteen horses have now been eaten, but the wolves are still hungry and going strong. There are hundreds of them, you see, and wolves have proverbially good appetites. Nothing will save the last sleigh but throwing the bride to the pack. This Miss Cather accordingly does, and so do half the other authors of tales. But it seldom happens that quite everybody is eaten. Somebody has to be saved, to give the narrator a chance to portray the survivor's life of shame and remorse through many effective pages that lead to a distant and friendless grave.

Such tales as Miss Cather's we usually consider to be "true in spirit" only, since they occur in novels, but we take them for sober fact when we read them in books of travel or in newspapers. The press stories excel the books in verisimilitude, for they tell us what is said to have happened yesterday or last week. They give the names of places that are on every map, they frequently mention the widow and orphaned children, they sometimes tell that the funeral of the fragments left by the wolves was conducted by the home lodge of Masons. There is every detail to prove that what you see in the *Sun* (or the *Bee* or the *American*) is really so.

If you look in the index to the news published by the New York *Times,* you will discover scores of authentic-looking wolf-pack stories. I have the space to reproduce here only a sample:

WOLVES DEVOUR 3 MEN IN
NORTHERN ONTARIO

An Elderly White Trapper and Two Indians Fall Victims to a Horde of Hungry Beasts

Port Arthur, Ont., Dec. 27—A great roving band of hungry timber wolves has devoured three men . . . Last Saturday an elderly trapper left his cabin in the woods seventy miles north of Ignace to mush down to the settlement for his Christmas mail. . . . There was no mail, however, and the old man said he would come back Christmas morning. At noon he had not arrived. The postmaster sent two Indians to follow the trail. . . .

About two miles from the settlement the Indians found a spot pounded down in the snow. There was blood. Bits of dog harness torn to shreds were scattered about. In the midst of them the Indians found human bones. They hastened back to report their discovery. The lure of the bounty on wolves, however, urged the Indians to take the trail again, with extra ammunition. They sped behind the dog team into the woods as the villagers waved good-bye. They did not return.

Yesterday a new searching party departed. They found another patch trodden in the snow, with much more blood, about two miles from the first. The two guns the Indians had carried were lying in the crimsoned snow. Scattered about were bones, bits of clothing and empty shells.

The carcasses of sixteen dead wolves—some half eaten—lay stretched in a circle about the remains of the two Indian hunters.

I quote from the New York *Times* of December 28, 1922. The story, from what is justly considered one of the world's greatest and most reliable newspapers, gives proof of the cunning no less than of the ferocity of the North American wolf. Judging from the evidence, the pack must still have been hungry when they got through eating the trapper (perhaps he was small and skinny), so they lay in wait to finish their meal on the search party, which they evidently knew was coming. Then, still hungry, and fearing the size and prowess of the second search party, they reluctantly ate a few of each other for dessert before retreating into the shadows of the forest. That was discretion and admirable generalship. They fought when there was a chance to win, and then withdrew before superior numbers.

139

There are plenty of such wolf stories in the papers, and now and then others even more impressive. During 1926, for instance, in the pages of the New York *Sun* packs of wolves held Italy under a reign of terror; a bit later in the New York *Times* villages in Siberia were barricaded against wolves. Two million cattle and many people were killed.

Thus stands the evidence for the affirmative—wolves *do* run in packs. They devour wedding parties in Russia and they eat trappers and Indians in Canada. They terrorize Italy and lay siege to towns in Siberia—in the papers, at least.

But there are skeptics who do not believe all they see in the papers or read in books of travel. These iconoclasts tell you that every story of a wolf-pack that you ever read or heard is fib, fiction, or folklore, and that there never has been a pack of wolves in Russia, America, or anywhere except in people's imagination. That seems a hard position to defend, but they go at it valiantly. Their defense lies in both logic and fact. For the logic they ask you to consider the caribou-hunting wolf as a sample.

Their argument begins with the generally accepted fact that there are more than ten million wild caribou in Northern Alaska, Northern Canada, Northern Siberia and the Arctic islands. From these at least two million caribou are born every year; two million must, therefore, die, or the numbers would increase. Certainly less than 10 per cent of these are killed by human hunters. None die of old age and very few of accident or disease, for if a caribou is old or sick it moves slowly and is soon overtaken and devoured. This means that wolves kill every year a good many more than a million and a half caribou.

140

In summer, when their puppies are being brought up, the northern wolves live in part on eggs, fledgling or moulting birds, and rodents. But in winter the birds have flown south, the rodents are safe asleep in their frozen burrows, and almost the only thing a wolf can find to eat is caribou. I know how wolves kill caribou, and I can offer some personal testimony on wolves in general, for I was born on Lake Winnipeg in a wolf country; I was brought up among wolves and coyotes in Dakota before it became "civilized" and was split up into North and South Dakota; I lived for some ten years in the Arctic, supporting myself most of the time by hunting. I have shot wolves with a rifle and have seen hundreds of them either trotting quietly along or loping steadily in pursuit of caribou. I have seen the tracks of thousands following game, and have found signs of hundreds of tragedies where they had killed some bird or beast. I have asked dozens of Arctic Indians (Slaveys, Dogribs, Loucheux) and hundreds of Eskimos about how the wolf hunts, and there has been no divergence between what they have told me and what I have seen.

A wolf cannot run nearly as fast as a caribou, and must capture it by tiring it out. That is the essence of all I have seen and all I have been told. It means that, before it is killed, each caribou has to be pursued by the wolves from several hours to several days—nobody knows exactly how long. All hunters agree that (except for newborn calves) the youngest caribou are the swiftest and staunchest runners. The ones killed by wolves are therefore chiefly the old bulls and old cows. A cow may weigh two or three hundred pounds, and a bull three or four hundred, live-weight.

Nearly half of that is waste. The wolves are, then, pursuing anything from 100 to 200 pounds of food. For, no matter how large the caribou herd may be when the chase begins, they eventually scatter, and the pack, if there is a pack, finds itself pursuing the single slowest animal.

Suppose, now, there are 200 or 300 wolves, as in Miss Cather's heart-rending story. She provided hers with six sleigh loads of Russians, six to twelve in a sleigh, and three presumably fat horses hitched to each. That would make a square meal for even 300 wolves. But it would be far otherwise if the 300 followed a single 300-pound caribou for three days, or even one day. They would be so hungry that the beast, divided by 300, would be to the pack no more than a tantalizing appetizer. There would be nothing for it but to resort to another well-known habit of the fiction wolf and use their whetted appetites on each other—eating, let us say, a dozen to correspond to the soup course, a dozen for the fish, and two dozen for the roast, with at least another dozen of the youngest and tenderest for dessert. But the continued practice of dining on each other like that would soon reduce a wolf-pack below fiction and movie standards. In fact, you might as well do without a pack altogether; for it is scarcely worth the bother to build one up to the required size, just to have it disappear again in a few weeks by the members of the troupe swallowing one another.

Those who are trying to prove that the wolf-pack really exists will perhaps admit that the abstract logic of pack hunting seems a little faulty, but will insist, and quite rightly, that logic does not amount to a hill of beans when contradicted by facts. The pack stories, they will tell us, are simple truth. Newspapers may exaggerate, but the better ones never invent. Besides, nearly everybody has an uncle or an aunt who had a grandmother or grandfather that was eaten or nearly eaten by a pack of wolves.

That brings us to the evidence—are the wolf-pack stories true? To save time, we shall take at once the testimony of a group of scientists and practical hunters who ought to know because they make the study of wolves their profession— studying also the testimony of everyone they ever heard of who claimed to have seen a pack of wolves. They are Americans, too, and within your reach, so you can write postcards to them tomorrow and see what they really think. Don't be diffident about asking. You are probably a taxpayer. They are your servants, for they work for the government that taxes you.

The branch of the government that studies wolves as a part of its business is the Bureau of Biological Survey at Washington, and the head of it is Dr. E. W. Nelson,* a lifetime student of wild animals. He was four years among Arctic wolves in Alaska (1877-81) and has himself studied wolves in Mexico and all over the United States. Further- more, he has under him other men who have studied wolves, among them Edward A. Preble, who has spent much time in the sub-Arctic and Arctic forests and prairies of Canada. But more significant still, there is under Dr. Nelson's suc- cessor's direction the wolf-killing service of the United States Government. This is a body of men who hold themselves in readiness for telegraphic appeals from stockmen, usually in the West, who find their animals being destroyed by

* Dr. Nelson died some five years after this paper was printed.

143

wolves. They come and exterminate the wolves "scientifically," and the flocks and herds are safe again.

In gathering material for a book I was writing about wolves, I consulted Dr. Nelson. We agreed, first, that the accepted meaning of the word pack, when applied to wolves is *a large number of wolves that have come together to help each other in hunting.* In other words, one mother with her puppies would not constitute a pack. Dr. Nelson felt so positive about the nature of wolves in North America, from Mexico to the Arctic, that he thought I would be safe in denying flatly in my book that any wolf-pack ever existed on our continent. But, just to make sure that no different opinion was held among people of authority corresponding to his own, we formulated a letter which he addressed to certain scientific students of wolves, and to all his wolf-killers.

As to how many wolves had been seen together, the various replies naturally gave different answers, for experiences varied somewhat. But they ranged only from two to five. They were unanimous in reporting that if several wolves were seen together then these were always the mother with her puppies, or conceivably the father and mother with their puppies, and never a pack in the usual sense of that word.

Then what about the story of the wolves that killed the elderly trapper and the two Indians on the front page of the *Times?* Surely that was no family of puppies—sixteen dead wolves, killed by the Indians; a few, presumably, killed by the old trapper, and enough left over to eat up one white man, two Indians and part of sixteen dead wolves. To make the inquiry into the truth of the story official and more

144

authoritative than if I were doing it myself, I suggested to Dr. Nelson that he write to Ignace, Ontario. For checking up, I wrote also to Mr. J. B. Harkin, Commissioner of National Parks, Ottawa, who was at that time (1922) in charge of the administration of the game laws of Canada, and therefore in a position to set in motion official machinery to find out about this wolf story. Thus I received the same replies from two directions, one through Dr. Nelson and the other through Mr. Harkin. They were, in substance, that no such man as the old trapper ever existed and that no white man had been killed by wolves. No such Indians as described existed there and none had been killed by wolves, whether in packs or otherwise, either in the vicinity of Ignace, or anywhere in the world, as far as anyone living in the vicinity of Ignace knew.

Hundreds of other tales about wolf-packs, published in newspapers or books, have been traced by the United States Biological Survey and by various students, including myself. In no case was evidence found to support them. Just try it yourself on the next American despatch you read. In spite of all the pretended details—the sorrowing family, the Masonic funeral—it will be reasonable odds to bet dollars to doughnuts that the story will turn out pure fiction, or at best will rest on testimony no court of law would accept as proof.

The case seems to be definitely settled against the wolf-pack in North America. But there still remains Russia. Well, why not let Russia remain? No one seems to have checked wolf-pack stories in Russia for everyone is so sure they are true. And perhaps they are. Besides, it is a distant country, and the fancy must somewhere have play.

145

The book on wolves which the July, 1927, *Mercury* said I was writing is still being written (1936), or, rather, the evidence for it is still being gathered. We use here from that accumulation sample case histories which give the trend of the material.

Under a date line of Winnipeg, April 16, 1922, many or most Canadian newspapers printed a story which I read in the Ottawa *Morning Journal* about the body of a trapper, Ben Cockrane, having been found torn to pieces north of Fisher River on Lake Winnipeg the previous Thursday. "He had been attacked by a pack of timber wolves. His bones and pieces of his clothing and a rifle with a broken stock were found nearby. Before being killed, Cockrane shot seven wolves dead and clubbed four to death, their bodies lying around his tattered remains being the **only** evidence of his fight for life."

That story had a personal interest. For I was born on Lake Winnipeg and might, therefore, seem to have had as a child a narrow escape from the ancestors of the pack which destroyed Cockrane—we were there in the pioneer days back in the late 70's, long before railways, when there was only an odd cabin along the shores of the lake and when presumably the wolves were even more numerous than now, and more predatory. Investigation would be simple, too, for I could write to some of our old neighbors or their descendants.

But the case was being handled so widely and with so much respect by the press that a formal approach seemed indicated, one above the suspicion of bias. Accordingly, two lines of inquiry were started, both of them official. Nelson,

at my suggestion, inquired on behalf of the logical department of the United States Government. In Canada, Harkin
was then in charge of wild-life investigation for his government and could use the machinery of the Dominion Parks
Branch. When I placed the newspaper report in their hands
I received friendly assurance that the case would be followed
up both in their own interest and because of their previous
association with me in similar studies.

Under date of May 22 Harkin wrote that an investigation
had been made and that "Mr. Cochrane has stated 'that the
report of his death was grossly exaggerated.' " On May 31,
Nelson, after like findings, wrote:

"This amusing climax to the ferocious wolf tale is similar to
that of many other newspaper accounts of the killing of human
beings by wild animals, which the Biological Survey has run
down during the last thirty years or more. Such stories are almost
invariably pure fiction."

A third inquiry, made by a friend in the Hudson's Bay
Company's office at Winnipeg, brought a statement that
when their representative interviewed Mr. Cockrane he
seemed annoyed and replied, I gather somewhat petulantly,
that as long as he could remember there had seldom been
so few wolves around as this year.

Sometimes when we trace the story of a pack devouring a
group of school children we find that it all started when a
small boy stepped on a dog's tail and was bitten in the leg.
There does not appear to have been even that much local
base for the Cockrane fabrication.

The Ignace, Ontario, story (given above in its *American*

Mercury form) has in my files considerable documentation. On January 2, 1923, I wrote Dr. Nelson in part:

"I wonder if you missed the interesting wolf story that appeared in the New York *Times* for December 28th. In case you did, I am enclosing a copy.

"I am writing an article for publication in *Collier's Weekly* about fake wolf stories and especially about the great wolf-packs that gallop through our books and newspapers. Just as this article is being prepared for publication out comes another story. I am so sure that this one also is a fake that I am not holding up the publication of the article. However, I hope very much that you will be able to put a tracer on it and find out whether there is any truth behind this particular version."

Dr. Nelson replied January 4:

". . . I saw the New York *Times* article copied in a local paper and at once considered it one of the typical wolf articles which appear in the press, particularly every winter.

"In order, however, to get definite information on the subject, I am writing to the postmaster of Port Arthur, Ontario, and also at San Ignace, sending them copies of the article and asking them what basis there is for a statement of this kind. I will let you know the results when they are received. . . ."

I had written similarly to A. Brabant, Fur Trade Commissioner, Hudson's Bay Company, Winnipeg, and to Harkin. Brabant, who later investigated for me more fully, gave preliminary reply January 6:

"I believe that the wolf story which was enclosed with your letter of the 2nd inst., is merely romance. . . .

"As you are well aware, there are few, if any, cases of wolves attacking people. . . ."

G. D. Russell, Postmaster of Port Arthur, Ontario, wrote Dr. Nelson 'January 17, 1923, in part:

"There have been similar stories circulated during the past years, but all have been found to be untrue, and while wolves are a serious scourge to wild animal life in the bush, and a source of annoyance to settlers in the back country, in so far as they are not averse to raiding their domestic fowl, yet the genuine evidence of men being killed by them has yet to be established.

"This recent story originated at Ignace, 200 miles west of Port Arthur. My personal opinion (and the consensus of opinion) is, that there is not the slightest foundation of truth in it."

The Postmaster of Ignace, John Davies, wrote Dr. Nelson January 18, 1923:

"Your letter to hand, RE: the killing of three men by wolves north of Ignace. We in Ignace know nothing about this affair excepting what we read in the papers. I don't think there is a word of truth in it. There are a lot of wolves which are doing a lot of damage among the wild game but so far as tackling human beings, I have never had any proof yet."

The press discussion of the Ignace story was voluminous throughout Canada, particularly in Ontario. On January 18, 1923, Harkin sent me a quotation from "one of our local papers, under date the 17th instant":

149

". . . The scene of the tragedy was laid on a trail seventy miles north of Ignace. The names of the victims of the wolves were not given. Several old timers in Northern Ontario have ridiculed the story and have claimed that wolves are not man-killers. A Toronto man . . . wrote to W. T. Thompson, dealer in furs at Ignace, asking as to the facts of the story.

"Mr. Thompson is quoted as replying: . . . 'Wolves are very numerous around here, but I have lived in this country for twenty-five years and have yet to hear of anyone being killed by wolves. During the past ten years, or over, I have been buying raw furs from trappers and Indians and have never heard any such tales that turn out true.'"

Reverberations of the Ignace yarn continued to reach me for several months. For instance, there came in a letter from an old friend, Inspector G. L. Jennings, of the Royal North-west Mounted Police (now styled Royal Canadian Mounted Police), dated April 20, 1923. We shall use the main part of it in another connection but print here extracts from a cutting he sent taken from the Edmonton *Journal* of February 10:

"Recently I read a letter concerning the habits of wolves. I had also read some time ago of a tragedy in the woods of our north country in which several men were pulled down and devoured by these animals," says Dr. J. S. McCullough, writing in the Toronto *Globe*.

"In the gold rush of 1897 or 1898, when so many men made an attempt to get into the Klondike country via Edmonton, Athabasca Landing, Great Slave Lake and the Mackenzie River, I was one of a party which attempted a traverse from the Mackenzie River to Fort Norman to the Stewart or McMillan

150

River over the divide. I was obliged to come back on account of sickness when we had got out about 60 miles on the trail. After dividing the supplies with my partner I made the trip back alone and as it was necessary that the onward-going party should have two tents I did not even have a tent to cover me on the return trip, but built little shelters of spruce, rolled in my sleeping bag with only boughs with a fire at my feet, and this slight windbreak to protect me from the winds and the wolves. Wolves there seemed to be in plenty, judging from the terrifying howls at night, but they were seldom seen. In my weakened condition from dysentery I made very slow time on my return trip to the banks of the river, six miles below Fort Norman, where there were several unoccupied, roughly-built log shacks. With 75 to 100 pounds on my sled I would drag along five or six miles, construct a stage and place my pack in safety, returning over the ground until I had all my stuff moved up. At this time of year and in this latitude I saw little of the sun, and frequently I made my move at night if the light was good and not much wind.

"I found the wolves very curious, following along on my snowshoe track, crossing and recrossing it, appearing at one side and ahead and then on the other side ahead or behind, always, however, in silence. I had been given to understand by Billy Paton, then of the Hyslop and Neaggel Trading Company, that the wolves never attacked a man, and so I traveled all alone, and very seldom with a weapon of any kind other than a light camp axe, and, although I was very lonesome and very weak and very down-hearted, I really never had any fear of the wolves. There was one that I became pretty well acquainted with, a very large and almost black fellow, who was afterward accidentally caught in a bear trap which had been set by an inexperienced miner by the name of Low Day. The trap was lost beneath the snow, and although Day knew about where it was, we were all afraid to

151

hunt for it for fear of getting into it ourselves. The large, almost black, wolf that followed my trail like a ghost in some mysterious way sat down on his haunches right in the jaws of this trap, where we found him dead and frozen stiff.

"I think that those of us who put in the balance of the winter on the bank of the Mackenzie were all more relieved that the trap was thus discovered than at catching the wolf. What I have said here makes a very negative sort of wolf story, but the fact that I was out night after night alone and that every time I went back over my trail I saw fresh wolf tracks, and that through the long Arctic nights one could almost always hear the howl or bark of the wolf probably chasing hares, for the big game was driven away by the 40-odd men who had gone over the country, leaving hungry wolves and little else but hares and ptarmagin, would seem to prove that if ever the wolf would attack a human being the conditions were right for them to do so as I plodded my slow course back alone over this trail.

". . . Personally I do not believe that the wolves of Canada ever attack a living human being. They would in time probably become bold enough to pick the bones of anyone dying or being frozen to death in the bush country. I have talked of wolves to many bushmen and never yet have I come across anyone who had bush experience but had an absolute contempt for the wolf so far as being attacked by him or them went. . . .

"I can quite believe that a person who had been fed-up on wolf stories might take to a tree in fear when the wolves kept appearing and disappearing as they will do on the trail of a woodsman as he marches along at dusk, but I believe that it is only the wolf's natural curiosity that leads to his follow-up tactics. The black tail or mule deer will often do the same thing if you pretend not to have seen him. . . ."

The Cockrane story, as said, never gave us investigators a trace of foundation. One version of a basis for the Ignace story was contained in a letter of January 12 from L. M. Gleeson, of 416 Victoria Avenue, Fort William, Ontario, who wrote me on the letterhead of the Fort William-Port Arthur Rotary Club:

"Replying to your letter of January sixth, re wolf story from Port Arthur. I would say that the story was just a rumor. It originated, I believe, by a trainman running between here and Ignace, Ont., and as the story was re-told it was enlarged upon. I do know that the newspaper here tried for sometime to get a confirmation of the story direct from Ignace, but they were unable to do so. This story did not appear in our local paper although it was telegraphed outside. . . ."

A theory of the Ignace yarn, published long after, makes it a fable devised for the good of a community. On January 16, 1933, the Portland *Oregonian* printed a letter from Ada Alice Tuttle, summarizing investigations which she had made or was familiar with, the occasion being that the "Ten Years Ago" column had revived the story:

"The occurrence was investigated by several persons, Dr. (William T.) Hornaday among them. The explanation reveals the resourceful boss of a lumber camp, solving an acute liquor problem. It seems that a number of his men were in the habit of going to the nearest settlement to get drunk. So, remembering the effect produced on the youthful mind by the adventures of 'Little Red Riding Hood,' he also invented a fairy tale, suiting it to his audience by introducing plenty of action and lots of gore.

153

... They swallowed the yarn, hook, line and sinker, and after that stayed where they belonged, with the most admirable docility."

As Dr. Nelson pointed out, the newspapers run dispatches on wolf-packs chiefly in winter. This, according to the stories themselves, is determined by laws of Nature. The rigors of the weather have banished or destroyed the wild animals on which the wolves customarily prey; besides, there is no doubt an increased metabolic rate, wolves, like people, needing some of the caloric energy from the food they eat for keeping themselves warm. In desperation the beasts gather in larger and larger packs and finally in extreme cases attack houses or even villages—the latter chiefly in some distant foreign country. In America they seem to confine themselves to attacks on people that are out in the woods. Usually we have to depend on word pictures by the survivors for information regarding these encounters, but on December 9, 1923, the New York *Times* was able to publish in its rotogravure section two photographs from Sudbury, Ontario, giving the supporting testimony of a camera. One of the pictures showed two men standing knee-deep in snow as they defended themselves against a pack of wolves. The caption was "A Tragedy Among the Snows of the Far Northern Woods." The summarized printed account said that, ammunition gone, two huntsmen were set upon by a pack of fifteen wolves. They fought them off, one using for a club the barrel of his gun, the other an axe. Before the battle came to a decision a third member of the hunting party arrived and was able to turn the tide with gunfire. The second picture has the description:

154

"The aftermath of a bloody battle in the wilds. Huntsmen binding up their wounds after hand to hand battle with pack of timber wolves from which they were saved by the timely arrival of a third member of their party."

When I sent these pictures to Harkin for investigation, if he thought well of it, and in any case for comment, he replied that he was fed up with tracing stories of wolf-packs. It seemed to him a study of the picture indicated that the wolves in the picture had all been dead for some time. Apparently they had been allowed to freeze stiff in various attitudes and had then been propped up in the soft snow to give the semblance of an attacking wolf-pack.

Doubtless the three hunters were too excited during the battle and forgot about taking pictures. So they had to re-enact the adventure for the camera next day. The chief difficulty about that explanation was that some of the "wolves" looked a bit like dogs.

Sure enough, time proved that the doggy look of the wolves had its reason. On April 12, 1927, the Utica *Press* carried a letter from B. H. Divine in which he said, in part:

"The New York *Times* published a picture a while ago of two men with clubbed guns fighting for their lives against a pack · of wolves. Following this up I received word from the Royal Canadian Mounted Police that the wolves in the picture were dogs very cleverly posed, and the whole thing was a fake."

During the next years there were few American stories of note although striking accounts of packs and their depredations were printed from Europe—these we shall discuss far-

155

ther on. The American scene brightened with January, 1926, when on the 17th the Chicago *Tribune* presented to its readers the desperate situation then facing one of the territories of the United States:

ALASKA TO WAR ON WOLF PACKS WITH AIR BOMBS

Shrapnel from Planes May Save Game

Juneau, Alaska—(Special)—Dropping bombs from airplanes upon packs of big timber wolves is a method for destroying these game-killing brutes, now advanced and approved by Governor George A. Parks. A trial of the idea is planned for next month, generally known as the hunger-month of winter, when wild life is at its lowest ebb and gnawing pangs grip wolves, lynx and owls.

According to reports received at the governor's office, female caribou, deer, and domesticated reindeers have been repeatedly attacked this winter by large bands of timber wolves. The destruction among the female caribou is appalling.

The bull caribou in winter round-up together, peacefully content, leaving the cows to protect themselves and yearling calves as best they can. All are antlered, but they lack the weight of caribou bulls, likewise the fighting strategy.

Air mail men operating in the Alaskan service have filed many reports of instances where packs of wolves, hearing and seeing the planes in the sky, gathered forces and raced the aviators, leaping and barking at the birdlike machines after the manner of dogs barking at pigeons. To the aviator it seemed that a large rock dropped into the packs would easily kill or maim many.

The plan proposed is to drop bombs loaded with shrapnel and

156

dynamite into wolf-packs powerful enough to wreak terrific damage even hundreds of feet away in all directions. Trappers and hunters believe that the animals, seeing a bomb dropped, would instantly run to examine it, thus bringing about their own destruction.

Timber wolves weighing 250 pounds, seven to eight feet in length, have been killed by trappers this winter near Fairbanks. The same breed of animal infests the territory from Ketchikan, far north in the tundra, where herds of reindeer forage. The native herders report many encounters with prowling brutes eager to pull down young reindeer.

A powder manufacturing concern has offered bombs free for the unique hunting expedition.

The *Tribune* account thus pictures not only a situation physically serious but paints a discouraging view of the moral deterioration of the Alaska bull caribou which were no longer willing to place at the service of the smaller and weaker members of the herd their superior antlers, greater weight and their fighting strategy.

But it was encouraging to read that the very head of the Alaska territorial administration, Governor George A. Parks, was in charge of the relief operations. I happened to know he was in Washington and wrote him there February 19. His reply came dated February 23 from the office of the Secretary of the Interior:

"Concerning the clipping from the Chicago *Tribune,* I am at a loss to understand how it originated. I left Juneau, December 16, 1925, and have been in Washington since early in January. I never have authorized any such statement. It may be a fact that

157

the bulls separate from the rest of the caribou herd during the winter, but my personal observation has been to the contrary. If any of the pilots in the Air Mail Service have filed reports as alleged in the newspaper account, these reports never have come to my attention. It would be most unusual to hear a wolf bark like a dog. There may be wolves in Alaska that weigh 250 pounds, but I do not know of any such records.* I believe that it is conceded generally that a wolf-pack usually includes only the members of the family—father, mother, and pups—and they separate about the beginning of the next mating season. I have no personal knowledge of any large bands of wolves, nor have I been able to find any authentic cases where bands of wolves have molested reindeer or caribou herds. Many times during my winter trips through Alaska, I have been told about the wolf-packs, but so far as I know the stories never have been founded on fact.

Geo. A. Parks
Governor of Alaska."

Logically the Bureau of Biological Survey was concerned with the situation and its Chief, Nelson, wrote me February 24:

"The other day I had a conference with Governor Parks on various matters relating to Alaska and he showed me the copy of the Chicago *Tribune* clipping of January 17, a copy of which you sent me, containing the weird tale of the plan to bomb wolves by the use of airplanes. Governor Parks was inclined to be somewhat exercised over the connection of his name with this absurd statement. . . .

"Of course, the whole thing is an absurdity on the face of it . . . there is no such abundance of wolves in Alaska as indicated in

* Most authorities consider 105 to 110 pounds as very large for northern male wolves.

this article. . . . The claim that timber wolves weighing 250 pounds have been killed near Fairbanks the present winter is another evidence of the absolute unreliability of the article."

This is trying to be a chronological statement but we are unable to resist the temptation to print from a Washington despatch of the *Associated Press* as it appeared in the New York *Times* of May 31, 1936:

"Plans for an airplane attack on savage packs of Alaskan wolves were worked out today by three Federal agencies. . . .
"Last Winter, Governor John W. Troy cabled for help. . . ."

It may have seemed a bit far afield in 1926 to go all the way to Alaska for stories of wolf-packs, so the *Associated Press* in 1927, with a Chicago date line of January 24, had a story which one paper used under "Hunters to Renew Search for Wolves Near Chicago. First Venture Fails to Disclose Marauding Pack Reported by Farmers." However, there was skepticism (that's the difficulty of having the stories too near home) and Leroy Davidson, former chief of the Cook County Highway Police, was quoted:

"Wolves—bah! Last summer there was a camp of Campfire Girls in the forest preserve. They had three dogs—the dogs were a mixture of Airedale and police dog. When the girls broke camp they left the dogs behind. I also had an Airedale. He ran away and joined the other three. These four dogs are the 'pack of wolves' that are causing all the commotion."

That pronouncement threatened at first to be a wet blanket. However, there is in my files a press cutting dated

159

February 4 with the heading: "Fliers Hunt Wolves on Edge of Chicago. Posse Has Had No Luck." So the story did keep going awhile.

When it requires ten days on the edges of Chicago to dispose of a wolf-pack, even with the assistance of the chief of the Highway Police, no wonder stories from Alaska have a considerable lease of life. Some of them promise to become, and to remain, a part of the source material of Alaskan natural history.

The year 1927 proved rich in American wolf tales, making up for the comparatively lean years since 1923. My favorite of that season, and of many years, I was able to trace through the help of my old friend Lee Smits, free lance writer and also columnist for the Detroit *Times*. It is not a story of a wolf-pack, but we digress a moment to place chronologically a striking episode of a lone Michigan wolf. We quote the St. Ignace *Enterprise* of February 3, 1927:

LARGE TIMBER WOLF

Entered the Home of Robert Alexander
and Attacked Woman and Children

Mrs. Robert Alexander and children were made the victims of a savage attack by a large timber wolf in their home in Brevort township last Wednesday. The animal, made desperate evidently by hunger forced its way through the doorway of the kitchen and made a rush at the children who were playing on the floor. Mrs. Alexander got between the wolf and the children and called to her husband to get a gun, and she also was leaped upon by the animal and borne to the floor. Before it could do serious harm

Alexander appeared with a gun and first kicking the wolf from the prostrate form of his wife fired as the wolf made its escape through the doorway and slightly injuring it. It was making towards the woods when Mrs. Lottie Page, a neighbor, hearing the shot came out of her home with a loaded shotgun in her hand and seeing the wolf made a lucky shot killing the animal.

While wolves have been reported as being numerous in Brevort and surrounding townships, and have done considerable damage, this is the first instance that one has been known to have attacked a human being. The Alexanders are of the opinion that the attack was caused by starvation as the animal appeared to be weak from exhaustion."

On seeing this gem, I wrote Smits, who replied April 29:

"State Conservation Officer George Gish, Jr., who patrols the area in which the 'attack' occurred, called at the Alexander home and was shown the dead wolf. It was a small mongrel of the collie type, with a bob tail, a white blaze, yellow in color, weighing not more than 40 pounds. There is an epidemic of 'running fits' or 'fright-disease' among dogs, and this dog may have rushed into the cabin while delirious, or it may have merely been cold, hungry and lonesome. It was a male dog. The rumor that the animal was a timber wolf started when someone in the neighborhood 'guessed maybe' there was wolf blood in the dog. Not because of its appearance, but because it came out of the woods and acted strangely. . . .

". . . The story is from a paper at the county seat. It was carried extensively over the wires. . . ."

Although chiefly known to the literary world for his novel *Spring Flight*, Smits is, among other things, one of

America's connoisseurs of un-natural history. So he could not resist going on:

"Not only can many bartenders and hotel clerks in the backwoods give you good wolf yarns—attacks on mankind—but old lumberjacks know, by direct hearsay, of some desperate encounters. The editor of the daily paper at Sault Ste. Marie, Ont., ... has for several years offered $100 for an authenticated report of a wolf attacking a person in the Algoma district of Ontario. No takers.

"The state prison at Marquette, Mich., fronts on Lake Superior and, although on the outskirts of a small city, is at the edge of a strip of wild country extending into rather large areas of swamp and timber and offering cover for a fugitive for hundreds of miles. Very few escapes are attempted, and the fear of wild animals is unquestionably a deterrent. One gang got loose and were rounded up because they made straight for roads and kept on them. They spent one night in the brush, with a few hares, porcupines and owls about them, and perhaps a fox or coyote, and said when they were caught that they all were sorry they ran away when darkness closed in on them. They had a terrible night. All city gunmen."

That there are at times very special motives behind wolf-pack stories appears from a letter from B. H. Divine, published in the Utica, New York, *Press* of April 12, 1927:

"To the Editor of *The Press:*

The following wolf story recently appeared in *The Press:*

'Huntsville, Ont., March 31—While making his way to a lumber camp near Algonquin Park, Elwood Bloss was pursued by a pack of wolves. He fled onto the open ice, where the animals, 16 of them, surrounded him. Their howling attracted the attention

162

of a game warden, who arrived before they closed on their intended victim. He shot seven before the pack fled.'

Upon writing to the authorities at Huntsville for the truth of the matter, I received the following letter from T. Muyhum, postmaster:

'This story was first published here early in January last, but since that time it has been pretty thoroughly exploded.

'The young man (aged 22) started out to walk six or seven miles to the railroad station early in the morning. The howling of some wolves at a distance frightened him so badly that he did not recover for some days. It was necessary to make some explanation of his condition, and the truth sounded so inadequate he built the story to suit his condition. It was soon into the papers, and after being contradicted from the pack end he acknowledged that much of it was not true.' "

For some reason there did not come to my attention until 1931 a support of wolf-packs by book reviewers and press commentators who relied on a volume published in 1929, *The Last Stand of the Pack,* by Arthur H. Carhart and Stanley P. Young. At last, said the reviewers, a distinguished biologist and student of wild life has spoken out, resentful about the sniping at wolf-packs by amateur naturalists.

Young was chief biologist of the U. S. Biological Survey, exclaimed the champions of the pack, in consonant triumph. They were right, for I looked him up in *American Men of Science* and found this substantial record:

". . . U. S. Govt. hunter, bur. biol. surv, U. S. Dept. Agr, Ariz, 17-19, in charge ground squirrel control work, 19, coyote control

163

crew, southeast N. Mex, 20, asst. leader predatory animal control, 20-21, leader, Colo-Kans. dist, 21-27, asst. head div. econ. investigations, Washington, D. C, 27-28, prin. biologist in charge div. predatory animal and rodent control, 28- . . ."

The reviewers did not notice, but I did, a sensational angle. To have Young opposing Nelson was like Roosevelt falling out with Smith—the chief of a division of the U. S. Biological Survey opposing that retired chief of the Survey who had brought him to Washington. It was a delicate situation but I had to get Nelson's view and wrote him discreetly April 28, 1932. He replied May 14 from California:

". . . It will surprise me very much if he has recorded a pack of any considerable size beyond that which you and I believe to be normal (mother with litter of pups). I will look up the matter soon after I return and talk to him about it. Will then write you. . . ."

An invalid, and busy though officially retired, Nelson did not communicate until March 22, 1933. There was to be no Smith-Roosevelt situation, it now appeared, for the retired Chief said:

"Under date of March 14, 1933, Stanley P. Young of the Biological Survey writes. . . .
" 'With regard to your question on wolves, I heartily agree with you that the great packs of wolves such as have been often described in books and newspapers exist only in the minds of writers. In my experience the typical wolf-pack consists of the two parents and their young of the year. One is apt to see this so-called pack in the late fall and up until the early spring. Also

164

it is possible in the formation of this so-called pack for two families of wolves to intermingle for a short time in the fall of the year, particularly if one family group is in close proximity to another, and a kill is in progress. My experience, even under these conditions, however, is to the effect that wolves of several families never unite in a long and friendly association. . . .

" 'It is therefore possible from the foregoing that newspaper writers and authors have in mind the family groups of wolves rather than the packs of adults. However, these writers usually give the impression that these packs are made up of adult wolves. The greatest number of wolves in one litter that I have ever seen totalled eight. This pack was made up of the eight young, which were apparently whelped in early March, and the old female and old male.' "

Nelson felt Young was a bit too generous "in explaining what the writers have in mind in their tales of big packs. Really they are drawing from an inexhaustible store of ignorance on the subject. Probably less than 1 per cent of them ever saw a wolf in the wilds."

The year 1933 closed on a note ominous for New York State. For the *Herald-Tribune* of December 30 reported:

"Lithgow Osborne, State Commissioner of Conservation, has assigned Ray Burmaster, game protector of the Saranac Lake district, to exterminate the wolves which have been seen in the northern counties in recent weeks. Ten dozen snares and traps have been set in the wolf-infested areas and seventy-five skilled hunters and trappers will be employed. Wolves recently attacked two farm hands near Fort Covington, in Franklin County. . . . The pack now at large numbers from twelve to fifty."

The New York *Times*, evidently not jealous, supported

its rival the *Herald-Tribune* by saying in an editorial of January 5 that: ". . . one pack hunting in Franklin County at this time is estimated at from twelve to fifty in number. . . ." They added that: "An application has been made to the Biological Survey at Washington for the services of an expert wolf trapper to rid New York of the unwelcome visitors."

I wrote the Conservation Department of New York at Albany January 5, and Lithgow Osborne, Commissioner, replied January 12:

". . . we do not have any definite information to indicate that the wolves which have recently appeared in the vicinity of Owls Head in the Adirondacks are running in packs. We are sending one of our field investigators, Mr. Darrow, into the region which the wolves apparently inhabit, in an effort to determine just what the situation is. I shall be pleased to request a report from him as to whether or not the wolves are actually hunting in packs, and to see that the information is forwarded to you sometime early in the spring."

The Commissioner's follow-up slipped and I did not remind him for two years. On July 13, 1936, came a letter from John T. Gibbs, Deputy Commissioner. He mentions several reports on the Adirondack wolves "all of which resulted in our deciding that there were no packs of timber wolves in the Adirondacks."

One of the reports was from E. A. Goldman of the U. S. Biological Survey. He had been in the region of the packs and "we crossed a fresh track of one of these canine beasts in a remote section of the forest. Owing to the softness and depth of snow it had been making slow progress. The track, about one day old, appeared like that of a rather small dog." Two animals from the supposed wolf-pack had been captured, but "general appearances indicated, however, that both are dogs." The skin and skull from another animal killed was sent to the American Museum of Natural History of New York. On February 15, 1934, H. E. Anthony, curator, reported that in his judgment the relics were those of a dog.

By 1935 the news magazine *Time* had already secured a wide public for its news radio broadcast. They had enough nobility or were secure enough to print in their "Letters" of January 21, 1935, an indignant protest from Manitoba against what the correspondent felt was their nature-faking. Axel Nielsen wrote them from Cranberry Portage, Manitoba:

"Your radio representation of the wolf story (Dec. 21, 1934), was most unconvincing. Don't let yourself be taken in by such stories. . . .

"For 15 years I have traded and prospected in the North, over a vast territory, a belt 1,200 miles long by 500 wide, the top of all the prairie Provinces and beyond. I have met wolves, traveled with them, trailed them. They have trailed me too; they're a curious lot. But my own sleigh dogs were ten times more dangerous. . . . Your terrified passengers were probably stretching the imagination valiantly, thanks to the nursery version of wolves in general. . . . In all my experience, all my questioning of Indians, whose language I speak fluently, I have never yet discovered a single wolf half as dangerous as the ordinary pasture bull, an irritable sow, or a gander."

167

THE WOLF PACK IN THE OLD WORLD

The *American Mercury,* July, 1927, statement on the wolf-pack closed:

"The case seems to be definitely settled against the wolf-pack in North America. But there still remains Russia. Well, why not let Russia remain? No one seems to have checked wolf-pack stories in Russia for everyone is so sure they are true. And perhaps they are. Besides, it is a distant country, and the fancy must somewhere have play."

For many years I sought and found reliable information on conditions in what is now the U.S.S.R. from a learned and far-traveled officer of the Russian Navy, Commander N. A. Transehe, who was doing scientific work in New York. One of our conversations dealt with packs of wolves.

Transehe had journeyed through recognized wolf districts of Russia and Siberia so extensively that few could have had more experience. He never saw more than single wolves or a pair (doubtless male and female), except when it seemed clear that the group was one or both parents with a litter. I suggested that doubtless the wolf-pack, then, existed in Russia only as folklore, but this he considered did not follow at all. "I have lived in New York several years," he said. "I have never been to Wall Street but I know there is a Wall Street. I have lived in the United States without seeing the Rocky Mountains but I know there are Rocky Mountains. It is that way with packs of wolves in Russia. They are of common knowledge."

This was the considered view of a Russian whose judgment I had often found good. Also there were two of the foremost authorities on wild animals in the United States, who had expressed to me the feeling that Eurasian wolves might be quite different from ours and that we had better not get too dogmatic about their not running in packs or in general about their being just behavior replicas of American wolves. These authorities were the above-cited Nelson, in several letters and conversations, and C. Hart Merriam in a letter of December 9, 1924.

In 1926, with the hilarious Lake Winnipeg (Ben Cockrane) and Ignace yarns fresh in mind, I found myself an after-dinner speaker at a New York banquet of the Western Universities Club where Kent Cooper, then recently elected General Manager of the *Associated Press,* presided. The opportunity was too good, and I dealt with press faking, spinning yarn after yarn and alleging, in some cases not correctly, that these had been carried by the *Associated Press.*

On July 8, 1926, I received a letter from Jackson S. Elliott, Assistant General Manager, saying that the *Associated Press* was making "use of the information you gave to us about the wolves not running in packs in order to have our own service as near accurate as possible."

Three things seemed to me: that the *AP* carried fewer American wolf stories during the next several years, that most American wolf stories in the press during that time were not of *AP* origin, but that stories of wolf-packs from abroad failed to decrease in number.

Magazines were active in European tales. Through an article, "Russia of the Hour," by Junius B. Wood, the

National Geographic Magazine, for November, 1926, p. 521, said:

"It is only a step from Moscow . . . into the wide open spaces. Wolves and bears still roam in the Moscow district, and when the dull winter dusk comes at 2 o'clock in the afternoon and the country is under its white mantle of snow, hunger drives them to prey on mankind.

"They boldly attack villages and, this year, even assailed a railroad train of cattle. No peasant ventures alone far outside his village, and one group of 20 men, fancying safety in numbers, was attacked by a wolf-pack. Several were killed and all seriously torn before the pack was driven off."

The author proved to be a correspondent of the Chicago *Daily News,* with broad experience of travel, including Russia. I wrote him July 14, 1927, with interest in his picture of Russia under the Soviets, asking several questions, mainly ones that would enable me to check on the reports further: On what railroad and near or between what towns was the cattle train attacked, whence did the information come, when did the attack take place? Could the author furnish corresponding information regarding the twenty men attacked? What further information could he give regarding wolves in Russia, as to their traveling or working in packs? What sources for still more knowledge could he suggest?

Wood wrote from Paris, France, August 31:

"Your letter of July 14, in which a certain unidentified group designated as 'we' requests further information concerning my reference to Russian wolves in an article in the *National Geographic Magazine* has been forwarded to me here. From time to time this coming winter when I return to the U.S.S.R. I will be pleased to send you what information I receive on this subject as wolves are as active a source of news in that country as bootleggers are in the U. S. A.

"This information was taken from Soviet newspapers. The attack on the cattle train standing on a siding was later corroborated from other sources. The attack on the villagers went into details to the extent of giving the names of those killed. Both occurred in the winter of 1926-7. As I do not have my papers here and do not remember the names of villages, railroad, casualties and other details requested in questions 1, 2 and 3, I must postpone answering further until I return to Moscow and have opportunity to look them up.

"Your statement 'You know, of course, that of all wolf-pack stories published by the American newspapers, more than 75 per cent are without any foundation whatever, and that most of the rest are based on some misapprehension' indicates a clairvoyance worthy of your fellow explorer 'Doc' Cook. It is the first suggestion which has come to me that I 'know', or even admit such a theory. It is far from proven. . . . (I) have serious doubts of your impartiality on the gregariousness of wolves. Though entirely personal, my humble opinion would accept the version of unscientific but not blind natives, including rural correspondents, who are living with wolves in preference to scientists' dogmas which appeal to publishers and lyceum managers. . . ."

The letter then goes on to valuable and no doubt accurately quoted statements by Russians on wolves, ending with: "Packs are reported as varying from 5 to more than 100 which, while leaving the figures open to doubt, cannot be entirely an optical illusion."

The promised letter of information from Moscow did not

171

come, but I secured Moscow and general U.S.S.R. information from other sources. Waldemar Jochelson, distinguished Russian traveler and anthropologist, was then in New York and wrote me twice concerning the Wood article, July 27 and August 11, 1927. The letters do not say it outright, but there is to be inferred from them a view that wolf-packs do exist, or at least may exist. In this Jochelson resembles most Russians whom I know. But, again like most, he holds this belief, or this willingness to believe, in spite of, rather than because of, his own experience. He says in the August 11 letter:

"As to my own observations in Siberia before the railroad was built and in places far away from the railroad after its construction I may say that I never saw a single wolf in my numerous voyages except puppies taken from wolf's den.

"I was told by my reindeer drivers of instances when single wolves attacking herds of reindeer seized calves in spite of the presence of the herdsmen. I remember one case when a reindeer of my team came running and fell exhausted at the entrance of my tent and the team driver told me that the reindeer was pursued by a wolf.

"Siberian hunters told me the following on the habits of the Siberian wolf. He does not like the woods, preferring the tundra and other open places, where he can see and smell his prey from a distance. Grown up wolves do not like company. Wolves have separate dens and she-wolves abandon their puppies when they become able to hunt for themselves."

The outstanding foreign wolf tale of 1927, not so much in itself as in what it led to, was printed as an *Associated Press* release by the New York *Times,* February 9:

CAUCASUS WOLVES BOMBED FROM AIRPLANE;
HUNGRY PACKS INVADE TOWNS, KILLING PEASANTS

GENEVA, Feb. 8 (AP).—Wolves in the Caucasus have become so numerous that the military authorities there sent an airplane to the infested districts, where poison gas bombs were dropped on packs, killing 200 of the invaders, say reports received by the League of Nations.

Wolves are becoming a menace to the lives of peasants in remote regions of Russia, Poland and some other countries of East Central Europe, the reports say. Ferocious from hunger, these beasts, which have multiplied surprisingly, are reported as frequently making attacks on villages, and in some cases have killed and devoured helpless peasants.

Austria reports that one farmer kept twelve wolves at bay with an axe, wounding them all with powerful swinging blows, and that he was finally rescued by villagers, who saved his life by quick bandaging of bleeding arms and legs.

In the district of Vilna, Poland, packs of wolves, maddened by cold and hunger, descended on the town of Ostrovsk and boldly attacked the inhabitants, who, during several hours, were obliged to put up an organized defense with rifle and shotgun before the savage enemy retired. Poland is reported to have mobilized several regiments to carry on an offensive against wolves.

From Russia come even more terrifying stories. In the rural region wolves by hundreds attack villages and even boldly enter the smaller cities in broad daylight. At Verchofourye five peasants were slain by the beasts before the packs were driven off.

At Orenburg three packs entered the town from different points, throwing the population into a panic and forcing all to barricade themselves in their houses, from which they launched a steady fire, finally killing all the wolves, which tenaciously refused to abandon their attack.

Perhaps through too much Edgar Wallace and E. Phillips Oppenheim I got on this story a slant which appears from a letter written by N. M. Stiles, Foreign News Editor of the *Associated Press,* to their Geneva correspondent, Joseph E. Sharkey, on February 24:

"Please recall your Wolf story which you sent us by mail. We used it on February 8, but before it got to the wires we sent out a note to editors suggesting its elimination for two reasons, the first being that the incidents described were so extraordinary, the second being that the statement that wolves travel in packs has been disputed. However, although the story did not get on the wires, two of the New York papers nevertheless printed it— the New York *Times* putting it in a box on the front page.

"Now comes a letter from Vilhjalmur Stefansson, in which he asks the following somewhat startling and curious question:

'Do you suppose the wolf dispatch you carried about two weeks ago from Geneva could possibly have been some sort of a cipher message on behalf of almost any sort of secret organization? If so, you are the people to do detective work on its origin. I am putting out two or three lines to trace it from the pseudo-natural history point of view.'

"As you recall we cabled you for confirmation of the story, and you replied that the reports were 'received unofficially leanations (League of Nations) circles also printed widely Swiss newspapers.' Now when you come to read this story with the thought in mind that the word 'wolves' might be a code word to identify some sort of an organization, as for instance an anti-Bolsheviki outfit, the dispatch does read most interestingly.

One can imagine that the organization was putting these messages over on the Swiss newspapers."

Meantime I tried to find out directly how the League was connected and wrote to the League of Nations Non-Partisan Association of New York City. Their librarian, A. G. F. Aylmer, replied February 24 that they could not understand how the wolf stories should interest the League, and while, like me, they had seen the press despatch, they had no direct information of any similar kind from Geneva. Their office would let me know if they found later that there had been some League connection.

The Stiles letter brought a reply from Sharkey, dated March 12. It puts the case reasonably and shows, particularly in the last of our quoted paragraphs, how normal it is in Europe to read, pass on, and believe wolf-pack stories.

"Answering your letter of February 24 concerning the wolf mail story let me say that this was founded on stories and despatches appearing in Swiss newspapers and on confirmatory talks with secretaries of the League of Nations. . . .

"The League interest in the wolf reports is chiefly economic. The reason was explained to me at the time by . . . member of the League information section. . . .

"He told me about recent cases of wolf-packs attacking peasants in the outlying districts. I have never before heard disputed the statement that Russian wolves 'carry on' in packs. When I was in Siberia in the winter of 1918-19 a detachment of the British Hampshire regiment which 'en-sleighed' from Omsk to Ekaterinburg was attacked by a pack of wolves. The soldiers killed most of them. Participants told me the story personally

175

and I wrote it at the time. The whole history of Russia shows that wolves, desperate with hunger, will attack in packs. The word pack means what it says.

"Since mailing you my story there has appeared a despatch from Constantinople declaring that wolves had attacked people in the outskirts. There is a general idea that the lack of arms in Russia (the Soviet government not favoring extensive arsenals in the outlying districts) has led to a big increase in wolves while the present severe winter has brought the beasts out into the open to secure food. I am sorry I have thrown away all my clippings. Certainly Mr. Stefansson's theory is startling and interesting and I shall follow any new wolf despatch from a new angle, letting you know, of course, the result.

"The wolf narratives have created no stir in Europe whatsoever because they are regarded as entirely probable, given the circumstances outlined above."

In due course a letter came from the Information Department of the League of Nations, dated Geneva, March 14, and signed by Arthur Sweetser. This letter vouches for the generally high character of the American press representatives at Geneva, the particularly high character of Joseph E. Sharkey, and the authenticity of the news conveyed by Sharkey so far as concerns its having been received by the League of Nations organization and passed on by them. The general tenor of Mr. Sweetser's long and careful statement is that, without being exactly able to prove the truth of the stories, he really knows them to be correct, and that therefore the League is neither a victim of propaganda nor indulging in any when it passes on information of this kind. One section of his letter reads:

". . . it is a fact that one of our officials has seen 6, 8, or 10 (he does not remember the exact number) despatches from Eastern European countries regarding the increasing depredations and boldness of wolves. . . . The official in question is a native of that part of Europe and his information, and the experience of his friends as to the habits of wolves, differs from that of Mr. Stefansson."

On June 1, Sharkey wrote me from Geneva:

". . . there may be an inherent difference in the wolves found in North America and those found in Russia, including, of course, Siberia. I personally spent three months in Siberia during the winter of 1918-1919, and persons who had long lived there frequently spoke to me about the depredations of wolves which seemed to run in packs. . . .

". . . I want to bring to your attention the testimony of a young Frenchman who with others was conducting an aeroplane trip over Ukraine during the latter part of the war. . . . He said: 'I think I can throw some light on that question, for when I and my colleagues were flying over Southern Ukraine we distinctly saw a pack of wolves marching slowly and somewhat solemnly through an opening in the woods. The band seemed to have a distinct formation with one wolf striding some feet ahead of the main pack as if he were their leader. Stragglers were seen in the rear, but the whole band seemed to have a distinct and almost military formation under a distinct leader.'

"I have talked again with the Polish friend whose father did a good deal of hunting of wolves, and he repeated that there is no doubt but that in Poland, where the wolves run over from Russia, the animals operate in packs or groups."

The *Associated Press* received as late as March 23 pack

177

despatches from Geneva, "where interest in news of wolf activity is chiefly economic." One of the despatches closed with these three paragraphs:

"There is a general belief here that the lack of arms in the Russian country districts has led to a big increase in the number of wolves, while the severe winter has brought the beasts into the open to secure food.

"Despite the assertions of many naturalists that wolves do not hunt in packs those who have personal knowledge of wolf hunting, particularly in Poland, assert that wolves, desperate with hunger, will attack in packs.

"In the winter of 1918-19 a detachment of the British Hampshire regiment in Siberia which went by sleigh from Omsk to Ekaterinburg reported an attack by a pack of wolves. The soldiers killed most of the animals by rifle fire."

These despatches, though I saw them through the kindness of the *Associated Press,* were not sent out to the newspapers—for the reasons given in the already-quoted letter from their Foreign News Editor. On June 22, Stiles wrote further:

"I have just read your article on wolves in the *American Mercury,* and am reminded that I intended to send you a mail story on the subject that we received some time ago from our then correspondent in Moscow, Mr. James A. Mills. We did not make use of it, as it was for the most part a denial of the wolf story that came from Geneva to which you called our attention and which we had already endeavored to 'kill.' "

The Mills contribution is valuable as a statement of the time from Moscow and is, of course, wholly authentic to the extent that it is a report of what was believed there then about wolves. We accordingly use more than three-quarters of it:

"Moscow, March 17.—Soviet Government officials were amazed at reports reaching the League of Nations recently that Russia was overrun with wolves to such an extent that in the Caucasus region the military authorities had to dispatch airplanes with poison-gas bombs to kill the invaders. The wolves had become so numerous and ferocious, the League reports said, that they devoured human beings and terrified whole cities and towns.

" 'A wolf story is always as good as a fish story,' said a prominent Soviet official to the correspondent. 'The more it is exaggerated, the better it sounds. But such stories ought to be left to those whom the late President Roosevelt called "Nature fakers." It is in poor taste for a dignified, serious organization like the League of Nations to issue them. The story about an airplane being sent in pursuit of packs of these wolves is pure fiction. Russia has its share of wolves, but they are no more numerous nor savage than those of any other country.'

"That Russian wolves are no more abundant or ferocious than their brother-wolves in other countries, is however, not strictly accurate; for statistics show that not only are wolves on the increase in Russia, but their depredations are much more extensive and costly than formerly. The animals are also considerably larger, stronger and fiercer than the average wolf. The increase in their number is attributed to the peasants' lack of rifles and shot with which to hunt them. It is only within the last year that the Government, yielding to complaints of the peasants that wolves were menacing their sheep and cattle, organized special detachments of professional hunters to extermi-

nate the wolves, giving a premium for each animal killed.*
"The loss in sheep, cattle and horses caused by wolves during
the last year is estimated at $6,500,000. A full-grown Russian
wolf can easily kill a horse, cow, or even a bull. But he rarely,
according to Russian authorities on natural history, shows sufficient courage to attack a man. Indeed, the wolf usually runs in
terror at the sight of a human being. Even when travelling in
large packs, these Russian experts say, wolves avoid meeting a
man in daylight; they become dangerous only at night, when
they may collectively attack a person along a lonely, dark road
in the country.

"Throughout the day they usually sleep, wandering and hunting in search of prey only in the dark. At such times, say the
Russian authorities, the most formidable weapon against the
animals is not a loaded gun, but a simple flare of artificial light,
like a burning match, a bonfire or an illuminated candle, wolves
having mortal fear of anything resembling fire.

"Wolves always live in families—the father, mother, two
young wolves born the previous year and two baby wolves born
in February or March. Throughout the Summer and Autumn
they never leave the neighborhood where their young were born.
It is only during the mating season in December and January
that the male wolves, seeking their female kin, form packs and
roam for scores of miles at night."

This statement would have been more convincing with
the last paragraph omitted. For perhaps the Russians might
err on packs when they were so wrong, or at least so far
from what naturalists think they know, about mating habits
and size of litters among wolves. The usual view is that

* The United States has long had this type of service. As mentioned, *ante*,
it is administered from Washington by the Biological Survey.

180

instead of being whelped in pairs, as these Moscow inform-
ants had it, wolves are born in litters ranging up to twelve,
and that they do not accompany the mother beyond six or
eight months. It is a fresh contribution, too, that wolf-packs
consist of males that are searching for females.

For the time being the packs had it—Sharkey's suggestion
(and Nelson's and Merriam's) that wolves might be different in Europe seemed to be carrying the day.

But there was the matter of wolves attempting to devour
the Hampshire regiment of British troops on its sleigh journey from Omsk to Ekaterinburg in 1918-19. Sir Sidney
Harmer of the Natural History Museum, South Kensington,
was a student of animal habits and of animal lore. He should
be able to get in touch with members of the Hampshire
regiment, and I wrote him June 23. The Museum's Keeper
of Zoölogy, W. G. Calman, replied on the Museum's behalf
July 21 that the Hampshire story was fading "as wolf stories
generally do when they are more definitely enquired into."
He forwarded a letter dated July 19 from H. M. Howgrave-
Graham, who is Secretary of the Metropolitan Police of
London and was (says *Who's Who*) "Captain in the 1/9
Batln. Hampshire Regiment in India and Siberia, 1914-19."

"I was in Colonel Johnson's Battalion (the Ninth Battalion of
the Hampshire Regiment) and it happens that I was in charge
of the only party which made any considerable sledge journeys
during the winter 1918-19.

"My party tried to get to Orenburg from Omsk but didn't get
so far. We went by train to Troitsk and from there we made two
sledge journeys, one to Verkhne Uralsk and back and one to
Orsk and back. I remember being told that we might see wolves

and had hopes of doing so as we travelled a good deal at night. But we were disappointed and never saw or heard any signs of wolves at all. . . ."

Junius B. Wood said in his above-quoted letter to me:

'Your statement 'You know, of course, that of all wolf-pack stories published by the American newspapers, more than 75 per cent are without any foundation whatever, and that most of the rest are based on some misapprehension' indicates a clairvoyance worthy of your fellow explorer 'Doc' Cook. It is the first suggestion which has come to me that I 'know,' or even admit such a theory . . . unless you can show that you have tabulated and checked the individual inaccuracies of 'all' the newspaper stories which you so sweepingly include, I am extremely sceptical of your '75 per cent' and have serious doubts of your impartiality on the gregariousness of wolves."

It had never been my intention to claim that three-quarters of all cases had already been studied and found without any vestige of truth. What I meant was that several students whom I know, among them the Chief of the United States Biological Survey, had been investigating for years the cases which came to their attention and that three-quarters of these had proved without foundation—while most of the rest, and perhaps all, were based on misquotations, misunderstandings, and the like.

Particularly with regard to a distant and vast realm like the U.S.S.R. it is hard to study all the cases reported. With increasing frequency through my investigations I began to run upon the name of Sergius Buturlin as a lifelong student

182

of Russian and Siberian wild life and as the foremost authority, among other things, on wolves. Accordingly, I wrote
him July 14, 1927, requesting as much general information
and as definite information as he felt like giving. He replied
August 18:

"I began hunting when about 8 years old, now—I am sorry to
say—some 46 years ago. And though my chief interest was always
with birds, and my first ornithological paper was published (in
Okhotnichia Gazeta or *Hunter's Journal*, Moscow) in 1888, I
was, and am still, very fond indeed of big game shooting (bears,
moose, wolves).

"I hunted much in the basin of middle Volga (governments of
Simbirsk—now Ulianovsk—Penza, Kazan, Nijny, Nijny-Novgo-
rod) in governments of Tula and Orel, in Livonia and Esthonia,
in governments of St. Petersburg—now Leningrad—and Nov-
gorod, in Kirghiz country (between Irtysh and Ob), Kulunda
steppe, gov'ts of Tomsk and Irkutsk, and in the north: Arkh-
angelsk and Olonetz gov'ts., Kolguev, Novaia Zemlia, Yakutsk,
Verkhoiansk, middle and lower Kolyma, some parts of Chuk-
chee-land and Kamchatka.

"As from 1888 on I was always an active contributor to almost
all our hunters' journals, Russian and German (we had *Baltische
Waidmann's Blätter*), and from 1898 always took part, as now,
in the editorship of our best hunter's periodicals, I had a vast
amount of correspondence with our most experienced shooting
men.

"I can fairly say that we have now too much wolves in our
country, but I remember years—for instance, about 1900—when
in my native Simbirsk gov. and Penza gov. they were as plentiful
as now.

"And never in my life have I seen more than 14 wolves in one

183

pack, and this only twice. And never have I heard a reliable account of such a case. And I have known many old and experienced professional trappers and hunters.

"Usual number is about 5-8.

"But I have seen—it was about half-past five in the morning on the 13th Oct. 1893, near my grandmother's estate Lava in the middle part of Simbirsk gov., Sura basin,—when a pack of 5 attacked a herd of about 10,000 sheep, frightened about a thousand of them in a narrow ravine and in a few minutes slayed 153 sheep—without even taking away a single sheep, as I drove them away.

"I suppose if I didn't happen to ride near by I would be informed afterward by shepherds that they were attacked by 50 wolves. It was of course too dark to see, but though there was no snow, the ground was soft from rains, and I could count all their footprints in the morning in the bush and woodland near this ravine.

"I am quite sure that wolves (at least in Russia and Siberia) hunt only in family packs, that is, papa, mamma, young ones of the year and often some ones of the previous brood. And this amounts to 5-8, more rarely 9-10, and quite exceptionally 14 specimens."

Privately we had disposed of the Russian packs of the winter 1927 but in the newspapers they continued to do well. There appeared in Miami, Florida, (and no doubt elsewhere), a despatch which we copy from the *News* of June 12:

"MOSCOW, June 11—Ten families were rushed to the Pasteur institute at Moscow from Kalujsky, a small village of the Kuban district, after a large pack of mad wolves had swept down the village street, invading gardens and even entering several homes, biting the residents."

By now the *Associated Press* was keen on wolves—indeed had been for six months when Stiles wrote on September 30 that there was in his office a Polish representative who believed stoutly in wolf-packs and that they had received (and, I gather, killed) a press despatch from Warsaw:

"Polish military patrol Russian border attacked by pack wolves dispersed them with gunfire."

I had long been thinking to write my classmate John B. Stetson who was Minister to Poland. This gave occasion, and he replied June 8, 1928:

"A long time ago I had your letter regarding the possible attacks of wolves. . . .
"While there is much talk about the danger of wolves attacking human beings and while people relate incidents which occurred to them when they have seen wolves which they thought were going to attack them, etc., it is extremely difficult to find specific instances when attacks have been made by wolves. . . .
"I asked the Chief of the Frontier Guards to make an investigation of the various border posts to see if any attacks had been noted along the 1500 kilometer front between Russia and Poland. This region is wild and not densely settled. I enclose herewith the letter which I have received from him."

The letter from General Minkiewicz had specific information on two cases of wolves, each time three in a group, that had been fired on by frontier guards.

185

As to whether wolves attack in large packs, the General says:

"Accounts of wolves attacking men sometimes appearing in the press have their origin in the phantasy of correspondents seeking sensational news.

"In a few cases, however, we have noted a very aggressive attitude displayed by wolves and, if they did not dare to attack me, it was only due to the fact that there were but few of them. . . ."

The general commanding the frontier guard, then, had apparently never heard that (around September, 1927) "Polish military patrol Russian border attacked by pack wolves dispersed them with gunfire."

Lee Smits had suggested my writing David C. Mills of the National Association of Fur Industries as likely to be informed on wolf-packs. Mills wrote from New York, December 9, 1927. A summary of his three-page letter is:

Vladimir Eitington (of Eitington-Schild Co., 226 West 30th Street, New York City) was once followed by wolves in Siberia until he camped and built a fire. He thought there might have been 15 or 25, "but he says that in the dark and under such circumstances, he could not make a rational estimate."

Many animals have the following habit. Mills cites from his own experience wolves (two), coyotes (several), and bears.

Writer's opinion, and that of his friend, is that wolves never kill people. Specially cited here is John B. Burnham, noted American authority on wild animals, former secretary of the American Game Protective Association.

186

Mills thinks that "common knowledge" of wolves and suchlike is usually wrong. Then he has his own summary:

"The information from Russian sources in re. the wolf myth is—

"1st There has never been a scientific investigation of the question.

"2nd That wolves, under ordinary conditions, do not attack humans.

"3rd That mad wolves sometimes enter villages and snap right and left at anything or anyone. I presume this means rabies, as that disease is also found in America among coyotes.

"4th That they have no knowledge of any authenticated case of wolves in packs attacking travelers in sleighs, etc., but do not know that it has never happened."

In 1928, perhaps for variety, the newspaper wolf-packs transferred their chief European activities to districts other than hackneyed Poland and Russia. The American papers informed us soon after the New Year (we quote the New York *World* of January 6) that:

"... eleven peasant girls of the Czechoslovakian town of Maramaros Sziget were devoured by wolves when returning from a neighboring village through the forest."

The Consul General of Czechoslovakia gave preliminary reply to my inquiry on January 10, warning that stories of wolves "especially stories from Vienna are always greatly exaggerated." On April 2 he wrote that "we have here the reply of the Administration of the Sub-Carpathian Ruthenia stating that the report of killing of eleven peasant girls by wolves in Maramaros Sziget is not true." Further on the letter says that some wolves were seen near Maramaros Sziget in January "and this was the possible foundation for the wild report of *Neue Freie Presse.*"

November 7 the *Evening Standard* of London, England, printed a Moscow despatch of even date:

"Wolves are becoming a menace to life in the country districts of North Russia and Siberia. . . .

". . . A pack of several hundred attacked a priest and his wife while they were driving from one village to another 100 miles south of Moscow.

"While his wife held the reins, the priest beat off the wolves with a whip. Suddenly a wolf bit one of the horse's legs. It lurched forward, throwing the priest from the wagon. He was killed by the wolves. The horse carried the woman to safety.

"Similar attacks on persons are reported daily from all parts of the country.—International News Service."

On this the Chairman of the Amtorg Trading Corporation, Saul G. Bron, wrote me November 25:

"These are termed in the Soviet Union as the 'big Russian cranberry tree' tales. Nevertheless, there is no doubt that malicious white-Russian propaganda agencies . . . are working overtime and that the comparative scarcity of reliable information about the U.S.S.R. in this country makes a fertile field for the circulation of stories about uprisings, wolves roaming the countryside, etc."

October 25, C. K. Ogden (whom H. G. Wells has since discussed in the Fifth Book of *The Shape of Things to*

Come) wrote me from the Royal Societies Club, London. He told that the De Reszke cigarette had small prize cards in their packages and that the one on The Wolf said "dogs and wolves hunt in packs." He wrote them and they replied:

"We are sorry that we cannot give you any zoological authority to maintain the view that wolves hunt in packs as stated on the back of picture No. 26 of our Zoological Studies. . . . The error will be corrected should we have a reprint of the series."

Through laxity, or real failure of the sources, my wolf record is blank for Europe and Asia during 1930 and 1931—there is no account of tenderly-nurtured wolf children from India, of babies devoured in Siberia, of forays of Rumanian wolves into Czechoslovakia. But in 1932 the times were more abundant and my records are bulky.

On January 10, 1932, Duncan Campbell Scott, president of the Canadian Authors' Association, descended to his more factual role of president of the Royal Society and wrote from Ottawa with concern for my wolf studies. He sent a press cutting headed "From Our Own Correspondent, Vienna, Sunday":

"While an express train from Bucharest was snowbound near Zloty and awaiting help, a pack of hungry wolves bore down upon it.

"Having no firearms, the train staff emptied a luggage van and threw into it raw meat from the restaurant car.

"Twenty or more wolves jumped into the van and began to fight one another for the meat. The doors were promptly locked and later the train proceeded on its journey to Kischinev, Bessarabia. On arrival 18 wolves were found alive, the rest having been torn to pieces."

189

In view of the style of this despatch I have looked up Karel Capek in *Who's Who* and *Britannica* but cannot determine from the brief sketches whether he was in Vienna during January, 1932.

How wolf stories rotate appeared two years later when C. K. Ogden sent me what is essentially the same tale—though with a new city of origin, a new date line, a few new frills. The cutting is unfortunately from an unnamed paper of London, England—I dare not guess which paper, though I think I recognize the style. It was from Budapest, December 19, 1933. Like the one of two years earlier it was "From Our Own Correspondent." It ran:

"An unpleasant adventure which overtook the direct train from Bucarest to Budapest is reported from Bucarest.

"During the night the train was held up by snowdrifts and obliged to stand nine hours in an uninhabited part of Roumania. To the terror of the passengers a pack of wolves surrounded the train, and the situation was only saved by the wit of a conductor.

"An order was given that the luggage van should be emptied, and some raw meat from the kitchen was then placed in the van and the doors thrown open. When all the wolves were safely inside the van the doors were shut, and the train continued its journey with these unusual passengers.

At the station of Chrisina, in Roumania, the wolves were transferred to cages which had been prepared for them."

It is usually difficult to trace stories from the Balkans, perhaps because their Ministers and Consuls there get tired of answering questions about all the strange things we print from their part of the world. For instance, I still covet the

190

real truth on what appeared, as Special Correspondence, in the New York *Times,* February 28, 1932, from Bucharest:

"Two peasants on the way to market in Oradea Mare were attacked on the highroad today by a pack of starving wolves. They were unarmed and, after a brief attempt to beat off the animals with sticks, were pulled down, killed and partly devoured."

I queried the Roumanian Legation on this but never had a reply.

I have had better luck with the northern countries, perhaps because there I know the ropes. The Director of the University Museum, Philadelphia, wrote March 21 on behalf of himself and one of his vice-presidents, passing on to me heartrending news:

WOLVES KILL GIRL IN FINLAND;
INVADE VILLAGES FOR FOOD
Wireless to The New York *Times.*

"HELSINGFORS, March 4.—Villagers in Eastern Finland were terrorized this week by an invasion of hungry wolves, roaming southward from the frozen plains of Lapland.

"The beasts entered villages and even the outlying districts of towns in search of food. The young daughter of a farmer in middle Finland was attacked and killed by wolves while she was walking on a highway near her home. Her parents found only bones and fragments of clothing after the tragedy. . . ."

I wrote Helsingfors, sending a copy of the *Times* despatch. The Intendent of the Zoological Museum replied March 20th:

191

"... it is not true that a young daughter of a farmer was attacked and killed. A similar notice was found in our press, so that the telegram to New York is therefore explicable. By an official investigation, the whole thing turned out to be a manifestation of too vivid imagination—somebody had found a bloody rag on the road, and thus the story was immediately given. In the same way it is a real nonsense that the wolves had penetrated into villages and towns. The whole thing was about a couple of animals which killed a number of dogs before they were driven away and killed."

The cruel ingenuity of man towards wolves is a defensive reaction to the cruel rapacity of wolves toward man. In fact, the wide dissemination of stories about packs is a necessity in justifying the extensiveness of the war we wage and the character of the weapons and tactics we use. We would not be half so successful in protecting the chickens of the farmer and the sheep of the rancher if we did not constantly circulate reports of how wolves will attack anything from a child playing on a cabin floor in Michigan to a regiment of British troops in Siberia.

Some of the methods used against wolves are commonplace, not worth describing, though we might name a few of them—trapping, shooting, the use of poisoned bait, the finding of dens and smoking out of the pups to be clubbed to death. One method is so peculiar that we describe it.

Under date of March 12, 1927, the *Associated Press* received, but did not issue to the newspapers, information upon the extent and manner of wolf hunting in Poland.

"... for centuries wolf hunts have been carried out by Poles

(1) by the aristocrats as a sport, (2) by peasants as a means of livelihood. The same method, which is gentle, as you will see, has been employed by nobility and peasant.

"A live pig is attached by a leather rope at the rear of sleigh or sled in which six or seven men take their places, all heavily armed. The sleigh is drawn by two or three horses. Two men devote themselves exclusively to protecting the horses from the onslaught of the wolves which, led from their lairs by the screams of the suffering and dying hog, rush in a pack after the swiftly moving sleigh. Two other men empty their rifles at wolves from either side and two others do their execution from the rear.

". . . (Our informant) said his father has often hunted wolves, which attack in packs, after this fashion."

I might have traced this account through my aforementioned classmate the Minister to Poland, and would have done so but for chancing upon remarks of Sir Albert Gray before the Royal Geographical Society of London as they are reported in that society's *Journal* for June, 1921, p. 445. They are to the effect that people continue holding strange, romantic, beliefs no matter how often these are exposed. He has in mind chiefly the idea that wolves run in packs and quotes the (for the time and place) annihilation of the idea by Baddeley in his *Russia in the Eighties, Sport and Politics,* (London, 1921). I was on the track of wolf-packs then and followed Sir Albert's clue. I found the author demolishing the pack to his own satisfaction and that he also pays his respects to various beliefs regarding the methods of hunting wolves.

John F. Baddeley spent in Russia, of which a large section of Poland was then a part, most of the decade following

1879 and much of those years in hunting and in the company of sportsmen and naturalists. After denying that wolves ever go in packs and after denying also that wolves are numerous in Russia, he says, beginning on p. 149:

"The idea that wolves are very numerous in Russia has gained substance, also, from the very natural tendency of certain sportsmen to exaggerate their performances; and more especially is this the case in regard to that form of sport in which wolves and sucking-pigs are supposed to play the chief parts. According to published accounts—I have one or two before me but will not pillory the writers—you have only to take a sucking-pig (in good voice) and drive along the highroad in a sledge any winter's night, trailing behind you a bundle of straw at the end of a string to represent piggy—who meantime must be made to squeal his loudest—to enjoy excellent sport with the numerous wolves that will assuredly come to the lure the first time of asking. Here again I am regretfully forced to say that I never knew a man of proved veracity who claimed to have bagged even one wolf by this method, while one honest friend assured me that he had tried it no less than seventeen times in places where wolves were known to exist, but had only once had a shot at what he thought might be one."

It may be, as claimed by this author, that wolves do not swarm in from Polish forests at the squeals of a pig, but the belief that they do is useful. Faraway, in Michigan for instance, stories detailing the alleged Polish ingenuities will tend to lead American woodsmen to cleverness of wolf-killing that, in the long run, saves the local farmers a good many chickens and lambs.

194

A reporter friend tells that the wolf-pack is a standard joke among the foreign correspondents in Europe, certainly in Vienna, and he has passed on to me a crystallization of their attitude, as expressed by the correspondent for a London paper:

The yarn is that the Orient Express was held up by a pack of wolves. They began at the front end, eating the engineer and fireman, and proceeded towards the rear, devouring everyone as they went until, in the last car, they came upon a correspondent whom they spared on his promise that he would give them adequate publicity.

CRUMBS FOR PACK BELIEVERS

The evidence has been, then, that wolf-packs which come up to motion picture and folklore standards do not exist. But there still may be a foundation of reality upon which the imaginative and inventive have built their fabrications.

Students who scout the pack as ordinarily defined and pictured have nevertheless agreed on certain things which, by multiplication, magnification and misinterpretation, could start the pack idea going, or at any rate might keep it going.

Obviously wolf pups will remain with their mother until weaned. Doubtless the family breaks up before the young are quite full grown, or when they are between five and eight months old. There may be as many as twelve in a litter, fourteen by some views. When you meet stories of packs with five to fifteen in them you can thus have a true report of a family hunting, traveling or living together. If the story describes a "gigantic leader of the pack" you may be sure that a family is involved. With the even-sized pups taken for normal wolves, mama looks colossal. If there are two gigantic leaders, then papa must be traveling along.

A foremost authority for America, Nelson, and a foremost one for Eurasia, Buturlin, differ on one point, though only in degree. Nelson is somewhere between thinking it rare and thinking it improbable that last year's pups will be found still traveling with their mother after this year's become large enough to hunt; Buturlin thinks it rare but sees no improbability. Accordingly, when Nelson credits a report of say twenty wolves he is inclined to think that two families have come together accidentally for a few moments, or are only following each other accidentally instead of really traveling together. Buturlin feels these are probably one mother's litters of two years and that they are in semi-permanent company.*

With such family groups for nuclei, the traveler's tale, the peasant's yarn which the reporter believes, become easy. Just multiply by ten and you have packs of 50, 100, 200. Zero is nothing. So what is a zero more or less in a good yarn?

There are methods other than simple multiplication which can lead reasonably to packs of great size.

In the Arctic and sub-Arctic I have stood at vantage points from which I could see in one, two, or several directions from me scattered wolves which, counted together, would

---

* J. Stokley Ligon, American student of wild life, says· "I am inclined to agree with Dr Nelson regarding young of a previous year not banding with parent animals and their young of a current year." (Letter March 17, 1928.) He writes in the same letter: "I have never observed the big packs of wolves one hears and reads about."

make a "pack." These are no more really a pack of wolves than the scattered and unconnected pickpockets of a city are a band of thieves. But assume the story is thrice repeated. First version: I saw 100 wolves from one place. Second version: Jones saw 100 wolves in one place. Third version: Brown says Jones saw a pack of 100 wolves.

It might happen that two wolf families scent a caribou or a band. Running up the wind they might so nearly come together, without really joining, that a careless observer seeing the two packs running in the same direction would take them to be one pack—this all the more because groups that are indubitably a mother with pups will sometimes string out half a mile as they lope in pursuit of caribou. But two families strung out, say a mile from the first to the last of them, would not make a pack in the sense of a band working systematically and semi-permanently together.

With considerations such as these in mind, we examine seemingly reliable testimony for considerable numbers of wolves having been observed together.

"Considerable" needs defining. The wolf-killing service of the U. S. Biological Survey were polled by Nelson and voted for two, three, and at highest five wolves being seen together, these always mother or parents with pups. Many have testified for seven in a family, however, among them the zoologist, Dr. R. M. Anderson, Chief Biologist, Ottawa, who has in Canada an official position similar to Nelson's in the United States. A few apparently good witnesses have testified to nine. We are, then, chiefly concerned in this section with numbers larger than nine and with their interpretation—were they really together and then in what sense?

197

How permanently were they together? Were they family groups?

My voluminous correspondence on packs was, as said, begun in 1922 when I realized that my own belief in wolf-packs, begun in *The Friendly Arctic* (see that book's index) was untenable. We have already used that part of the correspondence which attempted to trace packs reported between 1922 and 1936, finding all that could be traced wanting. We now canvass the rest of the evidence, using it in the main chronologically.

The Encyclopedia Britannica, Fourteenth Edition, says in its article on wolves that: "Except during summer when the young families of cubs are being separately provided for by their parents they assemble in troops or packs."

That edition is dated 1929. Seven years before, on March 27, 1922, Anderson wrote to Nelson that during several years spent in Arctic and sub-Arctic Canada and Alaska:

". . . I never saw more than seven wolves in any band nor did I hear of any larger bands than seven. A reliable Eskimo in my employ told me that he was once followed by nine wolves on a river near Herschel Island, and in the Joint Report, *Survey International Boundary, 141st Meridian,* 1918, there is a report of nine wolves seen in a band on the boundary.

"In that region the wolves are more often seen in bunches of two or three, or singly, and the bunches of five or more are probably an old female with her cubs of the year. Several that we killed out of such a band at Langton Bay were all immature. . . .

"I have heard occasional vague rumors of larger bands of wolves in more southerly parts of Canada, but have never been able to verify any such reports. . . ."

198

In passing on to me, November 25, 1922, the information given by Anderson, Nelson added:

". . . I am satisfied that the stories of great packs of wolves banded together to pursue caribou or any other game are based on the fertile imagination of the writers and not on observations in the field. It is common knowledge that the wolves pair more or less permanently and are in no sense gregarious animals. At the end of each breeding season and until well into the following winter, my field experience and the information which has come to the Biological Survey from its large force of hunters destroying predatory animals in the western states, coincide in enumerating packs of wolves not exceeding the ordinary normal number of the two parents and the litter of the season which may vary from three or four animals up to ten or twelve. Such bands of parents and their young of the year hunt together until well into the following winter but with the approach of spring they separate to mate. . . . There is a bare possibility that in pursuing bands of reindeer or caribou, several of these family packs of wolves might accidentally come together in pursuit but such union would be purely fortuitous and of very temporary endurance.

"My observations and personal information obtained at first hand extends from the mountains bordering the valley of Mexico, north to the Arctic circle in Alaska and also the observations of our large corps of hunters numbering several hundred men, who, during the progress of their campaign against predatory animals in the western states have killed between four and five thousand of these animals within the last six years."

Nelson wrote me January 4, 1923, after a fresh study of some Russian evidence, that clearly they have there the same situation as we have here, "the wolves running in family parties exactly as they do in North America, running in great bands only in literature and folklore."

On January 18 Harkin sent me a long quotation from a story he had found in "one of our local papers, under date the 17th instant." It is a long statement, generally claiming that wolves are not dangerous. A section bearing on our present theme is under the subhead "Whole Pack Fled." In northern Ontario the sledge was crossing a lake, on a winter evening, toward an island:

"We were just making the point of this island, and what should we meet coming from the other side but a pack of wolves. We just met there. The leader, a big, grizzled, long-legged old chap, looked me over from a distance of about twenty feet; the rest of the pack ranged behind and alongside of him, their tails straight out for just about as long as it takes to stiffen them out with fear. Then they broke. They just flattened out on the ice and flew—twenty-one of them."

We have used in another connection parts of a letter from Inspector Jennings of the R.C.M.P., Edmonton, April 20, 1923, one of the most informative of the whole wolf correspondence:

". . . it appears timber wolves are becoming more numerous in the McKenzie Delta, but do not appear to be running in packs. At Baillie Island where a number were killed in the winter of 1921-22 they appear to be running in packs of from four to seven. We have also paid bounties at Tree River Detachment for wolves killed in the Coronation Gulf. C. Klinkenberg, whom you remember, told me in 1921, when I was North, of a fight he had with a she wolf and five yearling pups. He was attacked by all of them, and only by the fortunate appearance of his son with his rifle was his life saved. . . . The general impression is that such bands, or what may be called a band, is generally a family, and that it is only occasionally, when hunting for food, that two or more families might come together and constitute a real pack.

"In regard to the McKenzie District, an old prospector who has travelled from the headwaters of the Thelon River to the British Columbia boundary in the West states that while east of the McKenzie River wolves may be plentiful when Caribou are numerous, he has never seen them in what may be called a pack, although at times in the open several wolves may be seen together, but evidently working independently. Below Simpson and also on the Liard River in the Foot Hills, he has seen as many as twenty under one leader, but generally the pack is from five to nine. The band of twenty was following a moose track. At another time he states that when his party had killed a moose, shortly after, a large grey wolf was seen on the opposite side of the river. This wolf called a few times and was soon joined by others to the number of ten. . . .

"One of my officers in February, 1916, while traveling on the McKenzie, about 30 miles below Simpson, came upon a band of seven, at a place where a moose had been killed the previous day."

December 19, 1924, Nelson reaffirmed his lack of evidence for believing that two or more families ever made up a "temporary pack." He also defined the terms under which, for sake of argument, he might concede theoretically, in the absence of evidence, that unions might take place.

"I am still skeptical about the formation of wolf-packs which are made up of two or more families hunting in companionship.

I have no knowledge of any such combination, and knowing the habits and characteristics of wolves doubt this occurring except under what might be termed fortuitous circumstances. Two or more family parties of wolves might incidentally come together in the pursuit of the same game animal and join in the kill; but if they did so I should expect a fierce battle to ensue between the different parties of wolves, strangers to one another, just as would happen in the case of strange dogs. Furthermore, I believe that should two or more family parties of wolves thus come together in the immediate pursuit of game, they would promptly spread into their original units as soon as the kill was made or the chase ended. Wolves have much the same nature as dogs, and the hostility that strange dogs show one to another is a good indication of what might be expected on the part of wolves. . . ."

C. Hart Merriam wrote January 12, 1925, quoting his own *Mammals of the Adirondacks* (New York, 1882):

"Comparatively few wolves are now to be found in the Adirondacks, though twelve years ago they were quite abundant, and used to hunt in packs of half a dozen or more. . . . The amount of noise that a single wolf is capable of producing is simply astonishing, and many amusing episodes of camp lore owe their origin to this fact. More than one 'lone traveler' has hastily taken to a tree, and remained in the inhospitable shelter of its scrawny branches for an entire night, believing himself surrounded by a pack of at least fifty fierce and hungry wolves, when, in reality, there was but one, and (as its tracks afterwards proved) it was on the farther side of a lake, a couple of miles away."

Merriam further quotes Theodore Roosevelt's *Hunting Trips of a Ranchman* (New York, 1885):

"According to my experience, the wolf is rather solitary. A single one or a pair will be found by themselves, or possibly with one or more well-grown young ones, and will then hunt over a large tract where no other wolves will be found; and as they wander very far, and as their melancholy howlings have a most ventriloquial effect, they are often thought to be much more plentiful than they are."

In its care to avoid nature faking the *Associated Press* refused to circulate a story which they received from Winnipeg and which Jackson S. Elliott, Assistant General Manager, sent along for my wolf files July 8, 1926. That account, however, runs well within family limits and so has the probabilities for it. The applicable section runs that "the hunter noticed a string of seven grey wolves crossing the prairie. He waited until they approached and was successful in bringing down five of them."

The story seemed probably correct and gave a lead to further information, so I wrote A. Brabant, Fur Trade Commissioner of the Hudson's Bay Company, Winnipeg, and received through him a valuable letter from their A. C. Clark, Norway House, Manitoba, August 3:

"Carl Sherman, the trapper who killed the wolves referred to, is at present in this locality, and I have been able to get the details of the story referred to.

"Sherman is trapping on the Hayes River, about 150 miles north of Oxford House Post. He was travelling north one day early in November . . . and saw about 14 or 15 wolves making for the point on which he stood. When they got to within 75 yards of him, he fired and brought down the leader. By the time

203

they got out of sight, he had killed five. . . . They were all full grown, and all males. The wolves were not dangerous, but made for safety, as soon as they got over the surprise of the first shot. The wind was in the wrong direction for the wolves to get the scent of Sherman.

"I can vouch for the above story being correct. . . ."

This, then, is a remarkable story. The reader will find several things in which it contradicts, or seems to contradict, Nelson, Buturlin, and Anderson in so far as he was quoted (above) by Nelson. It fits badly with the rest of our evidence but is nevertheless impressively vouched for.

Information similarly difficult came in an undated letter July, 1927, from Fred B. Kniffen of the Department of Geography, University of California, Berkeley:

". . . I have seen two wolf-packs.

"I had occasion to spend the winter of 1923-24 prospecting in the upper Tanana region of Alaska. I hunted considerably as caribou meat furnished an appreciable part of my diet and almost all of that of my dogs. One afternoon I was seated on a little hill about a quarter of a mile from a small lake. Through the natural pass below me the caribou had been passing at the rate of several hundred a day. As I watched, a file of wolves emerged from some brush on the opposite side of the lake, skirted the shore and went off in the direction the caribou were going. They seemed to be running roughly in a column of twos and I counted about twenty-eight in the pack.

"One night I was awakened by the howls of my dogs responding to those of some wolves. I stood in the doorway of my cabin and a little later could distinguish the forms of five wolves against the snow of the river, perhaps seventy-five yards away. The dogs were now growling, apparently in fear. One shot dispersed the wolves. . . .

"These events all occurred in late winter. It is quite possible that an old she wolf and her pups may have accounted for a large part of this but the large pack could hardly be explained away in this fashion."

Kniffen himself suggests a family explanation for his second pack. On July 14 I suggested in a letter to him that *possibly* the first set were not a pack, either,—in the sense of having banded together for cooperative hunting. I said that: "The wolves you saw following each other, though there were twenty-eight, were (then) no more necessarily a pack than eleven college men walking towards an athletic field are necessarily the college team."

The well-known and highly-regarded student of Canadian wild life, Tony Lascelles, wrote for the Winnipeg *Free Press* of April 25, 1936, an article, "The Mammals of Manitoba." A paragraph in it can be read as supporting the traditional wolf-pack—I did not so read it but thought others might. But Lascelles writes from Mistamick Lodge, Dauphin, Manitoba, May 15, 1936, with reference to his use of the key word, that "the pack is a family group and the maximum pack is a maximum family."

With this we close the section of our discussion which is written for those who like to believe that even the seemingly most absurd folklore tale has developed from a nucleus of fact.

WOLVES AND BABES

The misanthropy of wolves, dramatic in their pursuit of wedding parties and in the siege of stalled trains, is particularly horrible toward little children. They eat them all up, rather jocularly in Red Riding Hood, grimly in our newspapers. See, for instance, the tragic story "Copyright, 1928, by the New York Times Company. By Wireless to The New York *Times:*

"RIGA, Jan. 1.—A woman of the Unciany district of Lithuania, riding with a child in a one-horse sleigh and pursued by a pack of wolves, made a desperate effort to escape, but after a short, sharp race the horse collapsed.

"The wolves tore the child from its mother's arms, devoured it, and then fell on the mother. Some peasants, hearing her cries, hurried to the scene and rescued her, torn but still alive.

"As a result of the severe weather the depredations by wolves in many parts of Russia are unusually alarming. The Soviet authorities are carrying out an organized campaign against the danger by offering rewards for wolves' heads. In some districts detachments of the Red Army are used.

"Packs of wolves have appeared in many parts usually immune, especially in the Crimea."

Reporters naturally have time for cabling such stories but ministers at Washington and consuls-general in New York, though frequently kind and helpful, are at times so buried in humdrum that you cannot get them interested. I failed in tracing this despatch from Riga. Therefore we can but deal in likelihoods and refer to the Michigan story of February 3, 1927, reported *ante*—it was nearer home and so we were able to enlist the help of local investigators.

We are reluctant to pursue further this gruesome child-eating. The case against the wolf in this respect is indeed

206

black enough, what with the inclusion of many babes among the people devoured already in this chapter by the ravenous hordes. We turn with relief to a brighter side of the case. In warm contrast are the maternally kind and otherwise friendly wolves that have nursed and cared for children, sometimes even twins, as in the case of Romulus and Remus. In our present century there is never a decade, there is seldom a year, when newspapers do not bring us well-attested cases.

Through the *Associated Press* the New York *Times* reported October 22, 1926 (from London, October 21):

"Two little 'wolf girls' were found recently living in a wolf's den near an isolated village in Bengal, British India. The story is told by *The Westminster Gazette,* which received it from India, vouched for by the Rev. Jal Singh of Midnapur, Bengal, and Bishop Pakenham Walsh of Bishops College, Calcutta.

"Bishop Walsh relates that about the end of August, while visiting the Rev. Jal Singh's orphanage at Midnapur, Mr. Singh recounted how he discovered the 'wolf girls.'

"In a distant part of his district not long before, the villagers pointed out to him a path they avoided because it was haunted by demons. Investigation revealed a wolf den in which there were several wolf cubs and two girls, about two and eight years of age, both exceedingly fierce, running on all fours, uttering guttural barks and living like wolves.

"The supposition was that they were abandoned as babies by their mother or mothers and were found and adopted by the she wolf. With much difficulty, the children were rescued, but the younger died soon afterward.

"The elder child survived and is now at the orphanage. She was gradually weaned from her savage ways, but she fought fiercely against wearing clothes, and tore them off even after they were sewn on her. For a time she refused to be washed and ate with her mouth in a dish. Eventually she was taught to use her hands and say a few words.

"She still is weak mentally and neither cries nor laughs, but is gentle with animals, preferring the company of dogs to children."

Sir Sidney Harmer, British student of wolves, wrote November 15, 1926, that the *Westminster Gazette* had told him they knew the bishop of the story existed and believed the wolf children also were real. Sir Sidney closed:

"I have myself no information on the subject, and I do not know of anyone else who could help you. We are inclined to be a little sceptical."

I never did get farther with the investigation of this particular case.

Reports that were traced, though not by me, appeared several times the next year. The first, "Copyright, 1927, by The New York Times Company—Special Cable to the New York *Times,* Allahabad, British India, April 5," said that:

"Herdsmen near Miawana, seventy-five miles from here, found a small Indian boy supposed to be about 10 years of age, in a wolf's den. From marks in the den it was obvious that the boy had been living there. He was unable to talk or to walk properly, but went on all fours, lapped water and ate grass.

"The boy was brought here, put in a special lockup and supplied with food and medicine. At night he barked, bit himself and other people and had to be tied down. He is very thin and emaciated, but his limbs are otherwise well formed. He has a

208

terrible scar on one side of his face, as if he had been mauled by some animal.

"He has been taken to Bareilly for treatment at a mental hospital."

The *Times* furnished a supplementary note:

"This is the third case of Rudyard Kipling's 'Jungle Book' hero, Mowgli, in real life which has been discovered in India within the last ten months. Last September Bishop Walsh wrote to the Indian *Social Reformer* of Bombay of the case of two little girls who had been found by the Rev. J. Singh in a wolf's den near Bengal. They revealed the same characteristics as the boy described in the Allahabad dispatch. One of them soon pined away and died, but the other rapidly became 'humanized' in Singh's orphanage at Midnapur. It was supposed that the girls, as is sometimes the case in India, had been abandoned in the jungle by their parents on account of their sex and had been mothered by a she wolf which had just been deprived of her young.

"The same explanation would not account for the presence of the boy in a wolf's den near Miawana."

Further news, similarly special and copyrighted, came by wireless from London and was published April 27:

"Further information is now available about the so-called 'wolf-child' whose discovery near Miawana, British India, seventy-five miles from Allahabad, provoked so much discussion. Some travelers tell of similar discoveries extending back many years, but medical authorities are inclined to dismiss them as fables.

"The boy found in Miawana is judged to be between 7 and 12

years old and in general appearance is said to be little different from an ordinary child, but in his actions betrays signs that are declared to point to his bringing up with wolves. He can stand up and walk, but sometimes prefers to crawl, sitting on his haunches with legs curled up and propelling himself forward with the palms of hands. . . .

"He is said to display certain instincts even lower than those of his alleged foster parents. . . ."

On July 10, a long, undated communication marked "London," said that:

"News of the discovery of another alleged wolf-child in India has started a brisk controversy here over the authenticity of such children. No previous wolf-child has occasioned so much stir in scientific quarters as has the boy discovered by Indian herdsmen a few weeks ago in a wolves' cave near Miawana, seventy-five miles from Allahabad.

"Some of the best known medical men in London have called the story incredible. Old Indian army officers have replied by asserting that they have actually seen wolf-children. . . ."

whereupon the *Times* devotes more than a column to a statement generally in support of the India despatches. Among those in favor is:

"Rudyard Kipling, whose Mowgli of the 'Jungle Book' is the best known wolf-child in fiction, has for once withdrawn his veto on newspaper interviews, and is quoted as saying that wolf-children 'are by no means impossible.' The author goes on to say:

" 'There have been other instances of them. They say that the Miawana boy crawls on the hands and knees: I think it much more likely that it would be the knees and elbows. That was the way of the other children who, like Mowgli, were adopted by wolves and knew all the mysteries of the jungle. That way leaves their hands free to seize their prey and to defend themselves.' "

This long article, dealing with many cases of wolf-children, says that:

".... the one commonly known as the Secundra wolf-boy, is the best authenticated case within the memory of living man. This boy was captured in 1867 by a shooting expedition in the unfrequented jungles of Bulandshahr. The hunters surprised a stray wolf, which they followed to a small mound of earth with a flat-topped rock sticking out of the mound. A small, strange-looking animal was asleep in the sun on the rock. To the amazement of the hunting party, it proved to be a boy, who leaped from the rock as soon as he saw the hunters and, running on all fours, disappeared into a cave along with the startled wolf.

"The hunters were either unable or afraid to go further; but, feeling that something ought to be done, they returned to Bulandshahr and consulted the Magistrate. They were advised to go back to the cave and smoke out the wolf and its weird companion. This they did. The wolf was shot as soon as it rushed out and its companion was pounced upon and captured after a severe struggle, during which several members of the party were bitten. Two wolf cubs were also killed and the party returned to the Magistrate to claim a reward for the dead wolf and the dead cubs, and to exhibit the human being they had captured.

"The wolf bounty was paid and the wolf-boy was sent to the Secundra Orphanage. He was thought to be about 7 or 8 years old. For a long time he tore off the clothes that were supplied him and persisted in eating his food from the ground. As the years

211

went by he became more docile and eventually was baptized, taking the name of Sanicher, which is Hindustani for Saturday, the day on which he was captured. His head was small, his forehead low and narrow; his eyes were large and gray and restless. He squinted incessantly and when walking lifted his feet high like a man walking through wet grass, his entire body moving in a series of jerks as he stepped along."

Interest, sympathy, resentment were among the feelings commonly expressed by those who wrote "Letters to the Editor" during the outstanding wolf-child year of 1927. An undated cutting from the New York *Times,* probably around July 15 or 20, has a letter from Jacqueline Nollet:

"Have men for 'humanity's sake' the right to take this Miawana boy away from his mother-wolf and from his brotherly playmates, from the jungle's new and enthralling life, and to condemn him instead to an existence devoid of companionship and a life of utter misery. . . ?

"Since the wolf-man is no longer free to pursue his own mode of living and is considered as a near-animal, could not the Society for the Prevention of Cruelty to Animals interfere and have a law voted to the effect that a child saved from starvation, loved and protected by the wolves against ferocious beasts, might be left to live with his wolf family? And if the boy must be taken away from the wild, could not man take a lesson and be as merciful as a wolf and spare the life of the foster-mother and her cubs?

"Let us hope never to see repeated the act of the magistrate of Bulandshahr who planned and rewarded the murder of the wolf family of the Sanicher boy. . . ."

The scientists were more hard-boiled. For instance, Herman B. Sheffield, M.D., of New York City, wrote July 10, evidently fresh from reading the long historical summary in the *Times* of that date:

"Judging by the article on the 'New Wolf Child Found in India,' I surmise that there are still a large number of civilized people, including scientists, who seriously believe that 'wolf-children' exist in reality instead of in fiction. As a matter of fact, such 'wolf-children' are frequently met in daily practice and are nothing but microcephalic idiots.

"These children are born with small, often dome-shaped, heads in consequence of undeveloped, small brains. Owing to their extreme restlessness and awkward power of locomotion, their habit to hop from place to place often resembles that of a rabbit, goat or monkey."

As the *Times* reported, there was keen interest in London. The Over-Seas League was naturally concerned and published in their journal *Over Seas* a statement by "A Member" which says that:

"Valentine Ball (previously quoted) mentions that he asked an eminent surgeon of his day what he thought of all these stories, and the reply was, 'I don't believe any of them.' The medical profession of to-day seems to share this lack of conviction. . . .

"No one, apparently, has ever found a child living in an animal's lair and left it there, returning from time to time to observe how it was progressing and to find out how it was fed. There is no trustworthy evidence to show that the children so far reported as wolf-children have ever survived for more than a few hours or days away from human care before they were discovered and restored to such care. There is no recorded case which could not be explained on the theory that the child had wandered from

213

home or been abandoned within a day or two of its being rescued, and it is a well-known fact that Indian mothers will sometimes 'lose' in the jungle mentally defective children, which goes far to account for the imbecility of all so-called wolf-children. . . .

"All the stories of alleged wolf-children rest on native evidence, and native evidence is by no means always to be relied upon as faithful records of fact. The world of reality has its limits. The world of imagination, especially of Eastern imagination, is boundless."

Somewhere in the reports on most children nurtured by wolves there is comment that, even after they had been taught by their human captors to eat meat, they continued fond of roots, and even of grass. Is it possible, then, that the wolves which bring up children are of a kindlier disposition than ordinary wolves for the reason that they are vegetarians?

WOLVES FOR POSTERITY

As said at the beginning of this chapter on wolves, we write for every shade of belief. This last section is for a group first in our thoughts, because largest—the lovers of romance, the enemies of the cant of science, the vast multitude of free believers in the freedom to believe.

True, the attacks on the wolf-pack are numerous. But what do they amount to? They are not campaigns by great armies, they are at most guerrilla warfare. More accurately, they are sniping.

For example, the chief of a biological survey writes letters to a friend of his, poohpoohing wolf-pack stories, and the friend perhaps shows them around a bit. Not half of the few who see the letters will be affected—everybody knows what scientists are, a self-elected Brain Trust dictating to all of us as to what we may and may not believe. If the letter is shown in any place like a smoking room, it is talked down by several who know people who know other people who have been treed, pursued, or at the very least scared half to death by immense packs of wolves.

Or a pack story in the newspapers gets a large head on the front page; the denial comes a week later in small type on an inside page where no one reads it. Again the pack triumphs.

The disgruntled may have for a time the active support of a news-gathering organization, as above mentioned for the *Associated Press,* but the most they can do is to caution their own direct employees to be careful. They may not dictate to their affiliates, as, for instance, the *Associated Press* trying to dictate to the *Canadian Press* or to *Reuter's.* Besides, they could not hold their own as purveyors of readable news if they left to rivals the wolf-children of India, the sieges of trains by wolf-packs in the Balkans, or that increase of wolves in the U.S.S.R. which (everybody at that time agreed) resulted from the substitution of communism for capitalism.

You may manage, perhaps, to get printed a diatribe against packs in a highbrow journal, as I once did in the *American Mercury.* But you cannot make new disbelievers in wolf-packs by addressing the readers of such a magazine, for the badge of their sophistication is that they are disbelievers already in whatever the rest of the world believes. If you ever

215

made nearly everybody sceptical on wolf-packs the *Mercury* clientele would start believing in them—which is, of course, a digression.

We shall close this chapter with a triumphant, because sufficient, proof that wolf-packs are a reality. To accomplish this we use the democratic method, adjudication by majority vote.

We shall have support for wolf-packs from that most popular appeal to the people, our greatest of weeklies, the *Saturday Evening Post,* with its millions of sold copies and no doubt several readers per copy. We shall have on our side, too, the most orthodox and the broadest appeal to the scientists, which is through the American Association for the Advancement of Science and through their kind of affiliate *Science Service.* They do not have so large a membership as that of the *Post,* but it is effective since it overlaps but slightly the circle of the *Post's* readers. The members of the Association include most professors and other teachers of science in our various schools and colleges, most scientists in the employ of commercial companies (at least those in the higher brackets), and most of those employed by the national, state, and other governments. Their official journal, *Science,* goes to every library of consequence in the United States, and widely through other countries. *Science* is read for excerpts and for ideas on behalf of newspapers and magazines. Then a great many of the papers subscribe to *Science Service,* and even use it.

If we can show that the *Post* and *Science* (including *Science Service*) are on the side of the wolf-pack, we have it winning hands down.

216

On January 9, 1932, C. B. Ruggles had in the *Post* an article, "Neighboring With Wolves." We are told, or given to understand, in this and other of his *Post* contributions, that Ruggles yields to few in the extensiveness and intensiveness of his northern lore. He has not merely been in Alaska; he has actually lived there. He must have been way up north, for he tells about the sun that "it would, for one hour and fifteen minutes, skirt the earth's rim before sinking below the horizon for another twenty-odd hours of opaque-lidded slumber." We have been told a little earlier about a Light of Delusion—"The Eskimos call this kind of light Woosha Kua"—which plays strange tricks with your eyesight. Still, apparently, it was not, in the Ruggles judgment, due to the Woosha Kua that he saw wolves pursuing caribou in great detail and that "There were twenty-seven wolves in the pack."

About this time I happened to give a talk before a small group at the University Museum, Philadelphia. I must have said something about wolf-packs and the Director, Dr. Horace H. F. Jayne, must have given my address to Max C. Goodman, of 3143 West Diamond Street, Philadelphia, who in turn must have written to C. B. Ruggles, at Freedom, Oklahoma, telling that Ruggles and I seemed in disagree- ment on wolf-packs. These things are inference, for there is a gap in my records. I have, however, a copy of a letter from Ruggles, dated January 19, 1932, sent me by Goodman, which runs in part:

"Nature causes wolves to gather in monstrous packs in all parts of the wilderness the last part of December or the first part of

217

January. Eskimos call these large wolf-gatherings, 'KA-MA-CHUA' (Mate choosing season) for this is about four or five weeks prior to wolf mating time and the Eskimos as well as the Northern trapper believe nature has brought these gatherings about for the young and unmated wolves to choose their mates, believed for life.

"I am writing you the above for the sole purpose of you taking it up with the greatest and most noted naturalist that you might find. If you should find that Mr. V. Steffenson's statement is false, kindly investigate other positive statements that he has made regarding the Arctic. . . .

"I hope to hear from you again and in regard to the results of your investigation of my statement as well as the investigation of the statement of V. Steffenson."

Goodman was to submit the Ruggles statement and mine about wolves to "the greatest and most noted naturalist that you might find." So I wrote Goodman on January 25 a letter in about 90 per cent disagreement with Ruggles and taking substantially that position contrary to his which is stated in the first section of the present chapter. Goodman submitted this letter and the Ruggles one, which we quoted just above, to the often-mentioned Chief of the U. S. Biological Survey, Dr. E. W. Nelson. Nelson wrote Goodman from the Hotel Johnson, Visalia, California, February 10. Again we quote in part:

"Your letter came to me just as I was preparing to leave Washington for California—hence, the delay in my reply.

"I have been interested by the letters from Ruggles and Stefansson and am in complete accord with the statements in Stefansson's letter. Mr. Ruggles appears to be imbued with the old folklore idea about huge packs of wolves roaming wild regions of the North.

"In common with most people, as a young man, I had the same ideas derived from the commonly published misstatements on the subject. Then for more than twenty years as a field naturalist, much of the time in wolf country and later for more than that length of time administrating the field work of other naturalists and hunters in wolf country, I came to a definite knowledge that the typical wolf-pack consists of the two old wolves and their young of the previous spring. These 'packs' may number from three to more than a dozen animals, according to the number of survivors of the litter of young. Sometimes a wolf may have a dozen young. There is no doubt that, by chance, two or perhaps more litters might come together, but such association would be extremely brief. I have never known or had definite information of such an instance and it is given as a mere possibility.

"For many years, the Biological Survey in Washington investigated every published account of devastations and of the killing of people by wolf-packs in the United States and Canada by writing to the postmaster or others living near the scene of the alleged work of wolf-packs and without a single exception, they proved to be purely imaginary.

"Under my direction, one of the best field naturalists in the Government Service spent more than a year in the Tanana River country of Alaska in the very district where Alaska papers published accounts of great wolf-packs destroying caribou and although he traversed that country in various directions in winter, he saw only occasional wolf tracks in the snow and never a sign of the alleged packs. . . .

"My information is from my own observations and from hundreds of other reliable men in the field in wolf country."

219

Once more there is, superficially, a defeat of the wolf-pack. Really the pack won, for the *Post* is read by several million people of the type who believe what they see in that sort of publication, while the quadrangular Goodman-Nelson-Ruggles-Stefansson correspondence could have had an effect upon only one of the four. Ruggles knew already there were packs, so we could not convince him there weren't. Nelson and I knew there weren't any, so Ruggles could not convince us there were. Goodman remained the only one who may have been affected, and he may have swung either way. I believe Dr. Jayne saw the correspondence, but from his record I think he was likely enough prejudiced already against the pack. Perhaps a dozen or two of Goodman's friends saw the correspondence, and perhaps some of them were influenced. If so, they may have gone in either direction. Therefore, the balloting, *Post* readers against some of the letter readers, must have gone something like a million to one in favor of the pack.

The authenticity of the wolf-pack might have been secure for years on the strength of just the one Ruggles article in the *Saturday Evening Post*. But they have carried more articles by Ruggles, and may have carried further eyewitness testimony. Then certainly there are many journals, only a little down from the *Post* in their sway of the public mind which have borne witness. Packs are going strong in the movies and, as shown heretofore, they appear frequently in the daily press. The general verdict is, therefore, clear.

But we said above that we would range scientists with the true believers. This we do by referring to the previously described journal *Science,* from which we quote in part an item that appeared in the issue of February 28, 1936:

"Wolf fighters, skilled in warfare against these voracious pack-hunting beasts, are asked for in an emergency wire from Governor John W. Troy, of Alaska, recently received at the Department of the Interior. . . . Vicious gangs of wolves have been raiding the reindeer herds owned by natives of northern Alaska. . . . Native hunters have proved unable to cope with the animals, but it is believed that about four hunter leaders, each with a few assistants, could in a swift campaign break up the marauding bands."

Thus we have the official journal of a foremost scientific body vouching for wolves as pack-hunters, as being in gangs and in bands.

But a testimony from Canada is in a way more striking than any can be from the United States, for wolves are by common consent more numerous and widespread there. As in the United States, the Canadian Government takes special cognizance of them, for they prey on flock and fowl. There is, then, *Bulletin No. 13, New Series,* Dominion of Canada, Department of Agriculture, "The Habits and Economic Importance of Wolves in Canada," by Norman Criddle. On p. 6 we read:

"Parent wolves live in pairs during the summer months, but as the young develop they form with them small bands, which meeting with other families in their wanderings, acquire the proportions of packs. These packs break up again in February. . . ."

We close our case by repeating and insisting that attacks

221

on wolf-packs are not serious—they are no more than sporadic sniping.

The *Saturday Evening Post, Science Service,* and the Department of Agriculture of the Dominion of Canada, powerful and worthy of all respect and confidence, are in this relation spokesmen too for a popular and a scientific multitude. The wolf-pack, then, is secure even as things stand. But conditions are bound to trend steadily in their favor. As living beasts, wolves are getting fewer with the colonization of the wilderness, but wolf-pack stories do not thereby get fewer—witness how they come again and again from districts where wolves no longer exist. The fewer the living wolves the less the chance of their being so studied that evidence against the pack habit can be gathered. Finally there will be no wolves left, except in zoos. The belief in packs will have survived the means of refuting it. It will have become a truth.

CHAPTER VI.

BEYOND THE FRONTIER

THE FOLLOWING CHAPTER WAS ORIGINALLY A SERIOUS COM-
plaint against the schoolbooks of Canada, but, in the light
of more mature thinking along the lines of standardization,
it appears to us now that the points we have made against
the textbooks are really points in their favor. We have established (Chapter I.) that the standardization of error would
simplify our thinking, thus making life easier and, to that
extent, better. We must commend Canada for her pioneer
work in our theory, especially when, as we readily perceive,
it is done at the expense of her own development, therefore
in a spirit of true self-sacrifice.

The lower schoolbooks we shall quote in this statement,
for contrast with university teaching, are: *Ontario Public
School Geography,* authorized for use in the public schools
of Ontario; *The Teacher's Manual,* authorized for use of
teachers in Ontario; *Public School Geography,* authorized
for use in the public schools of Alberta; *Manual of Geography, I,* authorized for use of teachers and high school
·students of Alberta; Dent's *Canadian Geography Readers,*
Book II, optional or supplementary reading in several prov-

223

inces; *The Canadian School Geography,* authorized for use in the public schools of British Columbia, Manitoba, Nova Scotia, Quebec and Saskatchewan; *Canadian Readers,* authorized for use in the public schools of Manitoba, Saskatchewan, Alberta and British Columbia. Most of these books are dated 1928 or 1929. All of them were bought from displays for the present school season.

The observed temperatures about to be quoted in this article for contrast with the textbooks are, unless otherwise stated, taken from the records of the Dominion Meteorological Service. Some of the other facts used are from Government reports; most of the rest are from my own observation through ten winters and thirteen summers spent in the Arctic, during which I traveled there afoot about 20,000 miles—a good opportunity to see conditions as they are.

Studying the books purchased, I found that practically all of the geographies were still holding to the ancient Greek philosophical view that the farther north you go the colder it is, no matter what the time of year. One book expresses it, "The temperature steadily decreases from the Equator to the Poles," and the others have the same idea worded differently. The climate of the North is "especially unfavorable for both plants and animals." In the Arctic "terrible blizzards often rage for days together."

Postponing our discussion of the more important season of summer, what are the facts about the Canadian winter? One is that children in certain wheat-raising sections of Alberta, who probably shudder with sympathy for the poor Eskimos, are themselves living in a region that has minimum

224

winter periods colder than any Eskimo is known to have lived through. Few Eskimos have ever seen sixty below zero. The probable lowest temperature for the North Pole itself is twenty degrees warmer, say fifty-eight or sixty below. The lowest temperature recorded on the north coast of Canada is fifty-two below. But we have the following minima from the southern third of Canada: Quebec, sixty-three below; Ontario, sixty below; Manitoba, sixty-three below; Saskatchewan, seventy below; Alberta, seventy-eight below.

There is probably, then, no Eskimo living who has felt a temperature as low as thousands of our children face going to school in prosperous communities of southern Canada. If there are Eskimos who have felt cold equal to that of some of our farming communities, they belong to tribes that winter inland, well to the south of the coast dwellers.

As to blizzards and snowfall: excluding the Atlantic and Pacific coasts, the line of heaviest snowfall in Canada is approximately at the Canada-United States border. Storms are, on the average, fewer and milder in the Arctic than in any other equally large area on earth, as the great explorer, Nansen, pointed out more than thirty years ago. It is for these reasons among others that trans-Arctic flying is steadily pushing to the front as the practical solution of commerce by air between the Old World and the New.

However, from the strictly economic point of view, it makes little difference what we teach in the schools about the winter temperatures of Canada. Mining, for instance, can be carried forward in any climate, for among the successful coal mines are those of Alabama, 1,000 miles south of Winnipeg, and those of Spitsbergen, 2,000 miles north of

225

Winnipeg. In factory work the expenditure for fuel varies and is an important charge against operation, but still there are great industrial centers developing all the way from Birmingham to Montreal.

Blizzards are perhaps unpleasant. I have met in the Arctic numbers of Royal Canadian Mounted Police who had been stationed at Regina, in southern Saskatchewan, not so far from the United States border, and I don't remember finding one who did not think Regina blizzards as bad as any they had seen on the north coast of Canada. Yet Regina is considered one of the fine Canadian cities and its chief handicap of late years has been not the cold nor blizzards of winter—it has been the dryness of the hot summers. July temperatures are frequently higher in that part of Saskatchewan than in the Miami part of Florida.

Cold may distress you, but Montreal is larger than New Orleans. Of the two Red River valleys, the one in Louisiana is warmer, but the one in Manitoba is better for wheat. Winnipeg, which handles more wheat than any city in the world, has an average temperature for the year that is just at the freezing point—thirty-two F.

Winter temperatures, then, have little effect upon the prosperity of lands or the growth of cities, nor do blizzards signify. It is the summer temperatures that matter, and the length of the summer, for upon them depend the economic vegetations that give food to the people and feed to grazing animals.

The greatest economic damage to Canada that is wrought by the public schools is, therefore, in describing incorrectly its northern summers. For the schools teach as a principle

that the farther north you go the colder the summers become. They do further harm by misrepresenting not only
the summer temperatures of Arctic and sub-Arctic Canada
but also the length of the growing season.

As to the heat and length of the northern summer, and
some of their direct results, the textbooks approved by various provinces teach the following things among others: "In
northern Canada and northern Alaska . . . during the short
summer the very slanting sunlight is unable to raise the
temperature much above the freezing point," says a geography approved by several provinces. "There is no warm season (in the Arctic)," is how we are told the same thing in
a manual of geography authorized by a department of education for the guidance of teachers, and printed not by a
commercial house, but by a King's Printer. Every province
has some officially approved textbook that states or implies
that hot weather—eighty to ninety degrees in the shade—
does not occur in the Arctic at all, and that it occurs rarely
even in those parts of the Northwest Territories that lie
between the Arctic Circle and Edmonton—which is just
south of 54° and corresponds to Leeds in England, Copenhagen in Denmark, and Moscow in Russia.

This would be sad if true. But the summer temperatures
in the Mackenzie district of the Northwest Territories hard
up against the Arctic Circle really go to ninety-six degrees,
while the highest for Prince Edward Island, in southeastern
Canada, is only ninety-two. The highest temperature recorded since 1900 in Winnipeg is one hundred degrees and
the same temperature has been recorded in Alaska by the
United States Weather Bureau at Fort Yukon, north of the

227

Arctic Circle. Temperatures ranging from eighty to ninety degrees are common both in the Canadian and Alaskan Arctic.

Some of the lower school geographies give the real facts of Arctic summer temperatures, but do not correlate them so as to enable an ordinary student to realize that what the textbook says elsewhere about the summer never being warm must be incorrect. The texts state, for instance, that in mid-summer the sun delivers about half as much heat per hour in the Arctic as it does at the equator. Elsewhere they mention that the Arctic day is twenty-four hours long and the equatorial day only twelve hours long. What they do not draw attention to, thus failing to enlighten the careless reader, is that there is no difference between the result of half the heat-delivery for double the time and double the heat-delivery for half the time.

It is just because half the heat for double the time is as good as double the heat for half the time that you expect, and do get, tropical heat in those north polar lowlands (and they are extensive) where sea breezes do not seriously interfere.

Having described the climate in such unfriendly terms, perhaps it is consistency that impels the Canadian textbooks to make the vegetation correspond with it. "Much of this vast area," says one, "is a treeless wilderness of rock and swamp, covered with mosses and lichens which provide food for the caribou and musk ox." "In the extreme north," says another, "(there is) a cold desert where, however, vegetation is not entirely wanting; for in the marshes in summer the ground becomes covered with reindeer moss on which the

228

caribou and musk oxen feed." "Why cannot trees grow there?" asks a third, to which the general textbook reply is that the winters are too cold for them. A reading selection continues the work of the geographies with, "In that land there is little but ice and snow."

But what are the facts? One is that inside the Arctic Circle mosses and lichens are not so prevalent as they are inside the textbook covers. By tonnage they comprise less than ten per cent of the vegetation. The other ninety per cent is represented by flowering plants. In all my Arctic experience I have never found a region where mosses and lichens prevailed over the flowering plants. I had to visit a section near Churchill, Manitoba, 600 miles south of the Arctic Circle, to see that sort of country.

What about trees? A hundred miles north of the Arctic Circle in Canada the Forestry Branch of the Department of the Interior has reported trees seventy feet high, straight, and fourteen inches through. Similar trees go at least twice that height beyond the Circle in Siberia. Moreover, the textbooks imply in most cases, and specify in one, that winter cold limits the growth of trees; but the coldest known spot north of the equator—Verkhoyansk, in the Yakutsk Province of Siberia—has a dense forest of both evergreen and deciduous trees, although the recorded temperatures go down to ninety-three degrees below zero.* The Prairie Provinces which have approved this book are themselves in part treeless. Would they appreciate the intimation that this is

* Since this was written it has been ascertained that Oimekon, about 300 miles southeast and 200 miles south of the Arctic Circle, is colder than Verkhoyansk, and is therefore now the coldest known spot on earth. Like Verkhoyansk, the Oimekon vicinity is forested.

229

because of the cold? And if so, how can they reconcile the teaching of their schools with the fact that the largest treeless sections of the Prairie Provinces themselves are in their southern parts, the largest forests in the northern?

The Canadian textbook allegation that in the Arctic "there is little but ice and snow" conveys to the child among other things the idea that there is a heavy snowfall. Instead, the snowfall, as previously mentioned, is heavier in the most southerly hundred miles of Canada than in the most northerly hundred. Or again, the pupil may think the statement means that in July and August there is more snow or ice on the ground in the North. But the fact is that British Columbia has ten times as much snow in July (permanent snow) as the whole of the much larger section of our continent designated the Northwest Territories. The part of Alaska which lies in the temperate zone has a hundred times as much permanent snow as there is in the Arctic section of Alaska. In the south Alaska mountains the snow line comes down to sea level; in the north Alaska mountains it is 4,000 to 6,000 feet above the sea.

Lest the child may think that the desolation and worthlessness are largely confined to the Arctic Circle proper, a fifth-year Canadian reader instructs him in part as follows: "Long before the treeless wastes are reached, the forest ceases to be forest except by courtesy. . . . On the shores of Great Bear Lake—which is, of course, in the Temperate Zone—four centuries are necessary for the growth of a trunk not so thick as a man's wrist. . . . Still farther north the trees become mere stunted stems set with blighted buds that have never been able to develop themselves into branches; until, finally,

230

the last vestiges of arboreal growth take refuge under a thick carpet of lichens and mosses, the characteristic vegetation of the Barren Grounds."

The textbook editor borrows this heartening description, and much other cheerful information about Canadian resources and climate, from a book entitled, humorously enough, *Greater Canada*. If a country thus described be indeed a "Greater Canada," then we wonder what those may believe who are really pessimistic.

Against this "Greater Canada" view let us set the facts, uncontested by those who have lived on Great Bear Lake and have traversed the forest north of it to where it meets the Arctic prairie. Instead of being no bigger around than your wrist, the larger trees on Bear Lake are a foot and a half through, and a hundred feet high. There is no such gradual diminution in size as the author makes out. We have already mentioned, for instance, the Forestry Service report which describes trees seventy feet high a hundred miles north of Great Bear Lake and within five miles of the beginning of the Arctic prairie. Again there is Big Stick Island, northeast of Great Bear Lake, a clump really beyond the tree line. It is only a few acres, and yet the trees are a foot through, tall and straight.

I have come in from the Arctic prairie to the northernmost forest at various points on the thousand-mile front ranging from the Colville to the Coppermine, and I have never seen the peculiar trees of *Greater Canada* with "blighted buds that have never been able to develop themselves into branches." Once, for instance, when I discovered trees just a few miles inland from Franklin Bay in a section

231

where I did not expect them, I entered in my diary the unusually (for me) poetic description that I had seen "a little band of Christmas trees climbing the hillside." They were of such proportions as to branch and stem that they would have been saleable at Yuletide in any of our cities.

We have commented before on the textbook idea that the chief vegetation of the Arctic, or even of the "Barren Grounds," is mosses and lichens. Here we comment rather on the name itself—Barren Grounds. According to a bulletin of the Department of the Interior, the epithet "Barren Grounds" was originally applied to the prairie districts between Winnipeg and Calgary. When growing knowledge showed how absurd the name was for that section, it was not abolished as it should have been, but was, so to speak, lifted up and transported from the southern prairies across the northern forest to the northern prairies and there set down to do its part in holding back the development of the North as it already had held back for awhile the development of the West.

I was born and brought up in that West which was originally called "Barren Grounds," and have often said that had I been transferred in my boyhood by magic from the prairies, across which I used to ride as a cowboy, to the prairies of Banks Island, 200 miles north of the north coast of Canada, I should have known on waking up that I was not in my home district, but I could not have decided offhand that I was not somewhere in northern North Dakota or southern Saskatchewan. Dropping on my knees and playing Sherlock Holmes, I could have decided by careful study of the vegetation and soil that I was in a strange place, but looking off to

232

the sky line I should have felt at home. There would have been the same rolling prairie, with perhaps somewhat less grass but with a great many more flowers. Had it been winter there would have been snow on the ground in both places, but less in Banks Island than in Saskatchewan.

With such experience of the trees, grasses and flowers of southern and of northern Canada, it is easier for me to read the lower school textbooks as works of humor than of sober instruction. But children take them seriously, and it is difficult to look upon the results as merely funny.

The ground frost of northern Canada is made a handicap in the textbooks. But in real life as often as not it is useful. "Fields of ice and snow and a permanently frozen subsoil effectively limit man's movements in the Arctic . . . regions," says one of them, and that is a just sample of what most of them say or imply.

The first advantage of frozen subsoil is that there can be no dry season. The growers of cereals and vegetables now count on that in Alaska. So do the reindeer ranchers. For if the season has less rain than usual it means only that the ground will thaw deeper than usual, and the roots of the plants will reach farther down for their water. The only thing the rancher has to guard against is the trampling out of the forage vegetation by the animals, just as he would if he were an Australian sheep farmer. So far as dry seasons are concerned, he can graze the same numbers on a given ranch for any period of years, a thing the Australian cannot do, for his feed varies with the rains.

A second advantage, less important, but spectacular and about to come much into public view, bears upon flying. For where there is a frozen subsoil there is no underground drainage, and rain and thaw waters stay where they fall. This creates innumerable lakes all over the country, providing flyers with natural landing fields for pontoons in summer and skis in winter. That is one reason why accidents are fewer in the Arctic than in temperate or tropic flying. If you are a mile high and you develop engine trouble, you can always glide to a safe landing where the subsoil is frozen.

Those who have kept track of the advance of the Hudson Bay Railway from The Pas to Churchill, even if it be only through press despatches, are familiar with a third advantage, for the ground frost has simplified and made cheaper and easier the building of that important pioneer line. In so far as the cost of construction is derived from taxes, the people of the whole of Canada have benefited in purse from the very condition which they formerly thought would increase the building costs.

Coming back again to Arctic vegetation in the textbooks, we find a reader approved for school use in four provinces saying: "There are no trees in this cold land, but there is a kind of hard brown moss that grows under the snow." There are known to be more than 300 species of Arctic moss. These the textbook ignores along with more than 700 kinds of flowering plants. And why does this one moss that is known to the textbook compiler do its growing under the snow? Isn't it poor judgment for even a moss to wait idle during the hot summer and to begin to grow in the fall when snow comes? Or—and I gather this from the complete selection—perhaps the author believes that a snow covering is permanent in the Arctic. The fact is, of course, that Arctic land is permanently snow-covered only on or near mountains. Most Arctic lands are low and, like the Prairie Provinces, they have snow in winter and none in summer. In Peary Land, the most northerly land on earth, there are bees and butterflies in the rolling meadows of flowers and grass.

The textbook statement that musk oxen feed on moss is perhaps a minor error from the point of view of this article, but it shows how widespread are the inaccuracies. All those who have studied this animal report that it lives mainly on grasses, sedges, and browse.

Up to this point, the geographies have, in the main, agreed to disagree with the scientists. On the question of animal life they begin to disagree with each other. Some of them, having talked so convincingly of sparse vegetation, continue this idea. For, since many of the Arctic animals are herbivorous, if the text admitted that there are large numbers of them, the children might well begin to puzzle as to what they lived on. Therefore we find one author saying that the Eskimos live almost wholly on animals and that their "available food supply is scanty." A school reader has it that "there are very few (musk oxen) left. They keep them in a park with a high wire fence about it."

Others, however, report large herds of caribou and musk oxen, and some go so far as to mention polar bears, wolves, foxes, hares, seals and fish. But we gather from the texts that these animals lead a precarious existence.

As a fact, few known waters are richer in fish, whales and seals than those of the Arctic. The caribou of Arctic and sub-Arctic Canada number several hundred for each single

235

Eskimo, and yet travelers who have described bands of thousands, and even herds of a hundred thousand moving together, have never reported any noticeable depletion in the vegetation.

In the case of musk oxen, there are probably 4,000 wild for every forty that are in fenced parks. These wild musk oxen are in no danger of extinction at present, for most of them are on islands that are uninhabited, many of them never even visited by Eskimos.

Having invented a fictitious country and named it Eskimoland, the textbooks find it necessary to invent a fictitious people, and the Eskimos are misrepresented even more than the territories they inhabit. They are supposed to be all alike, though some of them live farther away from others than Canada is from Mexico, and have less contact. Their climate has only one description in most textbooks, although they really live in several different climates. The materials of the description of land and people, so far as they are not invented have, however, been gathered from many Eskimo countries, many Eskimo climates, and many Eskimo peoples. The result is a patchwork portrait which resembles no Eskimo who ever lived. Then they make this patchwork man live in a patchwork country. One is as real as the other.

The schoolbook accounts of the Eskimo presumably arouse in the child both pity and amusement. Here are some of the quotations:

"The Eskimo has an environment which forces him into constant conflict with Nature. He is in continual danger of freezing and starving to death."

236

"The Eskimo suffers from intestinal diseases, malnutrition and scurvy, and his resistance to disease is greatly lowered.

"The ravenous eating of tallow candles and soap by Eskimo children is well attested."

"When the Eskimo boy is thirsty, he drinks oil."

Against this picture stands in my mind my own experience of living more than ten years as an Eskimo among Eskimos. To me it seems that as a race they have more leisure than city dwellers, for instance. Some of the geographies mention their ivory carving and ornamental ceremonial dress, but they leave it a mystery how a people under terrific strain for a livelihood find time for such things. My observation has been that in many communities the needed work to provide food, shelter and clothing requires from the Eskimo less than half of our standard eight-hour day. Four hours of work and eight of sleep give him twelve hours of leisure. Accordingly, a man will spend a week carving an ivory handle which he could have made plain in half a day. A woman who could sew a warm coat in two days will spend two months making one not so warm (but in her opinion prettier) by cutting up whole skins and piecing them together in complicated designs. Entire communities spend weeks singing and dancing and listening to story-tellers spinning out long tales of adventure with spirits and with men. The winters, so frightful in the textbooks, are their holiday season, spent in carrying out elaborate festivities.

Most of the textbooks say or imply that most or all Eskimos live in snow or ice houses in winter. This is geographical hodgepodge. No Eskimos live in ice houses, or at least

I never heard of it. Some live in snow houses, but more than half the Eskimos in the world have never seen them. In the textbooks all snow houses are called "igloos," but the word *iglu* simply means house in general, or dwelling. It is misleading to imply that snow houses are known to all Eskimos and used by most of them. In many districts the snow house, being unknown, is not even represented by any word in the vocabulary. Many Eskimos live in houses built of earth and wood, or with bone rafters and walls of stone and earth. There are several other types of dwelling.

The case is worse about the use of oil. According to the above textbook quotation and many similar, they drink it. Before my recent study of Canadian lower school texts, I had heard that they did this for two other reasons—one that they liked it, and the other to keep warm. It remained for a Toronto textbook to advance the new explanation that they do it to quench thirst. But to have this true, the laws of both physiology and chemistry would have to be changed. Physiology teaches that thirst is quenched only by water, and chemistry that there is in oil no water which the human stomach is capable of extracting.

The Eskimo stomach is similar to your stomach. If you think he drinks oil for any reason, I would suggest that you take about a water tumbler of whatever oil you prefer. If you have a strong will you may be able to get it down, but the chances are three in four that you will not be able to keep it down. If you are the one in four who can keep it down, you will very soon wish that you weren't.

The truth is that Eskimos use oil with their food, as we do salad oil or gravy. They eat it but they don't drink it, and,

238

therefore, instead of being weird monstrosities, they are just like us in this respect, as they are in most fundamental human things.

One textbook says that a cold climate produces people who are stunted in mind and body. For body the Eskimo might be described as of average stature rather than small. Mentally their teachers usually report them to be near the European average.

That brings us to the question of the spread of European education in the Far North. A school reader says: "There are no books in that land and (the Eskimos) could not read them if there were." If this were true, it would bear out the allegation that the Eskimos are stupid, for the Danes began trying to teach them reading and writing about two centuries ago. They found them apt pupils, the knowledge gained by one or a few spreading by native instruction from house to house and village to village. The work since then has been shared by two governments, the Danish and that of the United States—Canada has, as yet, taken no direct educational action. Effective cultural work has been done by the churches, among them the Anglicans, Lutherans, Moravians, Presbyterians, Quakers, and Roman Catholics. It would be strange if the efforts of all these bodies, some going back two hundred years, left it still a justifiable criticism of Eskimos that they cannot read or write. As a matter of fact, more than half the total Eskimo population of Greenland, Labrador, Canada and Alaska can read and write some language, generally their own. They publish some of their own books and have (in Greenland) a magazine that has appeared regularly since 1867. Editors, proof-readers, type-

239

setters, engravers, printers, subscription solicitors and the rest have all been Eskimo through all that time. No other language has been employed in connection with the journal. It is as Eskimo as the *Spectator* is English.

Which, by the way, is more interesting, the fiction that "the Eskimo" does not know what a book is, or the fact that one of the older journals in the western hemisphere is in Eskimo?

That Eskimo children eat soap is ridiculous on the face of it. I have never seen Eskimos eat candles, nor heard of a case. But if they did eat tallow candles it would be no stranger than the eating of tallow in any other form. Tallow is only suet, and many a well-ordered meal in our country still includes suet pudding.

As for the "deficiency diseases and scurvy," the Eskimos are, as far as we know, free from them so long as they live on their own accustomed diets. Once they begin to live on white men's groceries and neglect to secure fresh meat, these diseases grow. Dr. William A. Thomas, of Chicago, found in Labrador, for instance, that the Eskimos who suffered most were those nearest the trading stations and most supplied with white men's food. In the sections beyond the reach of the traders, or little affected by them, the deficiency troubles vanished.

As to commercial dealings with the outside world, we are instructed by the geographies in contrary ways. On page 12 of one of them, the printed matter says: "The Eskimos have almost no trade with other people. They must depend on their own country to supply their wants." But on page 123 of this same book, there is a photograph of six power

240

schooners—not whaleboats—with the caption "Eskimo Whaleboats, Fort McPherson!"

It is, as a matter of fact, one of the important industries of Edmonton to supply Eskimos with power schooners. I have seen a photograph from the Arctic, sent me by an officer of the Royal Canadian Mounted Police, showing $100,000 worth of these in a single view. The same engines that produce electric light for these Eskimos on shipboard in summer are used by them sometimes to light their houses in winter. Some have separate Delco electric lighting systems for their homes.

But the teachers of Edmonton, the city which furnishes most of these supplies, use now, or did use recently, textbooks which state or imply that the Eskimos have no boats except skin canoes, and no light except seal-oil lamps. Nor can you defend the books by suggesting that they are talking of fifty or a hundred years ago. The context shows that these allegations are supposed to fit the present.

To balance all these unfavorable truths about the northern half of Canada, I have been able to discover in the school texts one—and only one—favorable mistake. A geography says, "Mosquitoes are found all over the North American continent except in the extreme north." Anyone who has been there will tell you that the contrary is the fact. Until you approach the Arctic you do not know how bad mosquitoes can be.

A thing which the incorrect schoolbooks are doing is to dampen that current enthusiasm about the Far North of Canada which is due to the beginning of actual mining in the Middle North, where Flin Flon and Sherritt Gordon are already words to conjure with.

241

For these mines are in the sub-Arctic, which, according to the textbooks, is almost as bad as the Arctic itself, a land barren because of the cold. Mining is expensive where food is not produced locally and where no one lives except the miners and their dependents. There is, in consequence, a fundamental need to colonize even the richest mineral districts with a food-producing population. Sunlight and rainfall are, therefore, the most important resources of any district, and the younger generation of Canadians should be permitted to grow up with a true understanding of how heat and water are distributed, and how these are used by nature for the production of those plants upon which all animal life, including the human, must in the last resort depend.

Canada is two things, a people and a country. We need truthful histories for a reasonable judgment of our past; we need accurate geographies for planning the future. The schoolboys and the schoolgirls of today, most of them without university training, will step into control of this land tomorrow. Their chief equipment for that task is their education. What the university courses teach in advanced geography and climatology is not propaganda but truth. Why not give the pupils of the common schools the advantage of the same correct description of the climate and its results, so that they, too, will know how to prepare for the great spread of settlements northward that must continue till inhabited Canada becomes as broad as it is long, a nation drawing power from all its territories, even the farthest islands in the northern sea?

242

CHAPTER VII

OLOF KRARER

IN THE SCHOOLS OF MANY LANDS, INCLUDING THOSE WHICH
speak English, the Eskimos are studied during the early
grades. In my youth I learned many strange things concerning them. We spoke of Eskimos and of Eskimoland as if the
people were all alike and lived in one place.

The Eskimos are a godsend to the schools. From their
simplicity you can get a parallel to the simplicity of our
own remote ancestors and also a contrast to the multiplici-
ties of civilization. It is easy to teach and to learn that, while
in our land it is sometimes hot and sometimes cold, there is
a district south of us where it is always hot and another
north of us, Eskimoland, where it is always cold. This im-
presses upon the child-mind that there is a balance and symmetry in nature, which has been a favorite doctrine since
Greek times.

Heat is life-giving (the school instruction went on); the
hot lands are luxuriant and beautiful. Cold is deadening; the
cold lands of the Eskimos are sterile, bleak, forbidding.
Things develop to large size in heat; cold has a stunting

influence. Therefore, trees become smaller and smaller as you go north until you come to the last cringing shrubs. Beyond them, in a treeless waste, are the Eskimos, a little people, themselves stunted by the cold. In their bitter struggle to eke out the scantiest of livings they cower, wrapped in furs, inside huts of snow which give them bare shelter from the furious Arctic blizzards. To keep warm they eat the most warming food, which is fat; so they live on blubber. They grease their bodies with oil as a further protection from the cold, and they drink oil. Though we need varied meals, a balanced ration, the Eskimos are strangely able to live on animal tissues alone and they eat their meat raw, usually warm from a recently slaughtered beast or else frozen. '

But, marvelous to relate, in spite of all these things, the Eskimos are a jolly, happy little people. They serve thus a double moral purpose. The gruesome view of their land and of their life makes us better contented with ours; we see from their happiness under conditions of misery that really it isn't so bad, in comparison, to be poor and jobless down here. We should all, therefore, be contented and happy.

In view of the large place held by Eskimos in our scheme of child training, the misfortune is serious that our educators, particularly the writers of our schoolbooks, have been forced to get their Eskimo material at second hand from the writings and lectures of explorers. The situation was made worse in that a good many explorers lacked the imagination and the literary gifts necessary for making possible the desired insight into the heart and soul of these present-day survivors of Stone Age man.

244

It is a major good fortune that American educators have had opportunity for close relation with at least one Eskimo, Olof Krarer.

The autumn 1912 I came south after four consecutive years in the Arctic, making several reports, one of them that among some hundreds of Eskimos who were not known to have been in touch with Europeans I had seen ten or more who were as light in complexion and eye color as if they were anything from one-quarter to three-quarters European. A reporter changed my statement to convey the impression that I had found near Coronation Gulf several hundred Eskimos all of whom were blond. This reporter has since claimed, probably with more right than anybody else, that he made me famous. Certainly there was a big newspaper hubbub.

In a barrage of letters to the press there came one from Ithaca, New York. The writer was a professor of Cornell. He tried to bring into an acrimonious discussion a quiet, urbane tone. It was not fair, he contended, to denounce Stefansson as a charlatan for having claimed to discover a new race of blond people in the Far North, for these people indubitably exist. But neither was it fair to praise his "discovery" vociferously, as some were doing, for blond Eskimos were so well known that they were, for instance, a matter of his own experience and that of his family. For he and his wife had had the pleasure some years ago to entertain in their home one of them who had come to Ithaca as a lecturer. She was a woman named Olof Krarer, small of stature like the rest of her people, with light hair and with blue

245

eyes of quite the Scandinavian type. She had made a favorable impression.*

The letter from Cornell stirred childhood recollections. I had heard my mother and the neighbors talk of a strange and pathetic girl who came with them on the emigrant ship from Iceland in 1876. She must have been nearing twenty but she was small for a child of ten, a dwarf. She was vivacious, ambitious, and talked of the opportunities for distinction and advancement which awaited her in the New World. Her fellow-immigrants did not know whether to laugh or weep. She was clever, but her physical handicap seemed more than her gifts could surmount.

The party of colonists landed in Nova Scotia. After a year in that province many of them traveled west through the Great Lakes and by way of the Red River of the North to Lake Winnipeg, where my parents settled and where I was born.

In 1880 our family moved to Dakota Territory and so did Olof's, but she had gone off on her own and was probably in Winnipeg. Some years later we heard in North Dakota that she was in a circus exhibiting herself as an Eskimo. The Icelanders (who until recently were proud of being about the least adulterated Nordics in Europe) were at first scandalized and inclined to attempt stopping the imposture. On second thought most if not all of them felt that little harm could be done to their nationality by the fraud compared to the tragedy it would be for this handicapped woman to be exposed and deprived of the one thing which

* Most things in this chapter are documented, but this letter is paraphrased from a vivid memory. Some details may be wrong, but the general trend is right.

gave her a livelihood and a tolerable life. We know now that she even won respect and affection—witness the above Cornell testimony and much shall be hereinafter cited.

There was presently in the Icelandic community in North Dakota a connected story of Olof Krarer. I do not know whether it was brought or whether it just grew. No doubt it was partly imagination; equally without doubt it was partly true.

Our North Dakota version of the story ran that Olof had been waitress in a hotel. Seeing how small she was, the guests asked about her and were told, sometimes by herself and sometimes by the hotel people, that she was an Icelander. The comeback was usually: "How interesting! We never saw an Eskimo before." Olof would then explain that Icelanders were not Eskimos and that their blood was chiefly Norwegian with a little mixture of Irish.* The interest waned. There were plenty of Norwegians around; the Irish were no rarity. That sort of dwarf was hardly a seven days' wonder.

But there were new guests in the hotel daily, new questions about Olof, and new accents for the tiresome: "How interesting! We never saw an Eskimo before." She became bored, annoyed, outraged. Finally she stopped explaining that Icelanders were not Eskimos and simply flounced off. The interpretation of that was, poor thing, she was ashamed of being an Eskimo. Her silence now gave consent.

* In 1904-06 I was fellow and assistant instructor in anthropology at Harvard. I had to read the examination papers but my seniors made up the questions. It was a standard joke with them to slip in somewhere: "In what country do the Eskimos live?" A good percentage of Harvard men, ranging from sophomore to senior, could be depended upon to answer: "The Eskimos live in Iceland." That, my colleagues thought, was a pretty good joke on me.

One day a local clergyman appeared. He said that the young people of his church had a mid-week meeting and they would be so interested if Olof would come down and talk to them informally about the Eskimos. They would be glad to pay her five dollars.

I go back to what my mother said of the pathetic ambition and anticipations of the dwarf. I imagine how, perhaps at first through embarrassment Olof did not correct the minister. When his invitation came to the five-dollar offer she was already realizing that her chance had come. She agreed to give the talk.

Combining testimony of the Cornell professor with that of my mother, I imagine further that Olof went to the town library next day, or to some bookish friend, and read up on the Eskimos. Then, to the best of her ability, she improvised a story of an Eskimo childhood and gave it at the mid-week church meeting. It was accepted and she was on that road which took her to the lyceum platform and the circus. As we shall see, it took her to other places, to fame and to a lasting influence upon American education and thought.

My memories, temporarily revived in 1912 by the Cornell professor's letter, had receded vaguely into the background when, in 1922, I had a secretary, Miss Dorothy Daggett. She came from a week-end one Monday morning and asked whether a young man whom she had met at the house party might come and consult me about an extraordinary yarn which he had picked up in Florida and which he had already sold tentatively to a magazine. She had urged him not to print without consulting me, for the story was about an Eskimo and seemed to her spurious. She did not think

248

that a young man ought to risk publishing that sort of thing at the beginning of a literary career.

In due course John Schoolcraft arrived and told the following story which I quote from notes made at the time:

THE STORY OF OLAF CRERAR

as told by

John Schoolcraft

The Eskimo woman, Olaf Crerar, says she was born on the north coast of Greenland in a village of thirty or forty houses, with an average of four people in each house. A family of eight children in that country is equivalent to one of twenty in this. The average family has two or three.

One day two big white men came into their village, the first big men they had ever seen and the first whites. The North Greenland Eskimos are blond themselves, but owing to the smoke in their houses they didn't know it. The two big men were Icelanders. After living in the village about a year, they persuaded Olaf's father to go on a long journey with them. He had no idea where he was going but he consented, and, as is always the case on long hunting trips, he took his family with him. They started across the ice and it took them something like three months to make the journey from northern Greenland to northern Iceland. When they came to the Gulf Stream it was partly open. There they went from one ice floe to another, like Eliza crossing the Ohio. They finally got to Iceland.

Olaf was about sixteen when she left Greenland (or perhaps she was twenty). She stayed in Iceland something like four and a half years. At the end of that time, all of her family were dead except herself and her father. They died from the change in climate. There was a missionary there who took a great interest

249

in her and baptized her into the (Lutheran) church. Her Eskimo name was Ahbo. The missionary, in giving her a Christian name, wanted to get one as close to the Eskimo as possible, so he called her Olaf. I don't know where she got her last name, which sounds like Crerar.

Olaf suffered so from the Icelandic climate that the missionary decided to send her and her father with some friends of his to Canada, thinking its climate would probably be better for them both than the Icelandic. He started them off on a boat with a company of Icelanders, and there may have been some Swedes and Norwegians. They landed at Quebec.

Olaf was knocked around from pillar to post in the United States and Canada for awhile, with this funny little father of hers. At that time she was 40 inches high, 45 inches around the waist, and weighed 136 pounds. Her father was smaller than she.

She told that she had been a nursemaid and implied that she had worked in hotels. On one occasion she was taken sick in a hotel in St. Paul and a doctor visited her who had been in Greenland and who knew a few words of her language.

Then Mr. Slayton of the Slayton Lyceum Bureau ran across her and thought she would be a good lecturer, so he took her into his home and together they worked up a lecture. She went around the country for something like twenty-five years (she is sixty-two now) lecturing. For the last few years of this time she was not only a lecturer but a sort of collector for Mr. Slayton. He would give these (lyceum) courses and she would be the last one on the course and would collect the money from those who had sponsored the course. The understanding was that at his death she was to have a home in his house as long as she lived. She did live with Mrs. Slayton for a number of years.

While in Florida she met the people named Stone who took her back to Michigan with them—Mr. I. K. Stone, Maple Street,

Battle Creek, Michigan. She is living there now and has been with them two or three years. She is always telling them how in Greenland people always tell the truth. It is a great shock to her, she says, to come into a civilization where they don't tell the truth. So in the household, when they aren't kidding each other, they have the saying, "This is Greenland."

Olaf says that the people up in northern Greenland where she was born continue to grow until they are thirty-five. When mature they are very small, like herself, and they mature slowly. They don't marry until they are twenty-five, and children don't walk until they are three. She says that the mothers do not nurse their children at all. As soon as a baby is born they give him a piece of whale meat and tell him to carry on. Many life processes there seem greatly slowed down.

However, a person of sixty is very old. They die off rapidly from what Olaf thought was something like tuberculosis. It was a wasting disease and usually ended with hemorrhage. She thought it was brought on by the change in going from the heated hut into the cold air outside.

North Greenland children are born either in the light time or in the dark time (the well-known six-month day and six-month night). When a child is born, the mother picks out a certain kind of bone. Since they live on polar bears, walrus and seals more than anything, it might be a bone from one of these animals. She has a little bag on the wall and drops into it a certain distinctive kind of bone for each child, and as each light time or dark time comes around she drops another bone of this same sort into the bag. In that way she can keep track of the children's ages. The children are forbidden to touch that bag, and if they do the punishment is severe.

Olaf said these people believed in one big good spirit and one big bad spirit, and there are also little good spirits and little bad spirits. The big good one sent the little good ones around, and similarly with the bad spirit. When a person dies he becomes a good or bad spirit according to the way he has lived. Asked what was their standard of good and bad, she replied that if during this sickness, which evidently came on them all, the man or woman was patient and unselfish, then he turned into a good spirit. Those who were cross and complaining turned into bad spirits.

If a woman is sick she is put into one corner of the hut and no one pays any attention to her. If she is given anything, it is given furtively. In the case of a man he is taken off and put in a hut by himself. The reason is that sickness is brought about by one of the bad spirits, and if you favor the sick person you bring the bad spirit's attention to yourself.

The language is extremely simple, with a great many words which by different intonations mean different things. They count up to ten and have one word which means ten and some more, which may be eleven or eleven million. The hardest thing for her to do in Iceland and in this country was to learn to think. The Eskimos talk a little about the fire and a little about the polar bear and walrus, but have no abstract ideas. The vocabulary is very small. There is absolutely no vegetation in North Greenland, with the exception of some seaweed. The reindeer there, which are very poor and which the people do not use for food purposes at all, live on fish.

. These Eskimos have no steel, and when a man goes on a long trip where he can't carry a fire, he makes a fire by striking a stone against a walrus tusk. He may work hours and hours to get a spark.

When a young man wants to marry, he picks out the girl he is interested in and stops hunting. He goes to the house of this girl and get his food there for some time. If the girl's parents continue to make him welcome, he knows he is acceptable. Then he has to get the girl out of that house into some other house in the village (it doesn't matter which one) without being seen. His success constitutes the wedding ceremony. If he fails, he is punished by death. Failures occur and the death penalty is actually inflicted.

The facts on Olof put Schoolcraft in a position from which he could find no escape. His literary conscience would not permit him to use the story in its original form, after he had found that it was a hoax; his humanitarian instincts would not allow him to expose the old lady, who was, after all, harmless in his view compared to the hordes of charlatans who get by. As long as her friends believed in her she would have a home, and these were probably her last few as well as her declining years. Schoolcraft, who needed both money and *kudos,* gritted his teeth and canceled his bargain with the editor.

You have guessed it. The young and high-minded author received his reward. Dorothy Daggett is now Mrs. John Schoolcraft.

No more than Schoolcraft could we publish, until Olof Krarer's death. But the responsibilities we feel towards that small minority who seek the facts, dictated eventual publication and therefore the immediate gathering of testimonies, documents, and explanatory theories.

The first step was to enlist the help of Miss Thorstina Jackson, a graduate student at Columbia University, whose father, Thorleifur Joakimsson Jackson, had been historian of the Icelandic colonization in North America—chiefly Minnesota, North Dakota, Manitoba, Saskatchewan and

253

Alberta, but also Nova Scotia and Utah. Many of his studies had been published, but there were others in manuscript. On canvass, these sources did not yield much directly, but Miss Jackson (now Mrs. Emile Waters) knew just how to follow up the investigation.

From the various replies to her letters it was possible to establish Olof's baptismal name, the names of her parents, her birthplace and date of birth. For a time we were following the wrong track on these points, for the first answer to our queries stated that Olof was the daughter of Jonatan Halldorsson. Jackson's pioneer sketches did not list Olof as a child of this family and a later correspondent, G. J. Hallsson, of Hallson, North Dakota, in a letter dated May 26, 1926, gave the right clue:

"... I feel certain I know the person you refer to. It must be Olof Solfadottir, from Langamiri in Hunavatnsysla. This girl was a dwarf in stature. ..."

At this time Miss Jackson made a trip to Iceland. While there she went to the Government library in Reykjavik and obtained from the *Kirkjubok* (Book of Church Records) a copy of Olof's birth certificate. We quote a translation of the Icelandic document which she forwarded:

BIRTH CERTIFICATE
Ólöf Sölvadóttir

Born 15 February 1858 baptized 17th of the same month.
Parents: Sölvi Sölvason and Solveig Stefánsdóttir, man and wife
of Outer Langamyri.

The above is correct according to the register of Audkul Parish.
Certified
The National Archives, Reykjavik, 13 July, 1926.
(Signed) Hannes Thorsteinsson.

The following year the identification was further confirmed and documented by B. L. Baldwinson, of 729 Sher-
brook Street, Winnipeg, Manitoba, as will appear.
All the accounts of Olof's early years in Canada, before
she assumed the character of Miss Krarer the Eskimo, swayer
of American educational destinies, are vague and the details
vary, but the general outlines are similar. As a continuation
of the above Hallsson letter, we quote a version, differing
somewhat from my memory of my mother's:

". . . She (Olof) had been living with her father in Winnipeg
and left him in 1880 to live with an English couple. They were
then resident in Winnipeg but I have no doubt they were really
traveling players who had some connection with a large company
of actors. I believe that shortly thereafter they left Winnipeg for
the United States, for (soon) after she got south across the line
she was recognized as the same girl, although she had then already assumed her Eskimo character. Why she did this, I am
unable to explain. I knew her very well and lived in the same
neighborhood. For that reason I would consider it remarkable if
she did anything seriously reprehensible so long as her conduct
was fully governed by her own desires. She seemed to have a good
and firm character and was intelligent above the average.

"According to my understanding, it seems clear that the
woman who adopted her came to be largely in control of whatever she did."

The most complete and thoroughly documented information came from Baldwinson, who enclosed with his letter on November 16, 1927, a statement which we quote in full.

"Olof Solvadottir

"Born at Ytri Longumyri in Blondudal in Hunavatnssyslu in Iceland about the year 1860 or 1861.

"Her father Solvi Sölvason, farmer.

"Her mother Solveig Stefansdottir: his wife.

"Solvi lost his wife in Iceland and remarried there; his second wife was Soffia Eyjolfsdottir, a widow. They emigrated from Iceland to Canada in the year 1876 and settled a short distance north of the town of Gimli in Manitoba and remained there for about 3 years until they moved to Winnipeg in or about the year 1879, where they resided for a period of 2 years. They then moved to Hallson in N. Dakota, built a house and resided there for several years, until they moved to Seattle in the state of Washington. There they built a house in Ballard and remained there until their death.

"Olof Solvadottir is a dwarf. She left her family while they lived in the Gimli district and went to Winnipeg to secure work. There she joined up with an American traveling tent show and has since been lost to all her relatives though she is known to be alive and well and in the care of wealthy benefactors in the United States. Her nearest relatives are:

(Here followed names and addresses of three brothers and a sister, in the U.S.A. and Canada, and of a relative in Iceland.)

"This information is given by Magnus Bjornson, 11 McDonald St., Winnipeg, who is a foster brother to Olof since she lost her mother in Iceland, and also by her brother at Westbourne as to names and addresses of her brothers and sisters. The two photos herewith enclosed are taken from photos the property of Magnus Bjornson."

The accompanying letter from Baldwinson said in part:

"... Magnus Bjornson, Olof's foster brother ... ran into Olof in a circus a few years after she had begun to exhibit herself. She then pretended not to recognize him, which he said suited him well enough, for he did not want to be the cause of her getting into trouble about her (pretended) nationality."

An earlier letter from Baldwinson contained an explanatory note on some photographs which were enclosed.

"I have also secured two pictures of her, one by herself, the other with the man that she is said to have been married to—both of them are wearing wedding rings."

This photograph shows the figures of equal stature. The body proportions are those of dwarfs.

Following these inquiries my activities in the Olof Krarer case were long suspended. And then, in Utica, New York (1932), I met Miss Frances A. Finch who, as a child, had known Olof Krarer in Florida. She told me something of her childhood recollections of this interesting character, and later confirmed them by a letter which I quote in part, dated from Skaneateles, New York, November 27, 1932:

"As you requested, I have gone into the question at home, but I think that the enclosed material (photographs) is all I have that would be of interest to you. . . .

257

"Print No. 1 is the one I mentioned as having been taken during the winter of 1917-1918. I was ten years old at the time. Miss Krarer and I are standing on the same step. I presume I was of average height, for now, at the age of twenty-five, I am about five feet two and a half inches tall. (The picture shows the girl of ten considerably taller than the old "Eskimo.")

"Miss Krarer was about fifty-eight years old when these pictures were taken, and print No. 2 shows Miss Olaf with a bouquet presented her at that year's celebration of her birthday. . . .

". . . The woman with whom Miss Krarer lived was Mrs. (H. P.?) Slayton. . . . Although Mrs. Slayton was considered the owner of the Seven Gables Apartments, rumor had it that Olaf Krarer had a substantial interest. I've been unable to verify the location of the Seven Gables Apartments, pictured in print No. 3, except that it stands at a corner of Williams Park in St. Petersburg, Florida."*

In November, 1934, my friend, Miss Gretchen Switzer, of Columbia University, told me that she was about to visit St. Petersburg. For reasons two or three paragraphs ahead, she was interested in the case of Olof Krarer. She followed up the information given by Miss Finch. In St. Petersburg she was able to verify the name and address of Mrs. Slayton (Mrs. W. P. Slayton) and the location of the Seven Gables Apartments. She also talked with the clerk of the Princess Martha Hotel, H. B. Boardman (now of The New Hotel Delaware, Ocean City, New Jersey) who said that Olof was known there only as Olof the Eskimo. To the best of his

* We have prints of the photographs described above and two additional ones—another of the apartment house and one that may be of Olof by herself, though it is most too good looking and may be of Miss Finch at the age of about 10.

knowledge she had gone to Battle Creek and at that time (1934) was in Chicago.*

Some years ago I became interested in the similarity between the Krarer tradition and the views about Eskimos held in Teachers College, Columbia University. I asked Miss Switzer, then a member of the New College staff of Teachers College, where she had obtained her ideas and it seemed she could trace a number of them to having studied in the lower grades a book published by Rand McNally and Company, *Eskimo Stories* (copyright 1902). A check showed that the author, Mary Estella E. Smith, of the Jenner School, Chicago, had for the last paragraph of its introduction, dated June 14, 1902:

"The author acknowledges her appreciation of the valuable suggestions made by Miss Olof Krarer, who read the book in manuscript, and whose interesting autobiography appears at the close of the volume under the title, 'The Story of a Real Eskimo.'"

A little earlier in the introduction Miss Smith says that

". . . various books have been consulted and drawn upon for basic material, but special acknowledgment is due 'My Arctic Journal,' by Josephine D. Peary, and 'The Children of the Cold,' by Frederick Schwatka."

Clearly Miss Smith did get a considerable part of her material from the dry-as-dust fact school, and perhaps three-

* We note here some of the ways in which this ties in with, and fails to tie in with, what Schoolcraft learned Olof told him that it was a Mr. Slayton who managed her lecture career, that after his death she lived with Mrs. Slayton for a number of years. See his account for why she left them. Then Olof met some people named Stone (I. K. Stone, Maple Street, Battle Creek, Michigan) who took her to Battle Creek where she had then (1922) been living for two or three years.

quarters of her book would be in humdrum correspondence with things as they physically are. But some of the more entertaining portions, likeliest to cling to the mind of a learner, are seemingly based on the "valuable suggestions made by Miss Olof Krarer." Though perhaps small in quantity, beside the contributions by Mrs. Peary and Lieutenant Schwatka, the Krarer section of the schoolbook was bound to impress itself, for the author says to the teacher at the head of the Krarer autobiography, *The Story of a Real Eskimo,* that "this story should be read to the children before they begin reading the book."

We quote portions of *The Story of a Real Eskimo:*

"I was born on the east coast of Greenland, the least known to civilization, about one thousand miles north and a little west of Iceland. I am the youngest of eight children. As nearly as I can remember,* my father's house was on a low plain near the seashore. . . .

"Our house was built of snow. . . .

". . . Outside of the door was a long, narrow passageway, just high enough for one of us little Eskimo people to stand up straight in. That would be about high enough for a child eight years old in this country; and it was only wide enough for one person to go through at a time. If one wanted to go out and another wanted to come in at the same time one would have to back out of the passageway and let the other go first. . . .

"Our fireplace was in the center of the house. The bottom was a large flat stone with other stones piled about the edge to keep

---

* Youthfulness at the time Olof left Greenland, as hereinafter stated, is said to have been useful in circus sideshow and on the lyceum platform—if challenged Miss Krarer used to say, modestly, that since she had for sources only vague childhood memories she might very well go wrong on particulars. But in general, she maintained, she was conveying an undeceptive first-hand impression of Eskimos and of Eskimoland.

the fire from getting into the room. When we wanted to build a fire we would put some dried meat and bones on the stone; then a little dry moss was put in, and then my father would take a flint and a whale's tooth and strike fire upon the moss. Sometimes it took a long time to make it burn. After the fire started he would put some blubber upon it. . . .

". . . Our food is eaten raw and frozen. We have only the salt ocean water, and if we had soft, fresh water we would not dare to use it, for it would be like poison to our flesh with the thermometer 80° or 90° below zero. So, when we eat, we take a piece of raw meat in one hand and a chunk of blubber in the other, and take a bite of each until it is eaten. Then we carefully rub the grease and fat all over our hands and face, and feel fine afterwards. My people have long hair, made dark by the smoke and grease.

"There was no chance to play and romp inside the snow house. We just had to sit still with our arms folded. It was in this way that my arms came to have such a different shape from people's arms in this country. Where their muscle is large and strong, I have but very little; and instead of that, I have a large bunch of muscle on the upper side of my arms, and they are crooked so that I can never straighten them.

"Sometimes we used to get very tired in the dark snow house and then we would try a little amusement. Two of us would sit down on the fur carpet, and looking into each other's faces, guess who was the best looking. We had to guess at it, for we had no looking-glass in which to see our faces.

"The one whose face shone the most with the grease was called the prettiest. If at any time we grew tired of it all, and ventured to jump about and to play, we were in danger of being punished. When a child was naughty, mother would place a bone on the fire, leaving it there until it was hot enough for the grease to boil

261

our. Then she would slap it on the child. She was not particular where she burned her child, except that she was careful not to touch the face. . . .

"But it was not always so that we had to stay in the snow house. Once in a while father would come in and say it was not so cold as usual, and then we would have a chance to look around outside the snow house. We never took long walks. There were some steep, jagged rocks in sight of our village, and during the long daytime enough of the snow would melt off to leave the rocks bare in a few places. . . .

"Now, in order that you may understand our way of living better, I will explain that we have six months night in Greenland, and during that time nothing is seen of the sun. . . . Before and after the night-time there was about a month of twilight. . . .

"In the long day we had the hardest time, for then the sun shone out so brightly that we would be made snow-blind if we ventured far from home. The day was four months long, and if we did not have food enough stored away in an ice cave to last us through, we would be in great danger of starving.

". . . My father's name was Krauker, my name was Oluar. On arriving in Iceland I was baptized Olof Krarer.

"One thing had a great deal of interest for us all. When the sun shone out at the beginning of the daytime, it marked the first of the year, as New Year's day marks the beginning of the year in this country. Then our parents would take out the sacks, each one of the family having one of their own. In each sack was a piece of bone for every first time that person had seen the sun. When ten bones were gathered, they would tie them into a bundle, for they had not words to count more than ten. In such a land was I born, in such a home was I brought up. In such pleasures I rejoiced until there were about fifteen bones in my sack.

"Then something happened which changed my whole life. Six tall men came to our village. They proved to be Iceland whalers who had been shipwrecked in a storm and who finally reached Greenland. When they returned to Iceland my father's family went with them. . . .

"Eskimos have no idea of a book. . . . They think, in their ignorance, they are the only people, and are consequently contented and happy.

"June 16, 1902.   "Olof Krarer."

By her own account Miss Krarer had been born an Eskimo in Greenland; those who claim to be her relatives state she was born an Icelander in Iceland. Both countries, and the sea between them, are hazy to the average reader and so a few remarks may be worth while.

Iceland is the largest country now inhabited by Europeans which had no aborigines when discovered. It is, too, the largest in the northern hemisphere of those islands which do not show, archeologically or historically, any evidence of pre-white human occupation.

The Irish discovered Iceland around or before A. D. 795; the Norsemen first visited the country around 850 and say they found ahead of them no people except the Irish. These things, so far as we know, are undisputed.

The part of Greenland, where Olof claimed to have been born around 1860, "a thousand miles north and a little west of Iceland," can never have been inhabited during the last several thousand years, since that distance takes you far into the interior, up on the inland ice where, so far as we understand it, neither humans nor the animals upon which hunters depend can have lived since prior to that Ice Age which,

263

millenniums back, gave the land its present cap of snow.

Be liberal with Olof and place her family on the seacoast of Greenland north and a little east from central Iceland. We then have a district that is believed by anthropologists and explorers not to have been inhabited by Eskimos at or anywhere near the time when Olof was born. If you wanted to be extremely generous, you might connect her story up with the few Eskimos seen by Clavering, near what is now Shannon Island, in 1823. Shannon is, true enough, some 500 miles south of Olof's claimed birthplace, but then it is also 500 miles north of where her alleged family claim she was born. That is kind of fifty-fifty.

The Clavering people were, by his account and that of Sabine, apparently just ordinary Eskimos, looking more or less as if they were Chinese. Olof tells that her Eskimo relatives were blond, but then she mentions that they did not know they were blond, they were so blackened with the smoke from their lamps. Most travelers have explained that Eskimos trim their lamps so carefully that they rarely smoke —but, if we start out to be generous, why haggle over a few smudges of lampblack?

Except Olof's there is no account of Icelanders going to eastern or northeastern Greenland near the time she says, nor ever any time for many decades before and after. So far as known, Europeans never visited northeastern Greenland (1000 miles north of Iceland) until after Miss Krarer became a prominent lecturer. Those Europeans were Danes, not Icelanders.

Olof seems to be the only person who has claimed that the sea was ever so frozen, or so filled with ice, between Green-

land and Iceland that people could walk across in the manner described by her, or in any manner.

I know of one Eskimo having been in Virginia; I cannot
find testimony, except Miss Krarer's, that any Eskimo ever
was in Iceland. Just possibly at some time during the Middle
Ages some Icelander may have brought an Eskimo from
Greenland, but, if so, there is no account of it. There is
one account of a medieval Icelander who did see Eskimos
on the southern east coast of Greenland, but the narrative
explicitly states that when he sailed from there he left the
Eskimos behind.

Iceland is among the countries which do not feel, or at
least did not until very recently, any such need for Eskimos
in their system of education as we feel in ours. You can see
through authorities such as Professor Ellsworth Huntington
of Yale, in his *The Character of Races,* that they are comparatively a learned people, so you would expect book
knowledge of the Eskimos which Olof might have picked
up. But other writers, for instance, Bayard Taylor in his
Egypt and Iceland in the Year 1874, have pointed out that
the Icelandic learning, next after dealing with their own
antiquities, is heavily preoccupied with Greece, Rome, and
the Mediterranean countries generally. The Icelanders tend
to be classicists in their schooling and reading.

It was, therefore, in one way unfortunate that Olof, when
she came to formulate the accounts of her Greenland childhood, had little groundwork derivable from her Icelandic
education or from the knowledge of her friends and family.
But in another way it was fortunate that she had to pick up
her ideas in America. For this made it simple to fit herself

to traditional beliefs, avoiding conflict with her hearers. So in Miss Krarer's account, as in the view previously common, the Eskimos are (for instance) a small people, they grease themselves with oil, they all live in snow houses, and they suffer long periods of uninterrupted darkness followed by long periods of uninterrupted light.

The Krarer version of Arctic lore does introduce a few novelties, as, for instance, where she says that:

"... we have six months night in Greenland. ... Before and after the night-time there was about a month of twilight. ... The day was four months long."

That replaced the six-month day and six-month night. After all, she had to contribute something novel or there could have been little advantage in getting knowledge for American textbooks and supplementary readers straight from a real Eskimo.

There is an almost tragic contrast between the Krarer division of daylight and darkness and the one which has recently forced its way into American school teaching, disturbing its symmetry. Like Miss Krarer's, this view attacks the even division between light and dark but (and here is the tragedy) where Miss Krarer arrived at a darkness period much longer than the daylight, the astronomers who are bothering the schools claim a daylight period much longer than the darkness. Their ratio is practically the same as hers, only reversed.

What a triumph it would have been for the little Eskimo had she only reversed the naming of her four-month and eight-month periods! The astronomers, right enough, are talking for the mathematical North Pole and Miss Krarer for a point only a thousand miles north of Iceland; but that discrepancy would not have been so hard to explain away. After all, Miss Krarer was born at a time when many geographers still believed Greenland extended to and beyond the North Pole, and she might so easily have been mistaken as to whether she was born one thousand or sixteen hundred miles north of Iceland.

As mentioned, it was the opinion among the Icelanders in North Dakota that Olof Solvadottir, the normally blond and blue-eyed Nordic dwarf, born in Iceland, had been induced by "the English couple" who adopted her to take the character of the Eskimo Olof Krarer, born in northeastern Greenland. The first the Icelanders knew of her changed status was when they discovered her as a freak in a circus. According to my mother's version of how Olof came to assume the Eskimo character, she went straight from waiting on table in a hotel to lecturing on a lyceum circuit—there was no mention of an intervening circus career. But there was a circus period, that seems clear. Perhaps the sequence was small-time lecturing, circus, big-time lecturing.

At any rate, there is no reason to doubt the testimony which connects Olof with a foremost bureau of lyceum's heyday.

Some of the leaders in the modern celebrity business are old stagers from the lyceum and Chautauqua days. Among these are O. B. Stephenson, head of the long successful Emerson Lyceum Bureau, Orchestra Building, South Michigan Avenue, Chicago, and the veteran field worker and at

267

present independent bureau manager, William H. Stout, Bluff Road 37, Greenwood, Indiana. From them and others we piece together the following:

At the crest of the lyceum and Chautauqua business one of the most successful organizations was the Slayton Lyceum Bureau, dating back also well among the pioneers. They ranked almost if not quite with such great institutions as the Redpath Bureau and produced some very successful managers who later branched out for themselves, as for instance, Charles L. Wagner, who was secretary for the Slaytons, a dominant figure with them at that time, and who is now a New York leader in concert management, with offices at 511 Fifth Avenue. It seems clear that the Slaytons had nothing to do with Olof's change of state but received her as a full-fledged Eskimo from those earlier patrons who may have been influential in changing her, or who at any rate may have been with her at the time she changed and thus familiar with the stages of the transformation.

The story of Miss Krarer's entry into and success in the big-time lyceum field is succinctly given by W. P. Slayton, son of the founder of the bureau, who writes from the Hotel Lorraine, Chicago, June 30, 1936:

"As I recall, my Father, Henry L. Slayton, made a trip to Minnesota to meet Miss Krarer with a view of making a contract for her appearance under the management of the Slayton Lyceum Bureau. At that time she was lecturing on Greenland with bookings arranged by a personal manager. This was back in the Eighties, I believe.

"She was glad to come under our management and we booked her for the next thirty years or until her eyesight failed and she

268

had to give up platform work. She filled over 2500 lecture engagements for us, of which over eighty were delivered in Philadelphia alone.

"The last two years of her life were spent at the Old Peoples Baptist Home in Maywood, Ill. She must have been over seventy years old. Her height forty inches. A very interesting personality on the platform and she had a host of friends all over the country."

From the time, then, when Henry L. Slayton discovered her, Miss Krarer was one of their chief and successful attractions. She was on the road pretty well constantly, lectured in schools, universities, churches, auditoriums, and under summer Chautauqua tents. Wherever she went she appears to have made a favorable impression personally and to have conveyed vividly her picture of that northeastern Greenland where she said she had been born an Eskimo.

We have further proof of Miss Krarer's success on the lyceum and Chautauqua platforms from S. Russell Bridges, one of the leaders in the lyceum field and now head of the Alkahest Lyceum Bureau of Atlanta, Georgia. He writes under date of July 31, 1936:

"Yes, I remember the little Eskimo lady, Miss Krarer, whom we had on one of our Chautauqua circuits, as I recall, in the summer of 1911. Then the following winter she came down and filled a few lyceum engagements. She was an excellent attraction who always made good with her audiences, and besides, she was a good box office feature.

". . . I recall trying to meet her when she first came down from Chicago to begin her tour for us but I missed her at the station and followed her on to the hotel where they had refused to give her a room until I arrived and identified her. . . .

"Another incident I recall is that she and William Jennings Bryan appeared on our Chautauqua at Newnan, Georgia, the same date, he in the morning and she in the afternoon, but they were both leaving at the same time and when the train pulled in at the depot, I took her baggage and went ahead and Mr. Bryan was following but when I got on the platform of the train, she was trying to reach the step but could not quite make it. Finally Bryan picked her up and put her up on the platform as you would a child."

The way in which Olof Krarer was presented to the public, the character of her service, and the impression she made upon her audiences, we try to show more concretely by quotations from a statement about her made by the Slayton Lyceum Bureau (then of Steinway Hall, Chicago). The document we have was likely printed in 1902 or 1903, according to an informant who was in touch with Miss Krarer then. It is, therefore, of about the period when The Little Eskimo was collaborating with Chicago educators and publishers along those lines which, through *Eskimo Stories* and otherwise, have had so profound an influence upon American schools. The statement runs:

"MISS OLOF KRARER has become one of the best known lecturers that ever appeared on the lyceum platform. She does not appear as a freak or a curiosity, but on her merits. The Bureau always guarantees that she will give entire satisfaction to any audience, however critical. Large sums of money have been made from her lectures by churches, charity organizations and lyceums.

Many a church debt has been raised and a weak lecture course freed from debt by the receipts from one of her lectures.

"For several years after the arrival of Miss Krarer in the United States it was very difficult for her to live through the summer months; she has, on the other hand, taken long rides during our coldest days in winter, with only her ordinary apparel, without the slightest discomfort, while those accompanying her were nearly frozen to death.

"The simple story of her life, as she tells it, is more interesting than a fairy tale. At the close of her lecture anyone in the audience is at liberty to ask her any proper questions concerning her life and native country. Some of the ablest legal talent in this country have taken advantage of this privilege, but Miss Krarer is always equal to every occasion and emergency. The Bureau, in her behalf, takes this occasion to thank the many hundreds of people and the press of the country for the uniform kindness and attention received at their hands. During the past Miss Krarer has delivered more lectures than her strength would really permit, and for that reason it will be necessary in the future to limit the number of her engagements, but first applications will receive most favorable dates."

That the general claims of managers were no empty sales talk is borne out by the specific statement that Miss Krarer had already (as of about 1902) lectured 85 times in Philadelphia, 16 times in New York, 14 times in Chicago, 6 times in Baltimore, 5 times in Jersey City, Cleveland, and Aurora (Ill.), and 3 times in Albany, N. Y., Syracuse, N. Y., Detroit, Mt. Pleasant, Ia., St. Louis, Cortland, N. Y., Toledo, O., Orange, N. J., Newark, N. J., and Dayton, O.

Before the close of her career she lectured several more

271

years; a corrected tally would give her more appearances in these cities than here listed.

The direct statement of the Slaytons is well supported by representative newspapers from the Atlantic coast to beyond the Mississippi. We quote them as they are quoted in the (1902?) booking circular of "Miss Olof Krarer, Esquimau":

"Newark (N.J.) *Evening News:* An appreciative audience greeted Miss Olof Krarer, the Esquimau lecturer, at the Irvington rink last night. She is a pleasant-faced little woman, only three feet five inches in height and weighing 120 pounds, who left Greenland with a party of Icelanders and was educated by missionaries in Iceland. She told many interesting things about East Greenland, of which so little is known. In her native land, she said, . . . There is only one social distinction—the man who owns a flint for making fire is looked upon as a big gun, but he is bound by custom to loan it freely and without remuneration. Water—that is, fresh water—is unknown. . . . The women of her country, she said, lived a life of pathetic idleness and helplessness, with no housework, no washing, no fancy work, no amusement and no cooking. All meat is eaten raw, and this is the sole food. The main occupation of the men was hunting . . . this being done mainly in the twilight period, lasting four months of the year. The remainder of the year is made up of four months of perpetual night, lighted by stars and moon, and four months of daylight. The latter is the hardest time for the Esquimaux, as large numbers of them are afflicted with snow-blindness, caused by the dazzling effect of the sun on the ice and snow.

"The only record of time kept by these primitive people is by means of a bone bag—one bone dropped into a fur bag on the day on which the sun is first seen each year. . . . Miss Krarer says her people . . . are becoming more stunted in growth and shorter-lived every generation. . . ."

"Holyoke (Mass.) Paper: Last night a large audience assembled in the city hall and listened to Miss Olof Krarer's talk on 'Greenland, or Life in the Frozen North.' Since her visit to this city two years ago Miss Krarer has increased her knowledge of English and entertained her audience finely. The lecture was the same as that given by her when she lectured under the auspices of the Scientific Association. Last evening, at the close of her lecture, Miss Krarer appeared in northern costume, a genuine polar bear skin from its natural state, which she had taken great pains to secure. . . . Miss Krarer still finds this climate trying, and during the summer months seeks the coolest spot she can find. . . . Tomorrow she speaks in Westfield, next in Warren. Almost every night she is engaged and business increases every season."

"West Chester (Pa.) *Republic:* Olof Krarer fairly captivated her audiences at the Normal yesterday afternoon and last evening. The story of the life of the inhabitants of Greenland became doubly entertaining when related in the quaint broken English of this bright and witty little native of that frozen land. The Normal School course of lectures thus inaugurated promises to be exceedingly popular and will no doubt have a large patronage."

"Manchester (Iowa) *Union:* The lecture on Greenland by Miss Olof Krarer at the city hall last evening in aid of the Orphans' Home was one of the most interesting and instructive lectures ever heard in this city."

"Vicksburg (Miss.) *Daily Commercial Herald:* Miss Olof Krarer's pictures of life from a Greenlander's standpoint afforded a very large audience at the opera house, last night, a unique experience, of which not the least entertaining feature was the personality of the speaker. She is scarcely taller than a ten-year-

273

old girl, a neat, trim, plump little woman, with very bright eyes and a countenance that has nothing unfamiliar in its appearance, such a one as might be seen anywhere in the United States and in no respect Mongolian or Indian. . . . Hers is a plain, unvarnished story, that of a sensible, educated woman, depicting the terrible conditions of life around the North Pole. It was deeply interesting, however, and the audience frequently applauded her. She sang . . . an Esquimaux love-song, which would no doubt impress a damsel of the frozen coast as something too altogether lovely. The lecture was given under the auspices of the Circle of the Silver Cross, King's Daughters, and was a financial success."

"Brooklyn (N.Y.) *Daily Eagle:* The hall of the Young Men's Christian Association was well filled last evening by an audience gathered to hear the lecture of Miss Olof Krarer, an Esquimau lady from the eastern shores of Greenland, her subject being 'Greenland, or Life in the Frozen North.' Miss Krarer is the only Esquimau lady in the United States and her lecture was unusually interesting. . . ."

"Detroit (Mich.) *Free Press:* The speaker's platform at Y.M.C.A. hall last evening presented a very Arctic appearance, covered with polar bear skins and white draperies, with a silver fox skin mounted over the speaker's stand. This was done to be in consonance with the character of the evening's entertainment, a lecture on the Esquimaux of Greenland, by Miss Olof Krarer, a native of that hypoborean region. . . . She was decidedly short, being only 3 feet 4 inches in height, and weighing 100 pounds. Otherwise her appearance did not vary strikingly from that of many a German maid, met with daily in Detroit. . . ."

"Sioux City (Iowa) *Journal:* At the Y.M.C.A. auditorium last night Miss Olof Krarer, the Esquimau woman, lectured on the customs of her people. The audience was intensely interested in the lecture."

"Mount Pleasant (Iowa) *Free Press:* As a psychological study, the little lady from Greenland, who gave her second lecture in this city last Thursday evening, is probably unexcelled on this continent; and as a study in heredity or the influence of vocation and environment for successive generations upon the body she is equally so. . . . Miss Krarer's person bears corroborative testimony to the claim of her being a native of Greenland, whose racial developments are as marked and as universal as color in Caucasia or Africa; and the indices of nationality in every unmixed people on earth. . . . But it is Miss Krarer as an intelligent and agreeable lady that is most interesting. The evolution from the national, natal condition of absolute non-exertion, into the consciousness of being a responsible, immortal, spiritual being; gracious in self-reliance, dignified in self-respect and potent in an intelligent, conscious, self-hood; attractive in demeanor, and gracious and punctilious in every point of social relations, she is certainly the most interesting personality to the student of mind that it is possible to find on this continent. The school people who failed to see and hear this speaker failed to see and hear a most suggestive object lesson in psychical development under the Christian idea of the nature of God and man. It is through Mr. Fred Hope that Miss Krarer was engaged to come to Mt. Pleasant. Having heard her in Washington, D.C., and knowing the interest she awakened in her audiences in that city, he induced the people of the Christian church to bring her here. Should she ever come again, let those who did not hear her upon this occasion be sure to do so."

Thus through half a century, nearly forty years of which were active, did Olof Krarer, blond Nordic dwarf who may never have seen an Eskimo in her life, continue to entertain and impress those who saw her and those who read about her. It does not appear from other sources, any more than it does from press comments, that her authenticity as an Eskimo was questioned by her friends, her managers, her audiences or her readers. On this we summarize representative testimony.

Obviously a great and careful house like the Rand McNally Company would not have accepted Olof Krarer as a collaborator on one of their schoolbooks had they not at the time believed her to be what their book says and implies, an Eskimo born in an Eskimo country. If possible, it is still more clear that Miss Mary E. E. Smith and her fellow educators were convinced of Miss Krarer's authenticity. Plainly the confidence of the educational world in Miss Krarer is still maintained for, as mentioned above, what is usually considered the foremost school of education in America, Teachers College of Columbia University, has on its staff teachers who until recently developed no suspicion either of Miss Krarer or of those views which at least some of them realized came from *Eskimo Stories.* Strongest proof of all that the faith still remains is the gratifying continued sale of *Eskimo Stories,* which employees of the Rand McNally Company report as late as July, 1936.

The testimony is the same from the lyceum fraternity. Not perhaps quite so meticulously careful as professional educators and the publishers of educational books, they nevertheless tried to maintain a high standard for their "attractions." Remember, those were the William Jennings Bryan and uplift days, when gate receipts were more likely to drop than they are now if lecturers or their management fell below ethical standards.

276

In a rather careful profession, then, the Slayton Lyceum Bureau stood high and in considerable part through the very influence of Miss Krarer. The Redpath Bureau, as well known in the lyceum world, has been at the very top in every requirement. I have a letter from Miss Amy M. Weiskopf, who was in close association when the Redpaths bought out the Slaytons, and who is with the Redpath organization still, or with its head, Mr. Harry P. Harrison. She says that she never doubted Miss Krarer's authenticity and that she never heard doubts of it.

An old friend of mine of high standing in the lyceum world and still active, is the aforementioned William H. Stout. He heard Miss Krarer lecture before the University of Indiana, had no doubts of her authenticity himself, and heard none expressed.

Those who knew her respected and liked Olof Krarer. Through charm of personality she confirmed the interest of the country, and particularly of the schools, in that frozen wonderland of the remote north where live those unique people, the Eskimos.

Olof died in 1935, but during the season 1936-37 teachers all over the United States are carrying on her work through continuing into its fourth decade of usefulness the book *Eskimo Stories,* which she read in manuscript, on which she "made valuable suggestions" and which contains her "interesting autobiography." The teachers who use the book are no doubt being careful to follow the author's directions that Miss Krarer's autobiography, *The Story of a Real Eskimo,* which we quoted, *ante,* should be read to the children before they begin reading the book.

277

Olof Krarer belonged to three cultural agencies that have had their ups and downs, the Chautauqua, the lyceum, and the circus. Chautauqua has faded; the lyceum is emerging slowly (we hear) from a temporary eclipse by the radio; the circus does pretty well, what with "Jumbo." But a greater cultural agency, the schools, in which Miss Krarer took her place 34 years ago, has never suffered eclipse. The teachers go marching on. In their ranks marches the forty-inch spirit of that good trouper, Olof the Eskimo.

CHAPTER VIII

THOSE VERSED IN FABRICATED HISTORY HAD MOMENTS OF SHEER
delight the forenoon of May 27, 1936, while listening to
Dr. Shirley W. Wynne, formerly Commissioner of Health
for New York City, as he spoke over station WEAF of the
National Broadcasting Company on the subject "What Is
Public Health":

"Even ordinary bathing, one of the simple factors in our personal hygiene, had a hard time getting inaugurated in our grandfather's day. The city fathers in the good town of Boston ruled
that it was unlawful to take a bath except on a doctor's advice;
and that law remained in effect from 1854 until 1862—think of
it. In Philadelphia they were a little more open-minded. The law
in Philadelphia was that you couldn't take a bath between November and March. The cities of Hartford and Providence discouraged bathing by raising the charges for water supply about
400 per cent for people who owned bathtubs. In 1847, in Newport, Rhode Island, a doctor tried to convert the people to the
habit of washing, though at the same time he conscientiously
warned them that the first bath or two might affect their hearts.
The American Medical Association immediately opposed him

279

and said that bathing was NOT compulsory to health, and the people needn't wash unless they just wanted to do so for some whimsical reason of their own. So you see our great-grandfathers and even our grandfathers all belonged in that category referred to inelegantly as the Great Unwashed."

The source of joy to the connoisseurs in hoaxes was that the learned ex-Commissioner of Health was reciting over the NBC what sounded a whole lot like an abridgment of a certain contribution to the history of the bathtub which was published in the New York *Evening Mail* of December 28, 1917. We have secured permission and herewith offer what, in spite of much quoting and discussion, is probably the first complete reprinting of this (the author is beginning to feel) overtenaciously successful hoax:

"A NEGLECTED ANNIVERSARY*
By
H. L. MENCKEN

"On December 20 there flitted past us, absolutely without public notice, one of the most important profane anniversaries in American history, to wit, the seventy-fifth anniversary of the introduction of the bathtub into These States. Not a plumber fired a salute or hung out a flag. Not a governor proclaimed a day of prayer. Not a newspaper called attention to the day.

"True enough, it was not entirely forgotten. Eight or nine

* The article was printed with an editorial note: "Here's a series of inspiring bath hour thoughts suggested by H. L. Mencken's discovery, through official channels, that America's first bathtub was built in Cincinnati and put in operation on December 20, 1842. Adam Thompson, its founder, got the idea on his visit to England, where Lord John Russell had started the custom of bathing fourteen years before. So, if any of the next best authors spring a freshly tubbed Englishman on you in a story of the revolution, you'll know he's phony."

months ago one of the younger surgeons connected with the Public Health Service in Washington happened upon the facts while looking into the early history of public hygiene, and at his suggestion a committee was formed to celebrate the anniversary with a banquet. But before the plan was perfected Washington went dry, and so the banquet had to be abandoned. As it was, the day passed wholly unmarked, even in the capital of the nation.

"Bathtubs are so common today that it is almost impossible to imagine a world without them. They are familiar to nearly every one in all incorporated towns; in most of the large cities it is unlawful to build a dwelling house without putting them in; even on the farm they have begun to come into use. And yet the first American bathtub was installed and dedicated so recently as December 20, 1842, and, for all I know to the contrary, it may be still in existence and in use.

"Curiously enough, the scene of its setting up was Cincinnati, then a squalid frontier town, and even today surely no leader in culture. But Cincinnati, in those days as in these, contained many enterprising merchants, and one of them was a man named Adam Thompson, a dealer in cotton and grain. Thompson shipped his merchandise by steamboat down the Ohio and Mississippi to New Orleans, and from there sent it to England in sailing vessels. This trade frequently took him to England, and in that country, during the '30's, he acquired the habit of bathing.

"The bathtub was then still a novelty in England. It had been introduced in 1828 by Lord John Russell and its use was yet confined to a small class of enthusiasts. Moreover, the English bathtub, then as now, was a puny and inconvenient contrivance—little more, in fact, than a glorified dishpan—and filling and emptying it required the attendance of a servant. Taking a bath, indeed, was a rather heavy ceremony, and Lord John in 1835 was said to be the only man in England who had yet come to doing it every day.

"Thompson, who was of inventive fancy—he later devised the machine that is still used for bagging hams and bacon—conceived the notion that the English bathtub would be much improved if it were made large enough to admit the whole body of an adult man, and if its supply of water, instead of being hauled to the scene by a maid, were admitted by pipes from a central reservoir and run off by the same means. Accordingly, early in 1842 he set about building the first modern bathroom in his Cincinnati home—a large house with Doric pillars, standing near what is now the corner of Monastery and Oregon streets.

"There was then, of course, no city water supply, at least in that part of the city, but Thompson had a large well in his garden, and he installed a pump to lift its water to his house. This pump, which was operated by six negroes, much like an old-time fire engine, was connected by a pipe with a cypress tank in the garret of the house, and here the water was stored until needed. From the tank two other pipes ran to the bathroom. One, carrying cold water, was a direct line. The other, designed to provide warm water, ran down the great chimney of the kitchen, and was coiled inside it like a giant spring.

"The tub itself was of new design, and became the grandfather of all the bathtubs of to-day. Thompson had it made by James Guinness, the leading Cincinnati cabinetmaker of those days, and its material was Nicaragua mahogany. It was nearly seven feet long and fully four feet wide. To make it watertight, the interior was lined with sheet lead, carefully soldered at the joints. The whole contraption weighed about 1,750 pounds, and the floor of the room in which it was placed had to be reinforced to support it. The exterior was elaborately polished.

"In this luxurious tub Thompson took two baths on December

20, 1842—a cold one at 8 a.m. and a warm one some time during the afternoon. The warm water, heated by the kitchen fire, reached a temperature of 105 degrees. On Christmas day, having a party of gentlemen to dinner, he exhibited the new marvel to them and gave an exhibition of its use, and four of them, including a French visitor, Col. Duchanel, risked plunges into it. The next day all Cincinnati—then a town of about 100,000 people— had heard of it, and the local newspapers described it at length and opened their columns to violent discussions of it.

"The thing, in fact, became a public matter, and before long there was a bitter and double-headed opposition to the new invention, which had been promptly imitated by several other wealthy Cincinnatians. On the one hand it was denounced as an epicurean and obnoxious toy from England, designed to corrupt the democratic simplicity of the republic, and on the other hand it was attacked by the medical faculty as dangerous to health and a certain inviter of 'phthisic, rheumatic fevers, inflammation of the lungs and the whole category of zymotic diseases.' (I quote from the Western *Medical Repository* of April 23, 1843.)

"The noise of the controversy soon reached other cities, and in more than one place medical opposition reached such strength that it was reflected in legislation. Late in 1843, for example, the Philadelphia Common Council considered an ordinance prohibiting bathing between November 1 and March 15, and it failed of passage by but two votes. During the same year the legislature of Virginia laid a tax of $30 a year on all bathtubs that might be set up, and in Hartford, Providence, Charleston and Wilmington (Del.) special and very heavy water rates were levied upon those who had them. Boston early in 1845 made bathing unlawful except upon medical advice, but the ordinance was never enforced and in 1862 it was repealed.

"This legislation, I suspect, had some class feeling in it, for

283

the Thompson bathtub was plainly too expensive to be owned by any save the wealthy. Indeed, the common price for installing one in New York in 1845 was $500. Thus the low caste politicians of the time made capital by fulminating against it, and there is even some suspicion of political bias in many of the early medical denunciations. But the invention of the common pine bathtub, lined with zinc, in 1847, cut off this line of attack, and thereafter the bathtub made steady progress.

"The zinc tub was devised by John F. Simpson, a Brooklyn plumber, and his efforts to protect it by a patent occupied the courts until 1855. But the decisions were steadily against him, and after 1848 all the plumbers of New York were equipped for putting in bathtubs. According to a writer in the *Christian Register* for July 17, 1857, the first one in New York was opened for traffic on September 12, 1847, and by the beginning of 1850 there were already nearly 1,000 in use in the big town.

"After this medical opposition began to collapse, and among other eminent physicians Dr. Oliver Wendell Holmes declared for the bathtub, and vigorously opposed the lingering movement against it in Boston. The American Medical Association held its annual meeting in Boston in 1849, and a poll of the members in attendance showed that nearly 55 per cent of them now regarded bathing as harmless, and that more than 20 per cent advocated it as beneficial. At its meeting in 1850 a resolution was formally passed giving the imprimatur of the faculty to the bathtub. The homeopaths followed with a like resolution in 1853.

"But it was the example of President Millard Fillmore that, even more than the grudging medical approval, gave the bathtub recognition and respectability in the United States. While he was still Vice-President, in March, 1850, he visited Cincinnati on a stumping tour, and inspected the original Thompson tub. Thompson himself was now dead, but his bathroom was preserved by the gentleman who had bought his house from his estate. Fillmore was entertained in this house and, according to Chamberlain, his biographer, took a bath in the tub. Experiencing no ill effects, he became an ardent advocate of the new invention, and on succeeding to the presidency at Taylor's death, July 9, 1850, he instructed his secretary of war, Gen. Charles M. Conrad, to invite tenders for the construction of a bathtub in the White House.

"This action, for a moment, revived the old controversy, and its opponents made much of the fact that there was no bathtub at Mount Vernon or at Monticello, and that all the Presidents and other magnificoes of the past had got along without any such monarchical luxuries. The elder Bennett, in the New York *Herald,* charged that Fillmore really aspired to buy and install in the White House a porphyry and alabaster bath that had been used by Louis Philippe at Versailles. But Conrad, disregarding all this clamor, duly called for bids, and the contract was presently awarded to Harper and Gillespie, a firm of Philadelphia engineers, who proposed to furnish a tub of thin cast iron, capable of floating the largest man.

"This was installed early in 1851, and remained in service in the White House until the first Cleveland administration, when the present enameled tub was substituted. The example of the President soon broke down all that remained of the old opposition, and by 1860, according to the newspaper advertisements of the time, every hotel in New York had a bathtub, and some had two and even three. In 1862 bathing was introduced into the army by Gen. McClellan, and in 1870 the first prison bathtub was set up at Moyamensing Prison, in Philadelphia.

"So much for the history of the bathtub in America. One is astonished, on looking into it, to find that so little of it has been recorded. The literature, in fact, is almost nil. But perhaps this

285

brief sketch will encourage other inquirers and so lay the foundation for an adequate celebration of the centennial in 1942."

Varying motives in the fabrication of history lead to varying methods. When the purposes are moral or political, as they seem to have been with Parson Weems in his handling of Washington, there is no deliberate straining at probabilities, there are no planted clues. But when the purpose is outright spoofing, as Mencken says it was with the bathtub, there is frequently a mendacious plant. Samples of these in Mencken are that he tells you the bathtub's first American home was at the intersection of Monastery and Oregon Streets, in Cincinnati, in the year 1842, and that a certain reference to bathing comes from Chamberlain's biography of President Fillmore. Now you can discover in any big library, or by writing the friendly librarians of Cincinnati, that while one of the two named streets, Oregon, may have existed there in 1842, the second, Monastery, is not listed until decades later. They will add that streets of these names have never intersected in that town. At your local public library they will report on the telephone that they cannot find any biography of Fillmore by Chamberlain.

Having in part given the victim fair warning, the Mencken type of spoofer proceeds to be reasonable enough to trap the unwary. Much of his tale of bathtub vicissitudes is, for instance, so reasonable superficially, so much in accord with what has actually been the history of the institution at other times and in other places, that not only are health commissioners liable to get caught but they have, on being caught, a pretty fair excuse. For, after all, you could, from so-called real facts, obtain approximately the same pictures and pretty roughly the same morals as you get from the fiction.

Indeed, one of the strongest arguments against troubling to fabricate history or science is that, with judicious manipulation and suitable reasoning, you can frequently extract from ordinary facts tales as pleasing and conclusions as ethical as are commonly based on those facts-by-definition which some call fictions.

Mencken probably felt that the numerous planted clews to his spoofing intent would keep "A Neglected Anniversary" from remaining long undetected. If so, he discovered presently that even he had overrated the public's discrimination. Then the initial delight with which Mencken had watched the poor fish biting, started to fade. By 1926 it seemed to him the yarn was getting altogether too firmly historical so he began trying to call it off. On May 23 of that year he owned up that he had invented the tale, pointing out its absurdities. This confession was printed simultaneously in thirty American newspapers. One of them, the Boston *Herald,* used the article on a leading page, under a four-column head; three weeks later the same paper reprinted, as a piece of news, the substance of the story as it had originally appeared in 1917.

We give below a classified list, which does not attempt to be complete, of some of the individuals, institutions and publications that took one or the other side of the ensuing controversy over the bathtub hoax.

ACCEPTING THE HOAX

Support from Journalists:

Scribner's, October, 1920.

A booklet entitled *The Story of the Bath,* published by the Domestic Engineering Company of Chicago, 1922.

New York Herald, Paris edition, September, 1925, mainly quoting an article in the *New York Sun* by Ruth Wakeham.

Chicago Evening American, December 7, 1926, under heading "For and About Your Home."

March 21, 1927, Colonel W. G. Archer, representing National Trade Extension Bureau of the plumbing and heating industry, in an address before the Clearfield, Pa., Commercial Club at the Jordan Hotel, Clearfield.

Chiropractor, 1927, an article called Splash, by A. J. Pufahl.

Cleveland Press, November 15, 1927, letter from E. Hershey, D.C., P.C.

A pamphlet entitled *Saga of the Bathtub,* by Walt Dennison, published by the LeRoy Carman Printing Company of Los Angeles, California, 1929.

American Baptist (Lexington, Kentucky), February 13, 1929, in an article headed Selected—probably indicating quotation from some other source.

Baltimore News, March 16, 1929, in a column headed "Baltimore Day by Day," by Carrol Dulaney (real name Richard D. Steuart).

House Beautiful, May, 1930, p. 535.

W. Orton Tewson, October 11, 1930, in a syndicated column, "The Attic Salt Shaker," quoting a Dr. Moody (possibly Dr. W. R. Moody, who had recently printed a life of his father, Dwight L. Moody).

Golden Book, early in 1931, article by Lenora R. Baxter.

New York Sun, February 17, 1931, review of *Puritan's Progress,* by Arthur Train, indicating the book accepted the hoax as fact.

Baltimore Evening Sun, May 22, 1931, letter signed S. A. Fact.

Tucson Daily Star, December 1, 1931, interview with C. R. King, manager of the Tucson branch of the Standard Sanitary Manufacturing Company.

New York Sun, December 22, 1931—quoting the *Military Engineer.*

New York Sun, October 12, 1933, advertisement of "Blue Coal," part of which advertisement was an illustration showing a policeman, ca. 1842, threatening to arrest a man in a bathtub.

United Feature Syndicate, April 27, 1933, illustration by Russ Murphy and Ray Nenuskay under the caption "How It Began"—illustration showing Adam Thompson in his first bathtub in Cincinnati.

New York Herald Tribune, March 4, 1934, reprinted portions of above article by Lenora R. Baxter, under heading "Baths in Disfavor for Long Periods, History Recalls."

New York Sun, January 6, 1935, news story.

New York Times, August 4, 1935, news story, "The Bathtub Wins Wider Patronage."

United Press Red Letter for September 26, 1935, "Bathtub Once Viewed as Curse."

J. Vijaya-Tunga, *New Statesman* (London), October 5, 1935.

Central Press Association, November 15, 1935, *Scott's Scrapbook,* cartoon.

Digest and Review, December, 1935.

Australia Age (Melbourne), December 31, 1935.

Liberty, March 21, 1936.

James N. Kane, *Famous First Facts,* published by H. W. Wilson & Co. of New York (no date).

Support from Leaders of Thought:

Dr. John H. Finley (former president of the American Geographical Society and of the College of the City of New York; now an editor of the New York *Times*), in an article in the *Survey*, July 15, 1927.

Alexander Woollcott, radio broadcast for February 24, 1935.

Dr. Hans Zinsser (professor in the Medical School of Harvard University), in *Rats, Lice and History*, Boston, 1935.

Dr. Shirley W. Wynne (former Commissioner of Health for the City of New York)—cited *ante*.

Support from Governmental Agencies:

Federal Housing Administration clip sheet, Vol. 2, No. 9, February, 1935, sent out to newspapers throughout the U.S.

Bulletin of the Department of Health of Kentucky, October, 1935.

EXPOSING THE HOAX

Exposure by Journalists:

Western Newspaper Union, November 28, 1930, syndicated article by Elmo Scott Watson, under the title "James, Draw My Bawth"—apparently printed in a great many small papers throughout the United States.

Martha's Vineyard Gazette, April and May, 1931.

Macon Telegraph, August 31, 1932.

Philadelphia Evening Public Ledger, January 15, 1935.

Editor and Publisher, February 2, 1935, Marlen Pew, commenting on the circulation of the bathtub hoax by the Federal Housing Commission.

Baltimore Evening Sun, April 16, 1935.

Wilmington Evening Journal, June 24, 1935.

Passaic Herald News, July 26, 1935.

New Statesman (London), November 2, 1935, a letter signed J.M.G., exposing the story as printed in the October 5 issue of the same magazine.

Mobile Times, December 28, 1935.

Chicago Times, January 23, 1936, editorial headed "A New True Story," first quoting a speaker who addressed the members of the American Institute of Banking in Chicago. The speaker had related the bathtub story; the editorial then went on to expose the hoax.

Exposure by Leaders of Thought:

Rev. Nolan R. Best, executive secretary of the Baltimore Federation of Churches, letter to the editor of *Survey,* exposing the article by Dr. John H. Finley. Paul Kellogg, the editor, wrote to Finley, who replied July 31, 1927: "The bathtub information was furnished me by a representative of the Cleanliness Institute."

Curtis D. MacDougal, editor of Evanston, Illinois, *News Index,* made an investigation of newspaper hoaxes, exposing, among others, the bathtub hoax. A summary of his report was printed in the *Editor and Publisher,* January 12, 1935. Later he embodied his material in an article for the *Journalism Quarterly.* A summary of that article was printed in the Worcester, Mass., *Gazette* for August 10, 1935. Dr. MacDougal printed a second article on the subject in the *Evanston News Index,* August 9,

1935; in it he discussed especially the apparent impossibility of putting such hoaxes down.

Exposure by Governmental Agencies:

Bureau of Municipal Research, Philadelphia. The Bureau's exposure of the hoax was printed in the *Philadelphia Evening Bulletin,* July 10, 1933, under the heading Bathtub Myth Exploded.*

History, whether real or fabricated, may lose or gain, may remain unchanged or may change with time. These things are handily illustrated by coupling statements from Mencken of 1917 and Wynne of 1936:

Mencken: "Boston early in 1845 made bathing unlawful except upon medical advice, but the ordinance was never enforced and in 1862 it was repealed."

Wynne: "The city fathers in the good town of Boston ruled that it was unlawful to take a bath except on a doctor's advice; and that law remained in effect from 1854† until 1862—think of it."

Mencken: ". . . the Philadelphia Common Council considered an ordinance prohibiting bathing between November 1 and March 15, and it failed of passage by but two votes."

Wynne: "The law in Philadelphia was that you couldn't take a bath between November and March."

Mencken: ". . . in Hartford, Providence, Charleston and

* Mencken's own summary of the first decade of struggle over the bathtub hoax is given in his *Prejudices, Sixth Series,* New York, 1927, pp. 194-201.

†The discrepancy between this 1854 and Mencken's 1845 may well be due to a mere transposition of figures.

292

Wilmington (Del.) special and very heavy water rates were levied upon those who had them (bathtubs)."

Wynne: "The cities of Hartford and Providence discouraged bathing by raising the charges for water supply about 400 per cent for people who owned bathtubs."

Mencken: "After this medical opposition began to collapse, and among other eminent physicians Dr. Oliver Wendell Holmes declared for the bathtub. . . . The American Medical Association held its annual meeting in Boston in 1849, and a poll of the members in attendance showed that nearly 55 per cent of them now regarded bathing as harmless, and that more than 20 per cent advocated it as beneficial. At its meeting in 1850 a resolution was formally passed giving the imprimatur of the faculty to the bathtub."

Wynne: "In 1847, in Newport, Rhode Island, a doctor tried to convert the people to the habit of washing, though at the same time he conscientiously warned them that the first bath or two might affect their hearts. The American Medical Association immediately opposed him and said that bathing was NOT compulsory to health, and the people needn't wash unless they just wanted to do so for some whimsical reason of their own."

That there is pleasant edification for believers in Menckenized history we infer from its popularity; that the employment of the many learned and famous commentators, disseminators and denouncers has been remunerative, we hope; that there is occasionally a spot cash return even to the man in the street we can show by an example:

A well-named periodical, *Liberty,* which encourages among other freedoms the one to believe, has a feature, "Twenty Questions." For those who, in view of the following, may desire to try making an honest dollar, we quote that "Liberty will pay $1 for any question accepted and published. If the same question is suggested by more than one person, the first suggestion received will be the one considered. Address Twenty Questions, P. O. Box 380, Grand Central Station, New York, N. Y." Some time before March 21, 1936 (for we quote from that issue) they had, then, paid one dollar for what appeared on that date, p. 39, as question No. 17:

"In which city of the United States was it against the law to take a bath in 1845?"

As directed, we turn to p. 48 and find under 17 the answer:

"In Boston, Massachusetts. It was then deemed unlawful to take a bath except when prescribed by a physician."

When, belated, I discovered this in *Liberty*, I wondered how the Bostonians were taking what must be a steady barrage, and wrote the Commissioner of Public Health, Dr. Henry D. Chadwick, who replied from the State House, Boston, July 16, 1936:

"The story which you quote from the magazine, *Liberty*, is periodically cropping out in various parts of the country.

"I obtained from W. J. Doyle, City Clerk of Boston, what I consider a true statement of Boston's attitude toward bathing in the early days, and I enclose a copy."

The Doyle statement said in part:

"In several forms during the past ten years an item has appeared in various publications stating . . . that the City of Boston at some time by ordinance forbade the use of bathtubs, or bathing except on the advice of a physician.

"The story has not the slightest foundation in fact. No such ordinance was ever adopted either by the Town or City of Boston from its settlement in 1630 up to the present time. . . .

". . . In 1843 an ordinance was enacted requiring that all prisoners in the Jail or House of Correction should be given a weekly bath. So much as regards bathing except on advice of a physician. The statement that bathtubs were prohibited is so silly as to hardly merit denial, but it is usually made referring to a mythical ordinance supposedly adopted in 1848 and not repealed until 1870. No such ordinance was ever adopted and no such ordinance was ever submitted to the City Council.

W. J. Doyle,
City Clerk."

I was evidently a long way from being the first to query Boston officials on Menckenized history, for the Clerk's original statement, of which I received the above copy, was dated May 24, 1929. Incidentally, that dating explains his reference to "the last ten years." For Mencken's "Neglected Anniversary" had been published less than twelve years before.

How the Mencken fabricated knowledge is being used towards the end of its second decade has cultural significance. We take a few samples.

Hans Zinsser, A.B., A.M., M.D., D.Sc. (hon.), is professor in the Harvard Medical School. During 1935 his *Rats, Lice and History,* a piece of trenchant writing, was a best seller, one of the much read books that was also much discussed,

295

filled with novel and startling facts. One of these (perhaps no longer exactly novel) is on p. 285:

"The first bathtub didn't reach America, we believe, until about 1840."

During February 1935, the Federal Housing Administration issued, in Clip Sheet, Vol. 2, No. 9, a statement on bathtub history:

"In 1842 Adam Thompson startled neighbors in Cincinnati by installing a box-shaped affair lined with lead in his home. Shortly after, in 1845, historians on the subject say the city of Boston passed an ordinance making it illegal to bathe unless a doctor had so ordered. Not until the early days of the Civil War was the act removed from that city's statute books. . . .

"Further indication of the manner in which early lawmakers viewed the matter of personal cleanliness is seen in a resolution introduced about 1843 in Philadelphia under which bathing would have been prohibited by the city fathers from November to March! As it turned out, the suggestion was tabled.

"When Millard Fillmore became President, the tide turned, due principally to his installing a tub in the White House. . . ."

But on July 25, 1936, Robert B. Smith, Assistant to the Administrator, Federal Housing Administration, wrote:

"After this story was published, we found that the statements made in it could not be substantiated so far as ordinances and laws against bathing were concerned. The Health Commissioners of Boston and Philadelphia both wrote us that they could find no trace of any anti-bathing ordinances in their records. . . .

296

"After this bathtub experience, we took care to have the statements made in the Clip Sheet double-checked. . . ."

August 4, 1935, the New York *Times* was celebrating progress in America's metropolis. East Side tenants had made "demands for the installation of that former luxury," the bathtub. This reminded the *Times* that:

"It was with fear and travail that bathtubs were introduced in these United States. One of the first bathrooms appeared in Cincinnati, Ohio, about 1850, and certain clergymen hearing of it preached that such luxury meant nothing less than degeneracy. The fading of the glory that was Greece and the collapse of the grandeur that was Rome were freely mentioned. The baths of wicked Caracalla also were cited."

The *Bulletin* of the Department of Health of Kentucky, October 1935, said on p. 75:

"The first bathtub in the United States was installed in a Cincinnati home in 1842. It was made of mahogany and lined with sheet lead. Newspapers denounced it as undemocratic vanity. Boston, in 1845, made bathing unlawful except when prescribed by a physician. Virginia soaked the rich by taxing bathtubs $30 per year."

A letter from J. Vijaya-Tunga was printed in the *New Statesman,* London, for October, 1935. We quote an extract as reprinted in the *Australia Age* (Melbourne) for December 31, 1935:

"The first American bathtub was built in 1830. It was made of

297

mahogany and was 7 feet long and 4 feet wide. It was lined with sheet lead and weighed more than 2,000 pounds. The invention was not popular. Boston authorities made bathing unlawful, and Virginia put a tax of $300 on each bathtub. Fifteen years later Boston declared bathtubs illegal, except on medical advice."

The *Age* did not fall for the hoax but the *New Statesman* apparently did.

The Chicago *Times* of January 23, 1936, quotes a speaker addressing a Chicago meeting of the American Institute of Banking:

"'The hardest job on earth for the average man,' he said, 'is to sit and think. He'll sit all right, but he won't think, and that is why the public always detests a new idea. Why, do you know that when the first bathtubs were introduced in America intellectual Boston passed an ordinance making it unlawful to bathe in a bathtub except on medical advice?' "

The *Times* treated this speaker editorially as the victim of a hoax which, perhaps naturally, did not influence Vice Presidential candidate Frank Knox's Chicago *Daily News,* which said July 11, 1936, under the heading "Bathtub Suffered Same Fate in U. S. as Most Pioneers," that

"America's first bathtub, according to a recent issue of *Architecture,* was built in Cincinnati in 1842 and was made of mahogany and lined with sheet lead.

"While still accepting the oft-quoted relationship of cleanliness and godliness, the people of the day were not receptive to such fantastic innovations, and the tub, suffering the fate of most pioneering ventures, was denounced as a luxurious and undemocratic vanity. Doctors, according to ·the magazine, termed it a menace to health.

"In 1843 Philadelphia prohibited by ordinance bathing between Nov. 1 and March 15, and Boston made bathing unlawful except when prescribed by a physician. Also, bathtubs were taxed $30 yearly."

A paper of which Knox is publisher stops in the heat of the Landon-Knox campaign to support Mencken as a historian; Mencken swerves from other forms of history-making the while to campaign for Knox as Vice President. With these things happening at and just after the Republican convention, we feel that God's in His Heaven and that all should be well at any rate with the making of history.

299